Choosing Sharia?

Choosing Sharia?

Multiculturalism, Islamic Fundamentalism and Sharia Councils

Machteld Zee

international publishing

Published, sold and distributed by Eleven International Publishing
P.O. Box 85576
2508 CG The Hague
The Netherlands
Tel.: +31 70 33 070 33
Fax: +31 70 33 070 30
e-mail: sales@budh.nl
www.elevenpub.com

Sold and distributed in USA and Canada
International Specialized Book Services
920 NE 58th Avenue, Suite 300
Portland, OR 97213-3786, USA
Tel.: 1-800-944-6190 (toll-free)
Fax: +1 503 280-8832
orders@isbs.com
www.isbs.com

Eleven International Publishing is an imprint of Boom uitgevers Den Haag.

ISBN 978-94-6236-634-3
ISBN 978-94-6274-447-9 (E-book)

Cover design by Siebe Bluijs

Printed in The Netherlands

TABLE OF CONTENTS

Introduction   **vii**

1   The Multiculturalist Ideology   **1**
Introduction   1
Identity Theory   4
From Identity Theory to a 'Politics of Difference'   11
Breaking Down Multiculturalism   17
1. Who Someone Authentically Is, Is Given by His Minority Cultural
Identity   20
2. Nonrecognition of Cultural Minority Identity Constitutes Psycholog-
ical Harm   24
3. Culture Is Good   29
4. Cultures Are Equal   31
5. Cultural Differences Are Good, But If Not, They Should At Least be
Tolerated   33
6. Minority Cultures Must Not be Criticised by the Dominant Culture
which Has the Positive Obligation to Preserve These   40
Conclusion   48

2   Islamic Fundamentalism   **51**
Introduction   51
Sharia as the Sacred Law of Islam   52
Political Islam Part I: Wahhabism   56
Political Islam Part II: The Muslim Brotherhood   59
Jahiliyyah   61
Sharia State Example I: Theocratic Saudi Arabia   64
Sharia State Example II: Islamisation in Malaysia   73
The Organisation of Islamic Cooperation and the Cairo
Declaration   79
Islamophobia   85
Political Islam Part III: The Middle Way to Establishing a Sharia State
in Europe   87
Conclusion   92

3   When Multiculturalism and Islamic Fundamentalism Coincide:
     Sharia Councils in the United Kingdom   95
     Introduction   95
     Distinguishing positions in the debate   98
     Multiculturalists' view of Sharia   100
     The Relationship between Multiculturalism and Islamic Fundamen-
     talism   108
     Behind the Islamic Sharia Council   111
     Sharia and Alternative Dispute Resolution   118
     What Happens at Sharia Councils?   123
     Marital Captivity   140
     Sharia Councils and Human Rights   143
     Batei Din: Jewish Councils   149
     The Arbitration and Mediation Services (Equality) Bill   152
     Secular Alternatives to Sharia councils   155
     Conclusion   158

     Concluding Remarks   161

     Bibliography   165
     Video Material   191
     Case Law   191

     Acknowledgements   193

Index   195

Introduction

There are several ways a state can deal with religion and religious believers. In 1918, for example, the Fifth Congress of Soviets officially proclaimed the Communist constitution. This marked the turning point in the creation of an anti-religious legal system, comprising the Communist atheist doctrine and laying the foundation for the subsequent legal provisions, which gradually and steadily crushed every religious institution.[1] Clergy and believers were actively prosecuted and sent to the Gulag camps for "counterrevolutionary activities".[2]

In this anti-religious political ideology, atheism is not regarded as a conviction privately held, but one that the state must achieve for all its citizens by all means and measures. The state, in a totalitarian effort, is committed to "liberate" people from religion and cleanse society from religious believers.

Political atheism is one of the five models for the relation between state and religion. A state can categorically reject religion, be agnostic, or neutral, towards religion, accommodate minority religions, prioritise one particular religion, and enforce one specific religion. This results in these state ideologies:

1) Political atheism; 2) political agnosticism, also known as political secularism; 3) Multi-culturalism; 4) State Church Doctrine; and 5) Theocracy.[3]

The model of political agnosticism stands for treating – or ignoring – all religions and non-religions alike. *Choosing Sharia?* focuses on the second model, multiculturalism, and on the fifth model, theocracy. The importance of the second model, political agnosticism, is embedded throughout this book.

It should not come as a surprise that eradicating religion (including believers) is irreconcilable with the central tenets of liberal democracy. A modern liberal democracy aims to secure justice for all citizens and does not persecute people for holding religious

---

1 Szczesniak, Boleslaw, *The Russian Revolution and Religion. A Collection of Documents Concerning the Suppression of Religion by the Communists, 1917-1925*, Notre Dame: University of Notre Dame Press 1959, p. 15.

2 See Pospielovky, Dimitry, *Soviet Anti-Religious Campaigns and Persecutions*. Volume 2 of A History of Soviet Atheism in Theory and Practice, and the Believer, Houndmills: MacMillan 1988 and Marsh, Christopher, *Religion and State in Russia and China. Suppression, Survival, and Revival*, New York: Continuum 2011.

3 See for a longer exposition of the five models: Cliteur, Paul, 'State and Religion against the Backdrop of Religious Radicalism', *International Journal of Constitutional Law* 2012, pp. 127-152. Cliteur defines multiculturalism as a state model for "treating all religions alike". I depart from that and define it as "accommodate minority religions".

beliefs. Democratic states uphold the principle of non-discrimination and respect liberty of conscience. The politically atheist state is not a model that should serve as a serious contender when we consider the possibilities of arranging state-religion affairs.

However, the opposite of political atheism is, unfortunately, indeed a serious contender: theocracy is *alive and kicking*. This political model determines the rights and duties of citizens in Iran and Saudi Arabia. Islamic fundamentalism, also described as Political Islam or Islamism, is a religious-political ideology that is not only limited to these particular countries. Due to oil trade in the past few decades, globalisation, and mass migration, Islamist religious leaders and followers have globally espoused a political doctrine firmly grounded in religion that aims to influence the lives of people worldwide. Karima Bennoune, Professor of International Law and author of *Your Fatwa Does Not Apply Here. Untold Stories from the Fight Against Muslim Fundamentalism* (2013), warns against "a creeping Islamisation" that transfigures lifestyles and limits individual freedoms – of both Muslims and non-Muslims – all over the world.[4] She laments Western left-of-centre responses to Muslim fundamentalism to talk about something else whenever the topic comes up:

> The anniversary of September 11 is a time to criticise the U.S. government. An Afghan women having her nose cut off by the Taliban becomes a platform for saying that there is violence against women everywhere. I think when we talk about Muslim fundamentalism, we have to actually talk about *it*. It exists.[5]

A part of this book is dedicated to Bennoune's message: we have to talk about Islamic fundamentalism; it exists. Not merely from a humanitarian point of view, also from an intellectual viewpoint it is important to seriously consider the consequences of a political ideology that challenges the relationship between religion and the state as we know in the West. The second chapter investigates the origin of Islamic fundamentalism, its consequences and the ways in which its adherents push for control. Sharia, the collected laws of Islam, lies at the heart of political Islam.

British German professor of Arabic and Islam Joseph Schacht (1902-1969), the leading Western scholar on Islamic law, described Sharia as the sacred law of Islam. It consists of

> an all-embracing body of religious duties, the totality of Allah's commands that regulate the life of every Muslim in all its aspects; it comprises on an equal footing ordinances regarding worship and ritual, as well as political and (in the narrow sense) legal rules.[6]

---

4   Bennoune, Karima, *Your Fatwa Does Not Apply Here: Untold Stories from the Fight Against Muslim Fundamentalism*, New York: Norton & Company 2013, p. 8.
5   Bennoune 2013, p. 24. Italics in original.
6   Schacht, Joseph, *An Introduction to Islamic Law*, Oxford: Clarendon Press 1982, p. 1.

One of the ways in which Islamic fundamentalism manifests in Europe is through Sharia councils, which since the 1980s operate in the United Kingdom as a legal order that stands apart from the British body of laws. The third chapter explores these Sharia councils in the United Kingdom and their relationship to Islamic fundamentalism, before stating the consequences that these minority legal orders have for individuals.

This book revolves around the implications of the political ideologies of multiculturalism and Islamic fundamentalism. And, more specifically, what the interaction is between these ideologies, with reference to the debate on Sharia councils in the United Kingdom. Modern and multicultural states struggle to respond to these religious-political challenges to liberal democracy, deliberating whether or not individuals should be allowed a choice to resort to Sharia councils.

One opinion holds that society itself may be diverse and *multi*-cultural, the legal order that regulates should be *mono*-cultural.[7] The sixteenth-century French political philosopher Jean Bodin (1530-1596) conceptualised the modern sovereign state as having the exclusive right to make laws and execute them within its territory.[8] "The rights, obligations, and democratic procedure are non-negotiable as they are based on a single body of laws and one language", as professor of Jurisprudence Afshin Ellian (1966) contends as well.[9] The idea is that there should be "one law for all". In addition, individuals may have the liberty to hold or dismiss religious beliefs, but the state should ultimately not favour religion over non-religion or vice versa. In establishing a legal order that oversees the social order of the entire population equally, the state should be "agnostic" regarding religious issues.[10]

A third contender for a model for state-religion affairs is thus political agnosticism. Rather than mildly favouring one religion over other sets of belief (as is the case for model number 4, the state church doctrine), the state should not take positions on religious questions, not in its daily administration and not in its laws, nor in its constitution. Political agnosticism does not view religion as something that is good which deserves to be promoted, nor does it see it as a dangerous force that needs to be contained.[11] Since the state represents all citizens, individuals who are religiously divided yet united under the

---

7   Ellian, Afshin, 'Emancipation and Integration of Dutch Muslims in Light of a Process Polarization and the Threat of Political Islam', *Middle East Program Occasional Paper Series* Summer 2009, pp. 15-23 (19).

8   Bodin, Jean, *On Sovereignty. Four Chapters from the Six Books of the Commonwealth.* Edited and translated by Julian H. Franklin, Cambridge: Cambridge University Press 1992.

9   Ellian 2009, p. 19.

10 T.H. Huxley (1825-1895), who coined the term agnosticism, said: "Agnosticism is not a creed, but a method". Almost a hundred years later Bertrand Russell (1872-1970) stated about whether we can know whether there is a god, that "The agnostic suspends judgement, saying that there are not sufficient grounds for affirmation or for denial". See: Cliteur, Paul, *The Secular Outlook. In Defense of Moral and Political Secularism*, Chicester: Wiley-Blackwell 2010, pp. 57-59.

11 See also: Laycock, Douglas, 'Religious Liberty as Liberty', *Journal of Contemporary Legal Issues* 1996, pp. 313-356 (313-314).

nation-state, social order and justice is served best when a formal position of equality is supported through religiously neutral laws. Part of being politically agnostic is that the state does not take a position on the idea that religion, whether from an individual or communal point of view, contributes to a positive or negative life. The state simply "does not know" and is insensitive to claims that are detrimental for or made on behalf of any religion. It should not have an opinion because it is not the role of the state to have an opinion about religion, religious believers or religious communities.[12]

In 2013, I visited the United Kingdom to do research regarding Sharia Councils. I have conducted numerous open-ended interviews with academics, activists, lawyers, and with a member of the House of Lords, who initiated a bill to restrict the legal remit of these councils. I consulted a *Beth Din* – a rabbinical council, visited the Nuneaton-based Muslim Arbitration Tribunal and attended hearings at the Sharia council of the Birmingham Central Mosque and at the Islamic Sharia Council in London.

Sharia councils are not universally viewed as "problematic" and in fact Islamic fundamentalists themselves favour the existence of such institutions, choosing Sharia over democratically established laws. But there is another significant school of thought that sees Sharia councils as a possibility, rather than a problem. Take for instance former Archbishop Rowan Williams, who was the principal leader of the British Anglican Church in 2008 and Baron Nicholas Phillips of Worth Matravers, the most senior judge in England and Wales that same year. Both made high-impact speeches about how Muslim minorities should be accommodated in their need for legal institutions based on laws that follow from the Islamic religion.[13] This is centred on the notion that religion and membership of a community is so vital for one's wellbeing that it should be accommodated into a minority legal order. This forms the foundation of state-religion model number 3: the multiculturalist model. Where does this notion come from? What are the implications of this political ideology?

Firstly, I discuss the foundations of multiculturalism. In the second chapter, I introduce the basis of Islamic fundamentalism. Finally, I bring these ideologies together in a case-study on Sharia councils in the United Kingdom. The development of British Sharia

---

12 "An agnostic has no opinion on whether God exists, and neither should the government. But an agnostic also believes that humans are incapable of knowing whether God exists. If the government believed that, it would prefer agnostics over theists and atheists. Agnostics have no opinion for epistemological reasons; the government must have no opinion for constitutional reasons. The government must have no opinion because it is not the government's role to have an opinion." See: Laycock, Douglas, 'Equal Access and Moments of Silence: The Equal Status of Religious Speech by Private Speakers', *Northwestern University Law Review* 1986, pp. 1-67 (7-8).

13 Williams, Rowan, 'Civil and Religious Law in England: a Religious Perspective', 7 February 2008. Available online at <http://rowanwilliams.archbishopofcanterbury.org/articles.php/1137/> and Phillips, Nicholas, 'Equality before the Law', Keynote speech at the East London Muslim Centre, 3 July 2008. A transcript can be found in: Ahdar, Rex and Aroney, Nicholas (eds.), *Shari'a in the West*, Oxford: Oxford University Press 2010, pp. 309-318.

councils is the result of the combination of multiculturalism and Islamic fundamentalism. These political ideologies combined are especially interesting, for determining whether individuals should be supported in their religious identity and making conclusions about the attraction of religious fundamentalism.

From a methodical perspective, it is important to bear in mind that each chapter could well be transformed into a book in itself. To that end, the chapters do not "read" homogeneously. The first is an in-depth analysis, critiquing one of the central tenets of multiculturalism. For this purpose, I have chosen to highlight the work of leading multiculturalist philosophers, namely Charles Taylor, Will Kymlicka and Bhikhu Parekh. In the second chapter, I explore the elemental structure of Islamic fundamentalism and have selected authors and sources that best explain the political implications of this particular ideology. While the first chapter is very analytical, the second is quite descriptive and taken collectively, they form the groundwork for the final chapter. In addition to a descriptive and a critical analysis of Sharia councils in the United Kingdom, this chapter is the result of extensive fieldwork and evidence was gathered from interviews and observation.

1   THE MULTICULTURALIST IDEOLOGY

INTRODUCTION

In the past few years, multiculturalism has become a popular target for politicians. All over Europe, political leaders have been calling for the bankruptcy of the multiculturalist model. At that time opposition leader, David Cameron stated in 2008 that "State multiculturalism is a wrong-headed doctrine that has had disastrous results".[1] German Chancellor Angela Merkel held a speech in 2010 in which she stated that multiculturalism has "utterly failed".[2] In 2011, then French president Nicholas Sarkozy responded to a voter on television: "Oui, c'est un échec".[3] Former Spanish Prime Minister Jose Maria Aznar also said "I'm against the idea of multiculturalism. Multiculturalism divides our societies, debilitates our societies, multiculturalism does not produce tolerance, nor integration".[4]

The fact that so many political leaders deemed it necessary to criticise the political ideology or public philosophy of "multiculturalism" is remarkable and shows that it is seen as an important perspective. It is experienced as a way of thinking with pernicious consequences; if this was not the case, these important political leaders would not have deemed it necessary to publicly take such a stance. But what is also clear from these reactions is that it is unclear *what* exactly it is that they reject; none mention the nature of their specific reservations about multiculturalism. Do they even all reject the same aspect of it?

The word "multiculturalism" has many meanings. There are many interpretations of multiculturalism,[5] and the term has become a "buzzword, a crusade, and a gigantic mysti-

---

1   Sparrow, Andrew, 'Cameron attacks "State Multiculturalism"', *The Guardian* 26 February 2008, via <http://www.guardian.co.uk/politics/2008/feb/26/conservatives.race>.

2   Weaver, Matthew, 'Angela Merkel: German multiculturalism has "Utterly Failed"', *The Guardian* 17 October 2010, via <http://www.guardian.co.uk/world/2010/oct/17/angela-merkel-german-Multiculturalism-failed>.

3   ("Yes, it's a failure.") Agence France-Presse, 'Multiculturalism has failed, says French president', *Daily Motion* 11 February 2011, via <http://www.dailymotion.com/video/xgzqs8_Multiculturalism-has-failed-says-french-president_news>.

4   'Multiculturalism 'a big failure: Spain's ex-prime minister Aznar', 27 October 2006, via <http://www.freerepublic.com/focus/f-news/1726950/posts>.

5   And many there are, Steven Vertovec and Susanne Wessendorf mention varieties within multiculturalism: "as represented for instance by Charles Taylor (1992), Will Kymlicka (1995), Bhikhu Parekh (2000), Brian Barry (2001) (who takes a critical stance), Tariq Modood (2007) and Anne Phillips (2007). A divergent set of civic programs might be labeled as 'radical Multiculturalism' or 'polycentric Multiculturalism' (Shohat and Stam 1994), 'insurgent Multiculturalism' (Giroux 1994), 'public space Multiculturalism' (Vertovec 1996), 'difference Multiculturalism' (Turner 1993), 'critical Multiculturalism' (Chicago Cultural Studies Group 1994) 'weak' or 'strong' Multiculturalism (Grillo 2005). Indeed, Steven Vertovec (1998) has pointed to at least eight different kinds of Multiculturalism while Garard Delanty (2003) suggests another list with nine types of Multiculturalism." See: Vertovec, Steven and Wessendorf, Susanne, 'Introduction. Assessing the

fication".[6] Some use it to indicate no more than cultural variety. So "multiculturalism" is prevalent in e.g. Sydney, if that city is home to many people from different cultural backgrounds. Others use the word "multiculturalism" to indicate a *positive attitude* towards cultural plurality. So you are deemed to be a "multiculturalist" if you believe that a multitude of cultures in one society is something that deserves to be cherished. There is a bewildering variety of uses of the word and a concomitant variety of associations people have with it.

Canadian political philosopher Will Kymlicka (1962), best known for his work on multiculturalism,[7] discerns three patterns of multiculturalism. Firstly, that there is state recognition, or as he labels it, 'empowerment', of *indigenous people*, such as the Maori, Aboriginals or Inuit. Secondly, that there are forms of granting autonomy to *sub-state national groups*, such as Scots in Britain, Frisians in the Netherlands, and Germans in South Tyrol. Lastly, that there are forms of multiculturalist recognition for *immigrant groups*.[8] Kymlicka, as well as other Canadian multiculturalist philosophers such as Charles Taylor (1931), drew their inspiration from Indian minorities in Canada. That said, their work transcends the early focus on indigenous groups into modern multiculturalism as we know it in contemporary Western Europe regarding Islamic immigrants and subcultures. It is this variant that this book ultimately centres around.

This chapter outlines the origins of multiculturalism, analyses this ideology and critiques it. I refer to the ideology of multiculturalism as a *normative* stance. Multiculturalism in that sense does not *describe* anything but rather, *prescribes* a course of action which dictates how states and society should deal with religious and cultural differences. I will break down the definition and evaluate its underlying assumptions. I define multiculturalism is the widest way possible as referring to

> a broad array of theories, attitudes, beliefs, norms, practices, laws and policies that seek to provide public recognition of and support for accommodation of non-dominant ethnocultural/religious groups.[9]

Backlash against Multiculturalism in Europe', pp. 1-31 (2), in: Vertovec, Steven and Wessendorf, Susanne (eds.), *The Multiculturalism Backlash: European Discourses, Policies and Practices*, London: Routledge 2010.

6   Higham, John, 'Multiculturalism and Universalism: A History and Critique', *American Quarterly* 1993, pp. 195-219 (208).

7   See: Kymlicka, Will, *Multicultural Citizenship. A Liberal Theory of Minority Rights*, Clarendon Press, Oxford 1995. See also: Parekh, Bhikhu, *A New Politics of Identity: Political Principles for an Interdependent World*, Palgrave MacMillan, Houndmills 2008; Parekh, Bhikhu, *Rethinking Multiculturalism: Cultural Diversity and Political Theory*, Macmillan Press, Houndmills/London 2000; Taylor, Charles, 'The Politics of Recognition', in: Taylor, Charles, *Multiculturalism. Examining the Politics of Recognition*. Edited and introduced by Amy Gutman, Princeton University Press, Princeton, New Jersey 1994, pp. 25-75.

8   Kymlicka, Will, 'The Rise and Fall of Multiculturalism? New Debates on Inclusion and Accommodation in Diverse Societies', *International Social Science Journal* 2010, pp. 97–112 (101).

9   Ivison, Duncan, 'Introduction: Multiculturalism as a Public Ideal', p. 2, in: Ivison, Duncan (ed.), *The Ashgate Research Companion to Multiculturalism*, Surrey: Ashgate 2010. This definition is borrowed from Ivision,

The definition of multiculturalism falls into two categories; 1) theory and moral attitudes, including political viewpoints; and 2) laws, practices, and policies derived from theory and corresponding attitudes.[10] I focus on the first category. It is important, because although political leaders have now denounced multiculturalism as state practice, its underlying ideology is very much alive today.

According to psychologists Fowers and Richardson in *Why is Multiculturalism Good?* (1996), "[m]ulticulturalism is a social-intellectual movement that promotes the value of diversity as a core principle and insists that all cultural groups be treated with respect and as equals". Moreover, it is a moral movement that intends to enhance the dignity, rights, and recognised worth of presumably marginalised groups, "[…] inspired primarily by a moral perspective on human life that values diversity, tolerance, human rights, and authenticity".[11] American Israeli Professor of Law Amos Guiora (1957) asserts that multi-culturalism is – philosophically, morally, and practically – "an embrace, or at least, 'understanding', by society of different communities, ethnicities and religions living in the nation-state".[12] Importantly, it is a social-intellectual movement lifted to the status of a political ideology, which has permeated contemporary society.

One of the most important and well-known critiques of multiculturalism is put forward by Susan Moller Okin (1946-2004), who questioned the compatibility of multiculturalism with feminism. Okin writes that, initially, minority groups, both immigrants and indigenous people, were expected to assimilate into majority cultures. That expectation is now considered as "oppressive", and Western countries have shifted to devising policies that are more responsive to persistent cultural differences. Yet, one issue which recurs across all contexts had gone virtually unnoticed in current debates (at the time of Okin's publication in the 1990s): "what should be done when the claims of minority cultures or religions clash with the norm of gender equality that is at least formally endorsed by liberal states (however,

yet is expanded by the incorporation of the elements 'laws' and 'religion', so that the definition of Multicul-turalism refers to 'non-dominant ethnocultural/*religious* groups' and 'practices, *laws* and policies'.

10   Regarding laws, practices and policies, according to Kymlicka, multicultural citizenship for immigrant groups includes a combination of the following policies: "constitutional, legislative or parliamentary affirmation of Multiculturalism at central, regional and municipal levels; the adoption of Multiculturalism in school cur-riculum; the inclusion of ethnic representation and sensitivity in the mandate of public media or media licensing; exemptions from dress codes, Sunday closing legislation and so on (either by statute or by court cases); allowed dual citizenship; the funding of ethnic group organisations to support cultural activities; the funding of bilingual education or mother-tongue instruction; and affirmative action for disadvantaged immigrant groups". See: Kymlicka 2010, p. 101.

11   Fowers, Blaine and Richardson, Frank, "Why is Multiculturalism Good?", *American Psychologist* 1996, pp. 609-621 (609-610).

12   Guiora, Amos, *Tolerating Extremism. To What Extent Should Intolerance Be Tolerated?*, dissertation Leiden University 2014, p. 74, available via <https://openaccess.leidenuniv.nl/handle/1887/21977>.

much they continue to violate it in practices)?"[13] She lists several clashing practices, such as the wearing of the traditional Muslim headscarf and full-face veils, polygamy, female genital mutilation, or child marriage or marriages that are otherwise coerced.

But the multicultural debate is not limited to feminist issues. Other real and pressing issues concern, *inter alia*, home-grown Islamist terrorism, practical limits on free speech (for instance, the Danish cartoon crisis, the murder of Charlie Hebdo cartoonists), legal plurality in the form of Sharia councils, a rise in anti-Semitism (including terrorist attacks on Jews), violence against homosexuals, and segregated neighbourhoods where Sharia patrols enforce Sharia law. Among Islam-rooted immigrants and later generations, we see a high level of adherence to Islamic fundamentalism and a greater rate of radicalisation. We also read about fundamentalist Imams, the influx of Saudi funds for mosques and education and young Muslims joining Islamic State to fight a holy war, where they commit murder, torture, and rape.

Yet, these issues do not address the critique on multiculturalism from an *analytical* angle, but more from a *practical* perspective. Multiculturalism is thus criticised mostly because of the practical problems connected to the ideal. But let us rather start at the basis. It is first fundamentally important to question the *focus on minority culture* itself and second to question why culture is considered as something worthy of our respect as such. Next, I discuss identity theory and the 'politics of difference'. The second part of this chapter is an analysis of the premises which form the basis of multiculturalist ideology. To make the analysis more convincing, I have added a fictitious case of minorities struggling with tradition, modernity, and undesirable practices in the country of Sealandistan.

IDENTITY THEORY

I now examine whether it is possible to trace the origins of the focus on culture by defining culture. Multiculturalists have a different interpretation of culture than anthropologists.[14] Needless to say, definitions range widely within any scientific discipline, and cultural anthropology is no different.

Nineteenth-century anthropologist Sir Edward Burnett Tylor (1832-1917) wrote:

---

13   Okin, Susan Moller, "Is Multiculturalism Bad for Women?", pp. 7-24 (9), in: Cohen, Joshua, Howard, Matthew and Nussbaum, Martha (eds.), *Is Multiculturalism Bad For Women?*, Princeton: Princeton University Press 1999.

14   See also: Turner, Terence, 'Anthropology and Multiculturalism: What is Anthropology That Multiculturalists Should Be Mindful of It?', *Cultural Anthropology* 1993, pp. 411-429 (412).

Culture or civilization, taken in its wide ethnographic sense, is that complex
whole which includes knowledge, beliefs, art, morals, laws, customs and any
other capabilities and habits acquired by man as a member of society.[15]

This definition, devised by Tylor in his 1871 book *Primitive Cultures*, is taken at the moment
the term culture came into play the way we are used to nowadays.[16] Later, anthropologists
included *shared values* in the definition of culture. A value is defined as "[...] an enduring
belief that a specific mode of conduct or end-state of existence is personally or socially
preferable to an opposite or converse mode of conduct or end-state of existence".[17] Values
are said to be acquired early in life, through family, environments, and school. Most
anthropologists would nowadays define culture as

[...] the shared set of (implicit and explicit) values, ideas, concepts, and rules
of behaviour that allow a social group to function and perpetuate itself. Rather
than simply the presence or absence of a particular attribute, culture is understood as the dynamic and evolving socially constructed reality that exists in the
minds of social group members. It is the 'normative glue' that allows group
members to communicate and work effectively together.[18]

It is the task of anthropologists to identify a group's culture in order to understand how
one's culture influences the way the world is perceived. This field of science concerns itself
with culture, the definition of culture and other aspects of it. Description is an end in itself,
which has no normative basis, no emancipation agenda and no political goals, nor an aim
for social change or cultural transformation. The choice of anthropologists to study culture
needs no explanation, much like biologists do not need to explain why they study flora
and fauna. Multiculturalists, on the other hand, fuse the study of minority cultures with
a political agenda.[19] Why is minority culture 'the chosen one', out of everything that forms
and influences individual experience? Is it really that self-evident as multiculturalist
philosophers would have us think? There are several ways to address this question and
one can *trace back* the origins of singling out minority culture, to *justify* this particular
focus.

---

15   Tylor, Edward, *Primitive Culture*, London: John Murray, Albemarle Street 1871, p. 1.
16   Straub, Detmar *et al.*, 'Toward a Theory-Based Measurement of Culture', *Journal of Global Information
     Management* 2002, pp. 13-23 (14).
17   See: Rokeach, Milton, *The Nature of Human Values*, New York, NY: Free Press 1973, p. 5, quoted in: Straub
     2002, p. 14-15.
18   Hudelson, Patricia, 'Culture and Quality: An Anthropological Perspective', *International Journal for Quality
     in Health Care* 2004, pp. 345-346 (345).
19   See also: Turner 1993, p. 412.

The idea of the unique value of cultures stems from the ideal of authenticity, which in turn is strongly influenced by the 18th-century German Romantic philosopher Johann Gottfried von Herder (1744-1803).[20] While earlier philosophers had tried to explain the phenomenon of difference, Herder was the one who accepted, and celebrated, diversity.[21] Bhikhu Parekh (1935), Indian-born British multiculturalist philosopher, writes on this:

> For Herder, the influence of culture permeated the individual's ways of thinking, feeling and judging, food, clothes, bodily gestures, way of talking, manner of holding himself or herself together, pleasures, pains, values, ideal, dreams, nightmares, forms of imagination, and aesthetic and moral sensibilities. Human beings felt at home and realized their potential only within their own culture and were awkward and profoundly disoriented outside of it, which is why Europeans, who displayed great civic virtues at home, often behaved with uncharacteristic brutality when travelling or living abroad. Not surprisingly every community 'holds firmly' to its culture and seeks to transmit it across generations 'without any break'. Its commitment to its culture was based not on rational conviction or utilitarian considerations but 'prejudice', an unquestioning and grateful acceptance of its inheritance accompanied by pride and confidence in its value. Prejudice 'returns people to their centre [and] attaches them more solidly to their roots'. Since no man could be human outside his cultural community, membership of it was a basic human need just as much as food and psychical security.
>
> All Cultures, for Herder, were unique expressions of the human spirit, incommensurable and, like flowers in the garden, beautifully complementing each other and adding to the richness of the world.[22]

Herder believed that individuals could only be 'truly human' if they were 'true to themselves'. "All peoples must be allowed to unfold toward their unique destinies, which requires resisting external pressure and other inducements to mimic and thereby become derivatives of another culture". His rejection of the ideal of individual equality has, indeed, been a guiding principle for the development of group identity.[23]

Identity theory is a result from that Herderian 'ideal of authenticity'. Sigmund Freud (1856-1939) formulated identity as the connection of an individual with the unique values

---

20 There are of course many more writers of influence, such as Jean-Jacques Rousseau (1712-1778), but Herder, who is taken as one of the founding fathers of nationalism, is considered the most important one.

21 Malik, Kenan, *Strange Fruit: Why Both Sides are Wrong in the Race Debate* (2008), Oxford: Oneworld 2008 (2009), p. 123.

22 Parekh 2000, p. 69.

23 See also: Fowers & Richardson 1996, p. 613.

which are fostered by a unique history of a people (he referred to Judaism). He mentioned it only loosely and did not tie it to any specific race or religion. Freud's disciple, German born American Erik Erikson (1902-1994) wrote this on the matter:

> It is this identity of something in the individual's core with an essential aspect of a group's inner coherence which is under consideration here: for the young individual must learn to be most himself where he means most to others – those others, to be sure, who have come to mean most to him. The term identity expresses such a mutual relation in that it connotes both a persistent sameness within oneself (self-sameness) and a persistent sharing of some kind of essential character with others.[24]

Erikson combined Freud's focus on the internal psyche ('personal identity') with a socio-logical approach ('social identity'). American researcher Seth Schwartz summarises these 'Eriksonian' concepts, claiming that personal identities are

> [...] the set of goals, values, and beliefs that one shows to the world. Personal identity includes career goals, dating preferences, word choices, and other aspects of self that identify an individual as someone in particular and that help to distinguish him or her from other people. [...] [S]ocial identity was identified as a sense of inner solidarity with a group's ideals, the consolidation of elements that have been integrated into one's sense of self from groups to which one belongs. [...] Aspects of self, such as native language, country of origin, and racial background would fall under the heading of group identity.[25]

'Identity theory', which is significant for the ideology of multiculturalism, has its origin in the American Civil Rights movement. From the 1890s onward, African Americans had been challenging the 'Jim Crow laws', laws which were devised to segregate blacks and whites when using public facilities, such as housing, medical care, public transport and schools. The 1896 landmark *Plessy v. Ferguson* case, in which the United States Supreme Court confirmed the *'separate but equal'* doctrine and thus reaffirmed the Fourteenth Amendment on citizen rights and equal protection laws, allowed states to uphold segrega-tion along the lines of race, provided that the quality of each group's public facilities was equal. In the case at hand, Homer Plessy (who was 7/8 white and 1/8 black) challenged his arrest after he refused to vacate his seat on a whites-only car of a train in New Orleans, as

---

24   Erikson, Erik, 'The Problem of Ego Identity', *Journal of the American Psychoanalytic Association* 1956, pp. 56-121 (56-57).
25   Schwartz, Seth, 'The Evolution of Eriksonian and Neo-Eriksonian Identity Theory and Research: A Review and Integration', Identity. An *International Journal of Theory and Research* 2001, pp. 7-58 (10).

the Louisiana state law required from him. The Supreme Court denied his appeal, stating that: "The object of the (Fourteenth) amendment was undoubtedly to enforce the equality of the two races before the law, but in the nature of things it could not have been intended to abolish distinctions based upon color, or to endorse social, as distinguished from political, equality (…) If one race be inferior to the other socially, the Constitution of the United States cannot put them upon the same plane."[26] From this we see that social inequality was used to justify legal and political segregation.

It was not until 1954 that a major achievement of African American emancipation was accomplished when the US Supreme Court ruled after the *Brown v. Board of Education* case that laws which enabled race segregation in schools were unconstitutional. Segregation in education was deemed to violate the 'equal protection clause' of the Fourteenth Amendment and did away with the 'separate but equal' doctrine. Following the spirit of the *Brown v. Board of Education* judgement, racial integration was now not only *legally* required, but largely *morally* required, even though it took decades more to abolish the Jim Crow laws. Yet, it was this event that deemed separatism incompatible with the innate equality of individuals.[27]

A year after *Brown*, an influential speaker delivered an address at America's oldest and most influential black history organisation of the day, the Association for the Study of Negro Life and History. He stated that *real* integration "[…] required changed minds as well as changed laws", and "legal gains and favorable court decisions […] cannot complete the work that must be done," he declared. "The spirit of legal justice must permeate the undercurrents of community life."[28]

An illustration of African Americans demanding equality is found in the 'textbook' problem. In the 1960s, 'pro-Black' activists lamented the content of educational material, either portraying coloured people as simple, ignorant individuals or excluding African Americans and black history altogether. Just as segregated classrooms, racist textbooks were considered to corrode "[…] Black self-concept, Black self-identification, and especially Black self-esteem." If textbooks did not provide a positive image of African Americans, Black children would continue to suffer from a sense of racial inferiority.[29] The campaign was successful; racist slurs were removed and new material about African Americans was added. Some activists even demanded the insertion of historical material that celebrated the 'gifts' of ethnic groups, and sometimes pressed for the inclusion of positive misrepresentations in the curriculum. This had the unintended consequence that some white con-

---

26 "History of Brown v. Board of Education", http://www.uscourts.gov/educational-resources/get-involved/federal-court-activities/brown-board-education-re-enactment/history.aspx.

27 See also: Wilkinson III, Harvie J., 'The Law of Civil Rights and the Dangers of Separatism in Multiculturalist America', *Stanford Law Review* 1995, pp. 993-1026 (994-995).

28 Zimmerman, Jonathan, 'Brown-ing the American Textbook: History, Psychology, and the Origins of Modern Multiculturalism', *History of Education Quarterly* 2004, pp. 46-69 (59).

29 Zimmerman 2004, pp. 47-48.

servatives demanded that negative material about their own past causing harm to *their* mental health, be excluded.[30] "So did every other racial and ethnic group, each seeking its own immaculate stripe in the multiculturalist rainbow. The result was a curriculum that celebrated "race" and "diversity" but downplayed racism."[31] This 'textbook revolution' aimed to create and protect African American nascent identity and the new 'identity politics' was deeply rooted in the belief that public problems should be defined in terms of individual mental health: "Prefiguring many multiculturalists today, textbook activists defined their politics along racial or ethnic lines in order to make each individual feel fixed, grounded, and proud."[32]

The idea of an extolled Black identity was fueled by intellectuals and community leaders, such as author and activist W.E.B. Du Bois (1868-1963), who inspired African Americans to embrace their African heritage. The idea that African Americans would not find equality with white Americans until a separate black community had been successfully built was elevated by Malcolm X and others. "Black power" became a new political agenda, and even though originally founded on the negative identity of cruel chattel slavery and racist violence, new phrases were adopted, such as "Black is beautiful" and "soul brother". Black power, a phrase originally coined by activist Stokely Carmichael (1941-1998), was defined as "a call for black people in this country to unite, to recognise their heritage, and to build a sense of community." To become "[…] an effective political force in the United States, […] blacks must achieve "self-identity" and "self-determination" as a group, not as individuals. The result would be a rising black consciousness or "an attitude of brotherly, communal responsibility among all black people for one another."[33] Thus, where *Brown* was founded on the conviction that skin colour and ethnicity were *irrelevant* in making public or private decisions, racial status was now back on the agenda. It was more and more used to *justify* public and private preferences in favour of African Americans, such as affirmative action, regarding different university admission standards or hiring and tenure procedures.[34] This was a paradoxical development, to be sure. Also, this 'identity politics' was not merely reserved for black Americans, as Native Americans, Latinos, Asian Americans and other groups appealed for inclusion within civil rights discourse as well. By using group identity discourse, community leaders established a sense of shared cultural values based on history, descent, and ethnicity. Membership of these separate subgroups led to certain entitlements, such as 'recognition' in a wider sense and changes in laws, policies and judicial decisions.[35] Moreover, social transformation itself was part of the

---

30   "If every individual retained the right to a "positive image," after all, no text could introduce a negative truth about anyone – including White people.", see: Zimmerman 2004, p. 68.
31   Zimmerman 2004, p. 50.
32   Zimmerman 2004, p. 68.
33   Herman, Arthur, *The Idea of Decline in Western History*, New York: The Free Press 1997, pp. 376-377.
34   Wilkinson III 1995, p. 1015.
35   Glazer, Nathan, *We Are All Multiculturalists Now*, Cambridge: Harvard University Press 1998, pp. 51-52.

political agenda. In *Strange Fruit: Why Both Sides are Wrong in the Race Debate*, British author Kenan Malik (1960) writes:

> Soon not just blacks but everyone had an identity that was uniquely theirs and separated them not only from the white man but from every other kind of man, too, and indeed from Man in general. Using the template established by Black Power activists, Native Americans, Puerto Ricans, Chicanos, Chinese Americans, not to mention myriad white ethnics, set up their separate cultural organisations. Women and gays became surrogate ethnics, each with their own particular cultures, identities and ways of thinking. 'The demand is not for the inclusion within the fold of "universal humankind" on the basis of shared human attributes; nor is it respect "in spite of one's differences", [...]. 'Rather, what is demanded is respect for oneself *as* different'. At the heart of the new politics of identity was the claim that one's political beliefs and ways of thinking should be derived from the fact of one's birth, sex or ethnic origins, a claim that, historically radicals would have regarded as highly reactionary and that lay at the heart of racial ideology. Yet, by the end of the 1960s, it was not the expression of identity but the language of commonality that [...] 'came to be perceived by the new movements as a colonialist smothering – an ideology to rationalise white dominance'.[36]

American sociologist Nathan Glazer (1923), author of *We Are All Multiculturalists Now* (1998), locates the abandonment of the ideal of assimilation in the failure of integration of blacks in American society, making them the 'storm troops' of the battles of multiculturalism in the United States.[37] It is actually the *lack of integration* that has inspired multiculturalism as a political doctrine. The idea is that if minorities do not fit in, the least we can do is praise them in words.

Writing at the time of the Civil Rights Movement, psychoanalyst Erikson warned against the development of a negative group identity, chosen for by young people who feel socially or personally marginalised within religious, ethnic and economic structures. He believed that the theory of identity could be useful when dealing with youngsters turning their negative energy into becoming "[...] exactly what the careless and fearful community expects him to be [...]".[38] This sounds familiar to us now. Regarding immigrants in modern day society, Canadian multiculturalist Will Kymlicka argues: "Without some proactive policies to promote mutual understanding and respect and to make immigrants feel

---

36 Malik 2008 (2009), p. 186.
37 Glazer 1998, p. 95 and 120. See also: Kristol, Irving, "The Tragedy of Multiculturalism", in: Kristol, Irving, *Neo-conservatism*. Selected Essays 1949-1995, New York: The Free Press, pp. 50-53 (51).
38 Erikson 1956, pp. 56-121 (118-119).

comfortable in mainstream institutions, these factors could quickly lead to a situation of a racialised underclass, standing in permanent opposition to the larger society".[39]

The inescapability of diverging cultures becomes particularly salient when individuals are confronted with another group's different culture and have to live together on a shared territory (hence *multi*culture). This is for instance the case with (mass) migration. Cultural diversity leads to a cultural awareness that would have been absent if it were a monoculture. Yet, one can still make a case for *integration* within the majority culture of the host society. Within multiculturalist thinking, however, this demands the unjustifiable sacrifice of one's cultural *identity*. In the aftermath of the Civil Rights Movement, the West gradually embraced the concept of minority identity and its consequential entitlements as something that could just not be denied. 'Recognition' of one's separate identity based on non-chosen factors, such as sex, sexuality, heritage, or ethnicity, and ultimately even *chosen* factors, such as religion, have become a *moral imperative*.

FROM IDENTITY THEORY TO A 'POLITICS OF DIFFERENCE'

The Civil Rights Movement and subsequent legislation (e.g. affirmative action) was 'identity politics in action'. The moral imperative of 'accommodating difference' entered the legal and political sphere. One of the most acclaimed political philosophers known for their work on multiculturalism is Charles Taylor, who emphasises the importance of recognition of culture for one's wellbeing.[40] In the opening lines of his essay 'The Politics of Recognition' (1994), he asserts

> The thesis is that our identity is partly shaped by recognition or its absence,
> often by the *mis*recognition of others, and so a person or group of people can
> suffer real damage, real distortion, if the people or society around them mirror
> back to them a confining or demeaning or contemptible picture of themselves.
> Nonrecognition or misrecognition can inflict harm, can be a form of oppression,
> imprisoning someone in a false, distorted, and reduced mode of being.[41]

This idea is grounded in the conviction that minority groups are authentic and unique and have a right to non-interference on their unique path to development. Individual

---

39   Kymlicka 2010, p. 109.

40   Who in turn was inspired by German philosopher Georg Wilhelm Friedrich Hegel (1770-1831). Hegel emphasised that recognition be the foundation of human conduct. See: Fennema, Meindert, *Van Thomas Jefferson tot Pim Fortuyn. Balans van de Democratie* (From Thomas Jefferson to Pim Fortuyn. Democracy's Balance), Apeldoorn: Spinhuis Uitgevers 2012, p. 98, 265.

41   Taylor 1994, p. 25. Italics in original.

members of these subgroups living in a nation with a dominant majority should be free from the imposition of majority norms and standards.

By now, we have identified two powerful moral foundations of multiculturalism. First, which results from the Civil Rights Movement, is the ideal of opposing racism, discrimination, and oppression endured by members of minority groups, perceived as weak, and caused by a dominant majority. (For instance, Jewish and Mormon minorities are not perceived as weak despite their status as minority group.) Second, we have the notion of recognising the uniqueness of individuals and cultures, and the right to follow one's unique path to self-realisation within that particular culture. These two moral foundations are tied together in the multiculturalist aim of *reducing suffering*. 'Celebrating difference' should be the norm, rather than ignoring difference. This implies exalting and exaggerating personal traits that do not belong to the domain of the majority American-European, white, heterosexual, (male) culture, which is considered oppressive. This approval of minority identity is considered vital for one's self-realisation, but even beyond the realm of discrimination, 'misrecognition' of one's identity in itself "[...] shows not just a lack of due respect. It can inflict a grievous wound, saddling its victims with a crippling self-hatred. Due recognition is not just a courtesy we owe people. It is a vital human need",[42] and "[e]veryone should be recognised for his or her unique identity".[43]

Everyone's uniqueness logically implies difference between individuals, or groups of individuals, and assimilation to or being ignored by the dominant or majority identity is considered "[...] the cardinal sin against the ideal of authenticity".[44] This uniqueness, it follows, should not merely be recognised, but also politically and institutionally accommodated through a *politics of difference*. Multiculturalist philosopher Bhikhu Parekh writes in *A New Politics of Identity* (2008), that he believes that "marginalised or denigrated groups" have poor self-respect and sometimes even suffer from self-hatred. It is not enough to merely enjoy equal rights, opportunities and access to requisite resources. Individuals "[...] need a sense of self-worth and self-respect if they are going to overcome the passivity and self-doubt generated by crippling self-images".[45] And, Parekh continues:

> [a]s Charles Taylor correctly observes, social recognition is central to the individual's identity and self-worth and misrecognition can gravely damage both. [...] Misrecognition, therefore, can only be countered by undertaking *a rigorous*

---

42 Ibid, p. 26.
43 Ibid, p. 38. Italics in original.
44 Ibid. Italics in original. Herder was actually blind to *individual* uniqueness. He espoused the idea of the diversity of cultures, not of diversity *within* cultures. See: Parekh 2000, p. 73.
45 Parekh 2008, pp. 48-49.

critique of the dominant culture and radically restructuring the prevailing inequalities of economic and political power.[46]

This lifts multiculturalism to the level of political ideology. Not denting self-respect is a wider social and political goal in itself, and one's self-respect is taken to depend on the opinions held by a nation's majority of Euro-American culture bearers. Taylor is aware that while a *politics of equal dignity* – the "old system", one could say – requires non-discrimination in the form of difference-blindness, the *politics of difference* actually defines non-discrimination as something that requires making individual and group distinctions the basis of *differential* treatment.[47] One particular example of this is affirmative action. This emancipatory program is for people whose heritage used to mount to discrimination and instead provides them with advantages on, for instance, the job market or educational access. Taylor is also aware that the politics of difference could be taken to violate the principle of non-discrimination. But, the author continues, the politics of equal dignity "[…] negates identity by forcing people in a homogenous mold that is untrue to them".

It is considered even more adverse that the mould is not a "neutral set of difference-blind principles", but a representation of the hegemonic culture. In reality, in a politics of equal dignity only minority or suppressed cultures are forced to adapt to its structure.[48] Taylor claims that such a difference-blind basis is inhospitable to difference and that a uniform treatment should make place for a system that acknowledges the demand of recognition of the equal value of all cultures: "[…] that we not only let them survive, but acknowledge their *worth*".[49] Multiculturalism, Taylor claims, extends the principles that the 'politics of equal respect' already established: "Just as all must have equal civil rights, and equal voting rights, regardless of race or culture, so all should enjoy the presumption that their traditional culture has value".[50] Parekh agrees that the value of a collective identity manifests itself in self-worth and social standing, in the sense of common belonging and collective empowerment, a moral anchor, and concludes that "[a] theory of politics that ignores this has only a limited appeal".[51] From the perspective of the five constitutional models that offer a way to deal with state and religion, it becomes clear that Parekh and

---

46   Parekh, Bhikhu, 'What is Multiculturalism?' Seminar Contribution (Multiculturalism: a symposium on democracy in culturally diverse societies), December 1999, via <http://www.india-seminar.com/1999/484/484%20parekh.htm>. [italics added]

47   Taylor 1994, p. 39.

48   Taylor 1994, p. 43.

49   Taylor 1994, p. 63-64. Italics in original.

50   Taylor 1994, p. 68.

51   Parekh 2008, p. 50. Although he does pay attention to the dangers of collective identity, such as "essentializing" identity and imposing a unity of views that is not shared by "all women, gay people, black people and Muslims"; see p. 35.

Taylor believe that the state should play an active role in acknowledging the worth of minority identity, rather than remaining agnostic towards it.

Culture is therefore a source of the *good*, and even when it encompasses undesirable practices, 'culture' deserves our respect as an abstract concept. Not just 'culture', but cultures (plural), and the many different lifestyles that different cultures offer humans, need to be respected. Bhikhu Parekh denounces the idea of 'moral and cultural monism' in his book *Rethinking Multiculturalism* (2000). Monism, he asserts, promises there is "[...] only one correct or best way to understand human existence and lead the good life".[52] He states that whilst different cultures present their members with different systems of meaning and visions of the good life, that does not follow that cultures cannot be compared and judged, nor that each culture is equally good for its members, nor does it mean that all cultural differences need to be valued. Culture can be best changed from within, as well as through a process of 'cultural dialogue' or 'intercultural dialogue'.[53]

Will Kymlicka, who is just like Charles Taylor a renowned Canadian multiculturalist philosopher, agrees with the foundations of the theory as espoused in Taylor's essay 'The Politics of Recognition'. Like Taylor, Kymlicka's work starts off with a focus on indigenous people; previously self-governing, territorially concentrated cultures such as Indians in Canada. Notwithstanding, the propositions he uses for indigenous people later develop into a multiculturalist ideology that fits immigrant minority cultures as well. In his book *Multicultural Citizenship* (1996), he laments traditional human rights thinking with its foundation of difference-blindness:

> Some liberals, particularly on the right, think it is counterproductive to pursue a 'colour-blind' society through policies that 'count by race'. Affirmative action, they argue, exacerbates the very problem it was intended to solve, by making people more conscious of group differences, and more resentful of other groups. This dispute amongst liberals over the need for remedial affirmative action programmes is a familiar one in many liberal democracies. But what most post-war liberals on both the right and left continue to reject is the idea of permanent differentiation in the rights or status of the members of certain groups. In particular, they reject the claim that group-specific rights are needed to

---

52 Parekh 2000, p. 47.

53 See: Parekh 2000, pp. 336-337. One of many definitions and purposes of international dialogue is given by the United Nations: 'Equitable exchange and dialogue among civilizations, cultures and peoples, based on mutual understanding and respect and the equal dignity of all cultures is the essential prerequisite for constructing social cohesion, reconciliation among peoples and peace among nations.' See: <http://www.unesco.org/new/en/culture/themes/dialogue/intercultural-dialogue/>. The idea that culture is best changed "from within" (and not by "outsiders") stands firm among multiculturalists. Yet, it is odd that attention to cultural "dissidents" is seldom brought forward by these thinkers.

accommodate enduring cultural differences, rather than remedy historical discrimination.[54]

Kymlicka opposes post-war liberals who do not agree with the notion that specific ethnic or national groups should be given a permanent political identity or an adjusted (legal) status. He believes that majoritarian decision-making renders cultural minorities vulnerable to significant injustice at the hands of the majority, which will exacerbate ethnocultural conflict.[55] A larger political, institutionalised structure is needed to *preserve* minority culture and protect it against the homogenising forces of the majority culture within a state. Besides peaceful co-existence as a multiculturalist goal, it is the importance of cultural membership for developing and sustaining self-identity, as well as individual wellbeing, that is the driving force behind Kymlicka's reasoning. In *Liberalism, Community and Culture* (1989), he writes that individuals make life choices from a spectrum of alternatives offered to us through a cultural framework. "People make choices about the social practices around them, based on their beliefs about the value of these practices (beliefs which, I have noted, may be wrong[56]). And to have a belief about the value of a practice is, in the first instance, a matter of understanding the meanings attached to it by our culture".[57] Each individual needs to feel a sense of security from the cultural framework(s) from which he makes his choices, he argues.[58] Practically, this implies that immigrants, who wish to isolate themselves from the majority culture, should be granted that space through non-discrimination policies and anti-prejudice measures, such as positive portrayals in textbooks and government materials. They are also morally entitled to legal exemptions, such as Sunday-closing exemptions for Jews and Muslims and exemption from restrictive helmet legislations for Sikhs. Regarding language development, Kymlicka is convinced that a unilingual focus – a focus on adopting the native language of the state – is harmful to members of minority cultures, "cutting them off unnecessarily from their heritage". It is also considered to be counterproductive from an integration perspective, as well as bordering on racism.[59] The old-fashioned approach to minority rights, meaning the lack of them:

---

54 Kymlicka 1995, p. 4.
55 Kymlicka 1995, pp. 4-5.
56 This is also part of Kymlicka's quote.
57 Kymlicka 1995, p. 83.
58 Kymlicka, Will, *Liberalism, Community and Culture*, Oxford: Oxford University Press 1989, p. 169, in: Waldron, Jeremy, 'Minority Cultures and the Cosmopolitan Alternative', *University of Michigan Journal of Law Reform* 1991, pp. 751-793 (786). See also: Taylor, Charles, *Sources of the Self. The Making of the Modern Identity*, Cambridge: Harvard University Press 1989.
59 "Moreover, there is an undercurrent of racism in the traditional attitude towards immigrant languages". See: Kymlicka 1995, pp. 96-97.

[…] has often been guilty of ethnocentric assumptions, or of over-generalizing particular cases, or of conflating contingent political strategy with enduring moral principle. This is reflected in the wide range of policies liberal states have historically adopted regarding ethnic and national groups, ranging from coercive assimilation to coercive segregation, from conquest and colonization to feder-alism and self-government. The result has often been grave injustices against the ethnic and national minorities in many Western democracies. But the failure to develop a consistent and principled approach to minority rights may have even greater costs in the newly emerging democracies. At present, the fate of ethnic and national groups around the world is in the hand of xenophobic nationalists, religious extremists, and military dictators.[60]

Respecting minority cultures is therefore not only the proper way to go about, as 'a moral right to authenticity' for people to become their selves (self-realisation), but it also serves another purpose, namely not endangering the lives of minority individuals under majority rule. Bhikhu Parekh, like Kymlicka, highlights several civil wars in the final pages of his book to illustrate the importance of multicultural citizenship.[61]

To summarise. Earlier, I asked the question 'Why focus on culture'? Herder had an important influence on the idea that we should value and celebrate cultural uniqueness as it is taken as vital to one's wellbeing. Freudian psychological theory – which is also from the Romantic era – established the notion of identity and argued it is 'important', making it a marker within psychology. Regarding culture, multiculturalist philosopher Charles Taylor asserted:

> [O]ne could argue that it is reasonable to suppose that cultures that have pro-vided the horizon of meaning for large numbers of human beings, of diverse characters and temperaments, over a long period of time – that have, in other words, articulated their sense of the good, the holy, the admirable – are almost certain to have something that deserves our admiration and respect, even if it is accompanied by much that we have to abhor and reject.[62]

Thus, as researchers Sniderman and Hagendoorn summarise Taylor's argument in *When Ways of Life Collide: Multiculturalism and its Discontents in the Netherlands* (2007):

---

60 Kymlicka 1995, p. 195.
61 Parekh 2000, p. 343.
62 Taylor 1994, pp. 72-73.

> People cannot flourish, the argument for multiculturalism runs, unless they
> can become who they truly and fully are. They – we – are not isolated atoms,
> each complete by himself or herself. We belong to larger communities, each
> with its customs, accomplishments, memories of what was, and images of what
> should be. For people to realize their full worth, they must appreciate the worth
> of their collective identity; still more, the majority-culture bearers they live in
> must recognise the full worth of their collective identity.[63]

Individuals have a moral right to authenticity, and not being able to live your life according
to the practices and beliefs of one's own (minority) culture is considered harmful to wellbeing. That is multiculturalism from a psychological perspective. From a political and
societal point of view, it is the multiculturalist objective to avoid a social division between
first- and second-class citizens, a division which is supposedly the result from misrecognition of minority cultures. Multiculturalism is an emancipatory project, aimed to relieve
minorities from the interference or dominance of the majority culture of the host society.
And, this ideology should deter the majority from persecuting minorities, to keep them
out of the hands of malignant leaders.

The multiculturalist political ideology gained formal currency as academia took it up,
as governments began to formalise its ideas in programs, and the "chattering classes"
adopted its views as Islam and Muslims became more salient in Western nations. It is
important we take it seriously and analyse and critique it.

BREAKING DOWN MULTICULTURALISM

In his article 'Why respect culture?' (2000), political scientist James Johnson questions the
special normative weight given to particularistic claims of cultural communities in our
political judgements and deliberation. He argues that many political philosophers, such
as Charles Taylor, Bhikhu Parekh, and Will Kymlicka, urge for the respect of culture up
to the extent of pursuing policies and designing institutions that actively promote and
protect cultural commitments. Yet, as Johnson states, these and other multiculturalist
philosophers and their discussants, simply presume that we should do so, without providing
convincing arguments what the moral reasons are for respecting culture in any direct
sense.[64] I subscribe to that judgement, and I would like to add that the works of these
authors, not seldom demonstrate a lack of clarity and coherence. Claims are posed and

---

63   Sniderman, Paul and Hagendoorn, Aloysius, *When Ways of Life Collide: Multiculturalism and its Discontents
     in the Netherlands*, Princeton: Princeton University Press 2007, p. 5.
64   Johnson, James, 'Why Respect Culture?', *American Journal of Political Science* 2000, pp. 405-418 (405).

one sentence later mitigated to a degree they basically counter the prior claims. Take for instance Kymlicka's view on the need for immigrants to integrate into the host society:

> The expectation of integration is not unjust, I believe, so long as immigrants had the option to stay in their original culture. Given the connection between choice and culture which I sketched earlier, people should be able to live and work in their own culture. But like any other right, this right can be waived, and immigration is one way of waiving one's right. In deciding to uproot themselves, immigrants voluntarily relinquish some of the rights that go along with their original national membership.[65]

We can distil Claim 1: Immigrants should be able to stay in their own culture. Claim 2: Immigrants' rights to stay in their own culture can be waived. How should the reader decide what is best according to the author? To echo philosopher Jeremy Waldron (1953): let us see "[…] how much substance there would be if various *determinate* communitarian claims were taken one by one, and their proponents were forced to abandon any reliance on vagueness and equivocation. In the end, that is the best way to evaluate the array of different meanings that are evoked in this literature".[66]

The objections to the foundation of multiculturalism can be formulated more easily once the theory is broken down into premises. These form the foundation of this political ideology:

1. Who someone authentically is, is given by his minority cultural identity.
2. Nonrecognition of this cultural identity constitutes psychological harm.
3. Culture is good.
4. Cultures are equal.
5. Cultural differences are good, but if not, they should at least be tolerated.
6. Minority cultures must not be criticised by the dominant culture which has the positive obligation to preserve these.

These premises of multiculturalism are primarily based on the theories of, Will Kymlicka, and Bhikhu Parekh, who I take as exemplary for multiculturalist thinking. They are part of a much larger socio-intellectual movement and political ideology that is multiculturalism. The following analysis on the doctrine of multiculturalism thus goes beyond these three thinkers. Like every comprehensive political ideology, its adherents and contributors

---

65 Kymlicka 1995, p. 96.
66 Waldron 1991, p. 757.

occasionally differ in opinion, demonstrate nuances, and can even mutually disagree. Nonetheless, in general, these six premises are the basis of multiculturalism.

Inspired by "practical ethics"[67], I present the reader with the fictitious case of the *Blueskins* and *Greenskins* living in Sealandistan. I hope that after at least 25 years of multiculturalist sensitivities a fresh case of cultural twists can open the mind for healthy judgement.

In the beautiful country of Sealandistan live two cultural communities: the Blueskins and the Greenskins. Blueskins value animal welfare. In fact they take great pride in it, and are hurt, shocked and offended when others don't. Therefore, all Blueskins treat all animals with great care. The Blueskins are also very satisfied with their loving attitude toward the elderly: traditionally, citizens over the age of 90 are administered a pill ending their lives. This way, the elderly will not grow any older stuck with bodily malfunctioning, worries about their upcoming death and being left to reminisce about the days which were, feeling lonely. They share their nation with the Greenskins. The Greenskins value life like nothing else, and are very much disturbed by the way the Blueskins, as they see it, "murder" their elderly and are frightened they will be required to follow that practice in the future. Luckily, they can relax a bit during their "feast of animal kicking". This festivity takes place every third Saturday of the month, when Greenskins assemble animals on village squares. Under the tunes of folklore music and the company of friends and family, they take turns kicking animals until the creatures die. The Greenskins take great pride in participating at the feast of animal kicking. It confirms their heritage, from which they draw cultural pride and a sense of belonging. Most would be hurt, shocked and offended if the Blueskins would make them abandon this practice.

We will occasionally come back to *Sealandistan*, but now we return to the ideology of multiculturalism.

---

67 "Instead of relying on an abstract theory to systematise and clarify these perceptions in practical deliberations, Aristotle recommends using a variety of less technical approaches to moral inquiry. For instance, in the *Rhetoric* he extols the power of well crafted narratives to engage our cognitive and affective sensibilities in a way that links the morally relevant features of a particular case to our existing moral commitments. He also extols the power of examples and analogies to highlight the way that appearances of value that emerge in one context are relevant to more controversial cases in which their presence or significance may not be as readily evident." See: London, Alex John, "The Independence of Practical Ethics", *Theoretical Medicine and Bioethics* 2001, pp. 87-105 (101-102).

1. WHO SOMEONE AUTHENTICALLY IS, IS GIVEN BY HIS MINORITY CULTURAL IDENTITY

To begin with the first premise: who someone authentically is, is given by his minority cultural identity. Those who are part of a cultural majority, are thus not 'defined' by their culture. Charles Taylor pleads for a politics of accommodating difference. He ascertains the need for state measures and a shift in attitude that shows respect for minority *groups*, not so much on individuals. From the multiculturalist perspective, a state should not have to let go of its universal affirmation of equality to accommodate *random wishes* of *randomly dispersed individuals* within a territory (John from Arkansas would like this, Mary from New York would like that). The founding principle of multiculturalism is that members of minority groups flock together based on a shared culture. Parekh states:

> People value their collective identity for various reasons: it is the basis of their sense of self-worth and social standing; it bonds them to those sharing it, and generates a sense of common belonging and the collective empowerment that accompanies it; and gives them a moral anchor, a sense of direction, and a body of ideals and values.[68]

Under a multiculturalist regime, people are entitled, and morally encouraged ("you are good the way you are", "become who you are", as well as politically stimulated (subsidised, exempted from laws) to live out this 'authentic' cultural group identity. Yet, culture and identity as concepts within political theory are difficult. 'Culture' in itself is a meaningless term. The same goes for 'identity'. Why the need to single cultural group identity out, lift it up and aim to preserve it *in abstracto*?

A helpful course now would be to make "cultural identity" less abstract. So I ask: *which* culture? Which cultural aspects within our identities warrant extra attention? People are 'members' of all sorts of 'communities'. For instance, we align ourselves based on shared professions (scholars, bakers, teachers), sports, sexual orientation, neighbourhoods, age group, educational level, arts, regional culture, and so forth. In a lifetime, we can switch identities and, for instance, go from a vegan Marxist to a fur-wearing capitalist (or from fur wearing Marxist to vegan capitalist). Yet, multiculturalists ignore most of these self-chosen allegiances. The community culture that multiculturalists deem important for one's self-realisation is subsequently always an *ethnic* and/or *religious* cultural identity.[69] No

---

68 Parekh 2008, p. 50. Again, as mentioned In a previous footnote, he does pay attention to the dangers of collective identity, such as "essentializing" identity and imposing a unity of views that is not shared by "all women, gay people, black people and Muslims"; see p. 35.

69 See also: Blum, Lawrence, 'Recognition, Value, and Equality: A Critique of Charles Taylor's and Nancy Fraser's Accounts of Multiculturalism', *Constellations* 1998, pp. 51-68 (53) and Waldron 1991, p. 777.

multiculturalist calls attention to the importance of a Rotterdam identity to citizens of Rotterdam.

So, multiculturalists elevate one's personal identity to the status of group identity and group identity is equal to the *ethno/religious*-identity.[70] If we consider the contemporary origins of multiculturalism, namely, the Civil Rights Movement, this becomes much clearer. An individual cannot change his or her ethnic roots and *thus* ethnicity is lifted (but only for minorities perceived as weak). Ethnicity is "authentic" and authenticity is good. In contemporary Western culture, multiculturalists have gone along with the idea that being a Muslim, like having an ethnic background, is given at birth, rather than a life choice.

An important point of critique is that this multiculturalist belief confines or guides individuals to a culture they were born into and not one which they have chosen after more options became available at a later stage in life. The act of "hypostatisation" or "reification" (to ascribe substance or real existence to mental constructs or concepts) actually *limits* individuals in what Kymlicka labels making life choices:

> In deciding how to lead our lives, we do not start *de novo*, but rather we examine "definite ideals and forms of life that have been developed and tested by innumerable individuals, sometimes for generations". The decision about how to lead our lives must ultimately be ours alone, but this decision is always a matter of selecting what we believe to be most valuable from the various options available, selecting from a context of choice which provides us with different ways of life.[71]

The selection of what is deemed best in terms of life options is, if multiculturalist ideology be accepted, constituted by the 'heritage' of those stemming from one's "own" ethnicity and religion. If multiculturalists were to encourage Redskin Indians to learn about family values from 8th-century Hanbali Muslims and would encourage Mexican Jews to check out Mongolian musical history, that would debase the idea that group identity is formed by a distinctive and traceable culture. Kymlicka does not stimulate humans to choose from options out of *general human history*. If that were the case, there would not be a need for focusing on preserving *multi*culture.

---

70 Amartya Sen also wonders how multiculturalists see human beings: "Should they be characterised in terms of inherited traditions, particularly the inherited religion, of the community in which they happen to be born, taken that unchosen identity to have automatic priority over other affiliations involving politics, profession, class, gender, language, literature, social involvements, and many other connections?" See: Sen, Amartya, *Identity and Violence. The Illusion of Destiny*, London: Allen Lane 2006, p. 150. See for another essay on the need for cultural criticism and individualism rather than religious communitarianism: Verhofstadt, Dirk, *De Derde Feministische Golf* (The Third Feminist Wave), Antwerp: Houtekiet 2006.

71 Kymlicka 1989, p. 164, in: Waldron 1991, pp. 751-793 (782-783).

The 'unique person' that one is today, is created within, and by, a culture. One can agree, but also because 'culture' is an abstract term without a specific substance. It cannot be refuted that we are all products of a, or 'our', culture. And if culture changes, so do we, as we are the ones who are the agents capable of changing culture. So, no matter *how* we act or *what* we believe, *that* what we do and think *is our culture*. Stating that individuals develop a cultural identity within a larger cultural framework is like saying 'humans breath oxygen' and may be an interesting field for psychologists (hence, Freud and Erikson), but is in itself an empty statement. It does not logically lead to a *particular* political theory of any kind. Moreover, ascribing anything to the empty category that is culture is rather vague.

Of all the options one has when composing a lifestyle, ethnicity is one element that is not optional. Yet, individuals still have the option to carry out that part of their genetic make-up into their sense of self. Individuals with a non-white ethnicity in a majority white society do not *have to* lift their ethnicity or religion as an important marker of their identity. But if we go along with multiculturalist thinking, members of minorities should be *encouraged* to highlight this part of themselves, because cultural authenticity is valued, rather than discouraged. This downplays the viable option to *not* make one's heritage a vital part one's life. It also assumes a cohesiveness in ethnical or religious heritage, as well as a group cohesiveness, that is not always there.[72]

Moreover, it negates the reality of culture as an ever-changing phenomenon. A focus on a return to ethnicity, as well as a focus on religious heritage, stresses continuity, community survival, and links throughout the generations.[73] Imagine the lives of our grandparents, or even our parents, and ponder over the changes in lifestyles and mentality. It makes no sense to state that, with the ideal of authenticity in the backdrop, we should be encouraged to be inspired by the lifestyles of our ancestors without asking ourselves whether that lifestyle conforms to modern standards. Moreover, even individuals who share the exact same heritage can diverge from one another significantly. But even beyond generational change, individuals do not seldom choose to leave their community, want to integrate in the host culture and are not merely looking for a sense of belonging to a collection of individuals sharing their heritage.

As Jeremy Waldron points out, "[…] Kymlicka is guilty of something like the fallacy of composition".[74] Kymlicka establishes that life choices are made in a cultural context, and options have culturally defined meanings. However, from this it does not imply that there must be a *particular* cultural framework, nor that membership in a culture is of a

---

72 Higham 1993, p. 205.
73 Higham 1993, pp. 213-214. Even though multiculturalist philosopher Bhikhu Parekh does not justify the idea of a static view of culture and calls preservation of culture in a more or less intact fashion, a mistake, see: Parekh 2000, p. 77.
74 Waldron 1991, p. 783.

particular relevance.[75] The question remains: *which* culture or which aspects of our cultural identity make us who we truly are? The answer "those which are deemed important" is circular and has no meaning.

Moreover, the tragedy for multiculturalists seems to be that blacks have much less culture in common with other blacks, and whites with other whites, than is necessary for upholding their multiculturalist ideology. Their tragedy is that some whites like Tolstoy and some blacks like Tolstoy; some whites like Bach and some blacks like Bach. The idea of a common culture for an ethnic group or religious group is increasingly a myth. So this common culture has to be "invented" or "imagined". Their assertions about this common culture often exude a sort of desperate and categorical tone. There is much more 'cross-cultural dialogue' and understanding than is compatible with multiculturalist premises. Secularist philosopher Paul Cliteur (born in the Netherlands) feels intellectually comfortable around Afshin Ellian (from Iran) and Ayaan Hirsi Ali (from Somalia), despite sharing his cultural heritage with Ian Buruma (Dutch writer who believes in the notion of Enlightenment fundamentalism[76]) and Maurits Berger (Dutch Arabist who endorses Sharia councils).[77]

These cross-cultural understandings are very difficult to understand on the basis of multiculturalist philosophy. That also explains the aggressive commentary on Hirsi Ali when she formulated a criticism of – supposedly – her own religion, Islam.[78] When she apostasised, she was assumed to be manipulated by angry white men. She was supposed to stick to her faith, because that would be "multiculturalist proof" that culture is valued by its members. As Hirsi Ali found her way out of her imposed cultural identity, she was labelled a "dissident" who "did not represent Muslim women" and was deemed unqualified to voice her opposition to minority issues and religion.[79] That someone who is Muslim can decide to become atheist and deliver cultural criticism is beyond multiculturalist understanding. Multiculturalists do not *actually* drive cultural change.[80] In that respect, in their attempt not to offend Muslims when formulating critiques, undeservedly viewed as stereotyping, "[…] Westerners may condescendingly think of other human beings as eternally sealed within their own cultural totalities and/or permanently condemned to live

---

75   Waldron 1991, pp. 783-784.

76   Buruma, Ian, *Murder in Amsterdam*, London: Penguin Books 2006.

77   Berger, Maurits, 'Juist blokkeren van shariaraad is dom' (Actually, blocking a Sharia council is stupid), *NRC Handelsblad* 15 June 2012.

78   See: Berman, Paul, *The Flight of the Intellectuals*, New York: Melville House 2010.

79   Hirsi Ali, Ayaan, *Mijn Vrijheid* (Infidel), Amsterdam: Augustus 2006.

80   See also: Chervel, Thierry and Seeliger, Anja, *Islam in Europa. Eine internationale Debatte*, Frankfurt am Main: Suhrkamp Verlag 2007.

their lives within the confines of their 'most authentic' systems of beliefs and values", wrote the Syrian-born academic Sadiq Jalal Al-Azm (1934).[81]

To conclude. Premise number 1 is: Who someone truly (authentically) is, is given by his minority cultural identity. Multiculturalists focus on groups, rather than on individuals. Individuals cannot be seen apart from their group culture and a group identity is vital to their sense of self. I expressed the view that a focus on "cultural identity" is so broad that it becomes meaningless. Therefore, multiculturalists cannot maintain a completely abstract view on "cultural identity", but ultimately must focus on ethnic or religious group identity. Other allegiances, such as profession or age, are of no relevance to multiculturalists. The act of focusing on a shared ethno-religious identity as something important becomes part of a balancing act in remaining vague on what that identity entails. For, the moment abstraction is exchanged for concreteness, factual group cohesion comes under pressure which diminishes the idea of a group identity.

I do not deny that (large) groups of individuals flock together. Orthodox Jews do so in Antwerp, and the Amish do so in Ohio. Neighbourhoods are filled with people sharing backgrounds and convictions. The question remains: why does group identity call for a particularly *positive* assessment, rather than merely establishing communities as sociological practicalities? Cultural diversity is a fact, yes, but it is unclear what the justification is for making it a political goal of moral importance that needs to be furthered.[82] For that, multiculturalists use the second premise.

2. NONRECOGNITION OF CULTURAL MINORITY IDENTITY CONSTITUTES PSYCHOLOGICAL HARM

Premise number 2 is that: *Nonrecognition of cultural minority identity constitutes psychological harm.* Crucial to multiculturalist thinking is taking one's identity to be of vital importance to the concept of self-respect, a form of a permanent psychological condition which should not be damaged (e.g. by critique), but respected (in word and [legal] action) and in some ways extolled, and secondly, that this identity is based on the minority group to which you belong to. From this perspective, one's identity is not chosen, but assigned at birth.

---

81 Al-Azm, Sadiq Jalal, 'The Importance of Being Earnest about Salman Rushdie', *Die Welt des Islams* 1991, quoted in: Mayer, Ann Elizabeth, 'Universal versus Islamic Human Rights: A Clash of Cultures or Clash with a Construct', *Michigan Journal of International Law* 1994, pp. 307-404 (386).

82 See also: Levy, Jacob, *The Multiculturalism of Fear*, Oxford: Oxford University Press 2000, p. 7: "[...] the preservation or perpetuation of any one cultural identity is not, by itself, a political goal of high moral importance".

In *Why Respect Culture?*, James Johnson identifies two multiculturalist justifications given for this. One is that we might intrinsically respect culture because we consider it valuable, and because individuals value culture. Or, two because we might respect culture on consequentialist grounds, meaning it contributes to the wellbeing of an individual or a group or perhaps to avoid civil war.[83]

Charles Taylor accentuates an instrumentalist justification for multiculturalist theory, viz. avoiding psychological harm, even to the extent of avoiding 'crippling self-hatred'. He has not described how recognition should be bestowed on the recipient, nor made explicit what constitutes interference at being what one truly is. He defines the importance of recognition by means of the *via negativa*: it not so much important to receive recognition, but to be free from *non*recognition or *mis*recognition. The latter two are presumed to constitute psychological harm and can even be taken as far to claim that identity is taken to be non-negotiable. "One says: 'I can give up many things for the social good, but I will not give up my identity. I should not be required to sacrifice who I am for the sake of the benefit to others".[84] Accommodating someone in their personal preferences which are presented as culturally originating, is crucial to showing respect, at least, that is the idea of it. Again, the emphasis lies on perceived weak minorities, on those who are viewed to suffer from a critical attitude towards their way of life. This presumed suffering is also presented as self-evident.

The foundation of Taylor's (and Kymlicka's and Parekh's) theory is: "people can suffer real damage, real distortion, if the people or society around them mirror back to them a confining or demeaning or contemptible picture of themselves"[85]. It *sounds* plausible. But to what extent is it *true*? Is it true that misrecognition is a form of psychological harm? Would no longer being categorised as a member of a particular community by outsiders constitute *harm*? Multiculturalist philosophers do not offer sufficient viable reasons why this should be the case. It is also not consistent with the accusation that members of the cultural hegemony exclude minority members. It seems to me that emphasising one's different position as member of a minority culture is not very "inclusive". This assumption of harm could be considered as an attempt to project emotions unto others. This also becomes clear when we ask the question: *who* should recognise *who*? Parekh writes:

> This feeling of being full citizens and yet outsiders is difficult to analyse and explain, but it can be deep and real and seriously damage the quality of their citizenship and their commitment to the political community. It is caused by,

---

83   Johnson 2000, p. 407.

84   Quote from: Waldron, Jeremy, 'Cultural Identity and Civic Responsibility', pp. 155-174 (158), in: Kymlicka, Will and Norman, Wayne (eds.), *Citizenship in Diverse Societies*, Oxford: Oxford University Press 2000 (2003).

85   Taylor 1994, p. 25. See also: Parekh 2000, p. 343.

among other things, the narrow and exclusive manner in which *wider society* defines the common good, the demeaning ways in which it talks about some of its members, and the dismissive or patronizing ways in which it behaves towards them. Although such individuals are free in principle to participate in its collective life, they often stay away or ghettoize themselves for fear of rejection or out a deep sense of alienation.[86]

Interestingly, what this also exposes is that there is no *general* moral duty to respect individuals for whom they truly are, as nonrecognition causes harm. I will elaborate as to why this is the case. Take, for example, "John". John is an Iraqi-born Muslim living in Birmingham who disapproves of people who do not follow his religion. In fact, an important part of John's identity is expressed through his dismissive attitude towards non-believers. He wishes not to recognise a non-believer for whom that person truly is, preferring to be critical or even dismissive of Western values. If we were to follow multiculturalist theory, we respect John's true nature. We should not even criticise John for criticising other people's life choices. John has the right to believe whatever he wishes, and we should be respectful and tolerant of his position. So far so good. But now we change John a little bit and this time, he is a white male citizen living in Liverpool. John does not recognise Muslims for who they truly are, in fact, he is quite dismissive of Islam. He regularly unfolds his critique on life choices inspired by that religion, stating that Islam is detrimental to individual wellbeing. He questions the merits of Islam-inspired practices, such as veiling and praying five times a day. Now, multiculturalists would label the latter as a lack of recognition as a form of causing psychological harm, as well as arrogant, condescending and eurocentric, possibly even racist and discriminatory. The moral duty of recognising an individual for who he truly is thus a one-way street.[87] That is what I mean with the fact that for multiculturalists there is no *general* moral duty to respect individuals for whom they truly are. Multiculturalist philosophers do not focus on the need for recognition of Inuit by a minority of Pakistani Shiite Muslims. Or recognition of Caribbean Africans by the Pennsylvania Dutch. Recognition should be bestowed on minority groups by the majority of white Euro-American culture bearers.

It assumes that members of the cultural hegemony have an enormous power and influence on the mental wellbeing of minority members, a power the latter does not have on the majority. It assumes that white Euro-Americans are psychologically immune to criticism, even to the accusation of being inherently racist, and, if not immune, at least they are considered adults who should be able to deal with it. Minority members, on the

---

86 Parekh 2000, p. 342. [italics added]

87 See on recognition as a one-sided act by the majority society only also: Joppke, Christian, 'The Retreat of Multiculturalism in the Liberal State: Theory and Policy', *The British Journal of Sociology* 2004, pp. 237-257 (238).

other hand, are considered dependent on the approval of white Euro-Americans for a sense of self-worth. Where does that idea come from?

In *The Tyranny of Guilt. An Essay on Western Masochism* (2010), French philosopher Pascal Bruckner (1948) dissects the idea that minorities suffer under misrecognition by a dominant European, white majority culture. The fixation some multiculturalists have on the duty to ensure the mental wellbeing of minority group members comes from a strong sense of *guilt*. He writes:

> Since 1945 our continent has been obsessed by torments of repentance. Ruminating on its past abominations – wars, religious persecutions, slavery, imperialism, fascism, communism – it views history as nothing more than a long series of massacres and sackings that led to two world wars, that is, to an enthusiastic suicide. Unparalleled horrors, the industrialization of death on a grand scale in the Nazi and Soviet camps, the promotion of bloodthirsty clowns to the rank of mass idols, and the experience of radical evil transformed into bureaucratic routine: that is what we have achieved.[88]

Bruckner formulates the consequence: "[t]hus we Euro-Americans are supposed to have only one obligation: endlessly atoning for what we have inflicted on other parts of humanity".[89] This is often adopted by multiculturalists. For instance, Will Kymlicka's *Multicultural Citizenship* (1995) ends with the message that "the fate of ethnic and national groups around the world is in the hand of xenophobic nationalists, religious extremists, and military dictators".[90] Therefore, not in the hands of members of minority groups themselves, we must conclude, who are docilely awaiting their fate. The history of slavery, colonialism and genocide is the proof that Euro-Americans are (potential or actual) perpetrators by default, uniquely capable of racism, discrimination and persecution. Members of minorities, on the other hand, are vulnerable and innocent by default and are in need of protection by the majority, yet awaiting their destiny of marginalisation by that same majority, a destiny only the majority can control. This is the psychological underpinning of the perceived relationship between majority and minority individuals. Bruckner asks:

> How can we fail to see that this leads us to live off self-denunciation while taking a strange pride in being the worst? Self-denigration is all too clearly a form of indirect self-glorification. Evil can come only from us; other people are motivated by sympathy, good will, candor. This is the paternalism of the

---

88 Bruckner, Pascal, *The Tyranny of Guilt*, Princeton: Princeton University Press 2010, p. 6.
89 Bruckner 2010, p. 34.
90 Kymlicka 1995, p. 195.

guilty conscience: seeing ourselves as the kind of infamy is still a way of staying on the crest of history.[91]

The Euro-American majority thus has the moral duty to make sure minority groups do not suffer psychological harm from nonrecognition or misrecognition of the worthiness of their cultures.

The indication that minority members are victims of unbearable psychological harm ("crippling") through the act of nonrecognition or misrecognition, does require some support. Also missing, is a clear view of what recognition, or lack of nonrecognition, entails. There appear to be two levels; the individual level and the institutional level.

Multiculturalist thinkers confuse the entities, that is the individual, the group or cultures themselves[92] which warrant protection or recognition; the individual from a psychological need to belong or not to feel degraded, a group that deserves protection against discrimination or a culture that is in danger of going extinct. But a 'group' is not an entity which deserves protection or recognition from any analytical angle. Groups have no feelings and fail as a unit to experience psychological harm.[93]

The same goes for cultures. Humans contain culture, cultures on their own do not exist and have no interests whatsoever. Of course, in normal discourse, and for sociological and political reasons, we constantly refer to groups, as well as to the abstract notion of 'culture'. But that does not defer to the fact that the only unit that actually values or needs something, is the individual. Another question is *how* the act of recognition, or absence of non- or misrecognition should be bestowed upon people. We have answered the question *who* should recognise *whom* (members of the majority should recognise members of the minority), but *how* does one recognise another human being? Should a white, Euro-American male approach a black American-Haitian, and say: "I recognise your ethnic heritage. (Now, let's do business together)". Or should the white man merely *think* that inside his head? Or is simply *not degrading* a fellow human based on his skin colour enough? Or does not abolishing harmful cultural traditional practices – for instance, ritual slaughter –

---

91 Bruckner 2010, p. 34.
92 See also: Blum 1998, p. 53.
93 As American author Ophelia Benson and British author Jeremy Stangroom describe: "But literally speaking, groups don't value things. Groups can't literally value anything, any more than nations or communities or families can, because groups don't have minds. It is only people (and some animals) who can value cultural practices, because it is only people who have minds, and they have them in a singular, one at a time. Their thoughts can't ever be added together to make a larger group thought, which then becomes 'what the group thinks'. Thoughts can't be poured into a large bowl to make soup; they can only be added to a pile of distinct entities, with the entities remaining distinct. The thoughts of people never melt into each other, no matter how high the heat." Benson, Ophelia and Stangroom, Jeremy, *Does God Hate Women?*, London: Continuum 2009, p. 99.

suffice for recognising a cultural *group*?[94] But where does one draw the line of tolerating harmful practices? To quote Jeremy Waldron: "I suspect that the popularity of modern communitarianism has depended on *not* giving unequivocal answers to these questions".[95]

3. Culture Is Good

To be clear, none of the multiculturalist philosophers claim that minority cultures are purely 'good'. Culture is important as multiculturalists consider it to define one's identity – that is, if you are a member of a cultural minority. Culture is thus important to people, and, therefore, culture is good, the justification goes. The idea behind the sense that culture is important has some vagueness to it which many authors fail to analyse adequately. Does it mean "inevitable"? Does it mean "favourable"? What I take from it is that "important" implies that people hold certain beliefs and act in a certain matter, because they want to. This is a form of circular reasoning: why do people act in a certain way? Because they want to. Why do people want to act in a certain way? Because it is important to them. Why is it important to them? Because they want to. But we must not forget that some people also want to kill their daughter for having a non-Muslim boyfriend or value their membership of the Ku Klux Klan. That individuals want to, value, or find something important for their identity is not sufficient when answering the question of whether something deserves respect, recognition or toleration.

The fact that cultures encompass reprehensible practices is widely accepted. However, that acknowledgement does not affect the conclusion that *overall* minority culture is important to members and *therefore* good. Especially "traditional" cultures have value, as Taylor claims: "Just as all must have equal civil rights, and equal voting rights, regardless of race or culture, so all should enjoy the presumption that their traditional culture has value".[96] Because culture is the source of identity, and living one's minority identity is crucially important to one's wellbeing, cultural membership is good, and culture is thereby a source of good. Even when a collection of individuals demonstrate 'bad' or 'abhorrent' practices – e.g. forced marriage, we should not draw the conclusion that culture is bad, because even the bad practices are valued (otherwise these practices would logically be

---

94   Taylor does at a given point somewhat specify *where* the act of recognition should take place: in the educational system. As Blum summarises: "Valuing the recognition of ethnocultural difference provides an obvious underpinning for educational Multiculturalism. Educational institutions should recognise the ethno-cultural (and ethno-racial) identities of their students. This recognition can take curricular form, as when the historical experiences and contributions of ethno-cultural groups are studied. But recognition can take other forms as well – for example, school assemblies for cultural presentation, or teachers' informal acknowledgement inside and outside of class of their students' ethno-cultural identities." See: Blum, Lawrence, "Recognition and Multiculturalism in Education", *Journal of Philosophy of Education* 2001, pp. 539-559 (540).

95   Waldron 1991, p. 756.

96   See: Taylor 1994, p. 68.

abandoned). That those practices are harmful to *the victims* is not recognised in the same way as nonrecognition of the culture is conceived to be harmful to the perpetrators. Thus: forced marriage, bad, condemning it, worse, as it rubs off negatively on all members.

Community cultures can and do have a negative effect on individual wellbeing.[97] Interests between community members do not seldom conflict. Take, for instance, the relatively high suicide rate among south-east Asian girls in the United Kingdom: male members value their culture of protecting modesty by means of restricting the girls' freedom to choose how they want to live.[98] This causes disproportionate (and lethal) depressions among these women. In this sense, culture is not valued, not by these women. Now, a multiculturalist can say that this is merely *a part* of South-East Asian culture and that *in general*, their culture provides a meaningful framework for making life choices. However, that focus is revolting if that framework prompts suicide.

Multiculturalists do acknowledge the fact that cultural frameworks can cause harm to members, and it would be a misrepresentation of multiculturalism to say that such acknowledgements do not exist. However, the general statement of valuing and respecting culture from a general perspective stands.

How is life in Sealandistan? If we follow multiculturalists we must conclude that both Blue- and Greenskin cultures are good, offering the individual members a sense of belonging and enabling them to live according to their authentic heritage. This creates an identity from which they make their life choices. In Sealandish reality though, not every member is happy and some elderly Blueskins are unsatisfied and Greenskin animal rights activists are unhappy with their monthly feast of animal kicking. Moreover, both Green- and Blueskins are not convinced the *other* culture is good. In fact, generally speaking, both communities believe that they themselves have a refined and joyous culture and that it is the other culture whose practices are malicious and cruel. It is important to recall that internal dissent is not appreciated, either. The debate is tense and people wonder how to solve cultural tensions. Who is right? Who should change? And as the tension builds, more and more elderly and animals have an early meeting with their creator. Sealandistan's multiculturalist elite calls for more dialogue, yet, whenever issues are discussed, multiculturalists say that the debate actually worsens tensions. They are not much help. Their viewpoint is that both cultures serve as valuable frameworks for identity, are an invaluable moral anchor, and are considered equally good.

---

97 This brings us to the "minorities within minorities-debate", see: Spinner-Halev, Jeff and Eisenberg, Avigail (eds.), *Minorities within Minorities. Equality, Rights and Diversity*, Cambridge: Cambridge University Press 2005.
98 Hasan, Rumy, 'Critical Remarks on Cultural Aspects of Asian Ghettos in Modern Britain', *Capital & Class* 2003, pp. 103-134 (106).

4. CULTURES ARE EQUAL

We now arrive at premise number 4: *Cultures are equal.* That is, cultures are not *factually* equal, but they are *morally* equal in the sense that cultures will provide its bearers with equal value; no culture is better than anyone else's. In 1996, for example, the Dutch cabinet sent out the message that "the debate over multiculturalism must be conducted from the starting principle that cultures are of equal value".[99]

In *Culture and Equality: An Egalitarian Critique Of Multiculturalism* (2001), philosopher Brian Barry (1936-2009) asserts that it is logically impossible to recognise all cultures as equal. This is because cultures have, as he phrases it, 'propositional content': "It is an inevitable aspect of any culture that it will include some ideas to the effect that some beliefs are true and some false, and that some things are right and others wrong. The demand for cultural equality runs into conceptual problems of a kind that are not inherent in the demand that we should find equal value (or any value at all) in every cultural artefact such as a painting. This is, indeed, an absurdly inappropriate demand. But the reason is simply that, unless discriminations are made, ascribing value to something ceases to have any point".[100] Barry believes affirming everybody's culture simultaneously is as tenable as stating that "everybody has won, and *all* must have prices".[101] Or as Italian political scientist Giovanni Sartori (1924) explains: "To attribute "equal value" to all cultures [...] destroys the very notion of value. If everything is of value, nothing is of value: the value loses its content".[102]

Truly, even multiculturalists draw the line of equality and value somewhere: the value of culture for minorities should be duly recognised by members of the majority and not doing so is a *bad cultural trait* and should be changed. Imposition of majority norms at the cost of authentic minority culture is *bad.* Being from a white majority and not, or not fully, recognising someone's non-white minority identity, is *bad.* It is arrogant, condescending, intolerant, and bordering on racist and discriminatory. Interestingly, this bad, or to some abhorrent, practice of nonrecognition is part of a culture, a culture which, assuming Herderian philosophy underlying multiculturalism to be correct, is important to its members, and is thus a source of *good.* This contradiction makes it difficult, if not impossible, to found multiculturalism as a worthwhile ideology. That is, if nonrecognition of minority culture is an inherent part of the (dominant) culture, why should we not respect *that*? Is multiculturalist theory in that sense not *self-defeating*? In a sense it is. If all cultures

---

99   See also: Caldwell, Christopher, *Reflections on the Revolution in Europe: Can Europe be the Same with Different People in It?*, London: Allen Lane 2009, p. 70.

100 Barry, Brian, *Culture and Equality: An Egalitarian Critique of Multiculturalism*, Cambridge: Polity Press 2001, p. 270.

101 Barry 2001, pp. 270-271.

102 Sartori, Giovanni, *Pluralismo, multiculturalistismo e estranei*, Milano: Rizzoli 2000, in: Joppke 2004, p. 242.

are different yet equal and are entitled to recognition, than the phenomenon of culturally-based nonrecognition of minorities should be respected. This is the case, because, as the theory goes, even if it is accompanied by an abhorrent practice, culture deserves our admiration and respect. We should admire and respect the dominant culture, even though it supposedly imposes psychological harm on others by not naturally recognising the worth of minority cultures.

This contradiction might be lifted, if we adjust the maxim: members of *minority* cultures should be respected by members of the *majority* culture.[103] Multiculturalist theory is about restoring a power imbalance, which aims to contribute to peaceful coexistence of a plurality of people in one nation. Although *formally* multiculturalists state that all cultures are equal, or of equal value, the focus on respect *for minority, by majority*, actually leads to the conclusion that "some cultures are more equal than others". In no theory of multiculturalism is the act of recognition reciprocal.[104] Members of a majority culture, who are in a more powerful position (at least, that is the assumption), are not presented as individuals that might claim authenticity, but as humans who are expected to be able to do away with some of their cultural beliefs (e.g. reject the belief that refusing to shake a woman's hand is unacceptable) and practices (e.g. give leeway to the violation of animal rights in the case of ritual slaughter) in order to accommodate those for minority cultures. It also means that multiculturalist theorists present their audience with the moral instruction to hold their own culture against the light, while members of minority cultures have the moral right to keep their culture intact. The Euro-American dominant majority confronts their "own group" with a cultural critique (e.g. "you are descendants of slave own-ers/colonists/bystanders during the Nazi regime"), a critique which is not deemed to cause psychological damage. It is only members of minority cultures which are allegedly suscep-tible to getting hurt. That conclusion, albeit unintentionally, demonstrates the implicit superiority of the dominant culture; the power to change for the good and to show benevolence to members of minority groups, as Bruckner also argues.

Multiculturalists are actually mainly concerned with *rhetorically* stating cultures are equal. It is a way of not causing offence and doing away with the idea of the host majority's superior culture. They believe that a cultural hegemony owes respect to minorities. This notion is incompatible with the notion of equality of cultures. If cultures are considered equal, because they provide members equal utility, then all members of all cultures should be respected and cleared from interference. This is obviously not the case, as the responsi-bility to adapt is expected to come from the host society: those members are apparently not affected by psychological harm from misrecognition.

---

103 Or respected by 'the state', but that is backed by the idea that 'the state' is made up out of individuals from the dominant culture.

104 As Joppke formulates it: "[…] the winner is asked to recognise the loser, in what amounts to an act of repa-ration and restitution". See: Joppke 2004, p. 243.

In the meantime, in Sealandistan, unfortunately, even though there is a degree of intermarriage and both groups are interspersed throughout the territory, both members of the Greenskins as the Blueskins encounter intercultural rivalry and suspicion. In other words, they are dealing with opposing visions of the good life and a good society, leaving both communities with the feeling of an environment in danger of existence.[105] This is not uncommon. American political scientist Robert Putnam found that ethnic diversity tends to reduce social solidarity and social capital.[106] This effect of several cultures co-existing in an environment in danger of existence is of the utmost importance to multiculturalists. Softening the feeling of cultural endangerment is considered even more important than the wellbeing of the elderly or animal welfare. Multiculturalists are not likely to dive into ethical discussions on specific cultural practices, but call for *respecting difference*.

5. Cultural Differences Are Good, But If Not, They Should At Least be Tolerated

We now come premise number 5: *Cultural differences are good, but if not, they should at least be tolerated*.[107] It would be a good idea if we were to agree on at least the basic point that some practices are good, and some practices are bad. Progression is possible through identifying differences. Every society recognises difference. We socially recognise the young apart from the old, men apart from women, we notice skin colour, the successful, the beautiful, the ugly, the rich, the poor, and the psychically and mentally handicapped. Societies acknowledge relationships of marriage and kinship, and work with the difference between employer and employee status and therefore simply living life means encountering *differences galore*. Sometimes we wish to exacerbate those differences, for instance, by investing in an education, writing literature, train for a sports career, in short, to achieve something that will make us stand out (and be less equal to others).

The fact of difference is universal and so is its social recognition. Yet, despite its universality, especially in contemporary Western society does differentiation tend to be more complex and more 'optional' than in their traditional societies. Barry attributes this to our consumer ethic and the whole concept of lifestyle.[108] For example, in *Why the West is Best: A Muslim Apostate's Defense of Liberal Democracy* (2011), author Ibn Warraq (1946) tells

---

105 See on opposition and authenticity also: Waldron 1991, p. 761.

106 Putnam, Robert, "E pluribus unum: Diversity and Community in the Twenty-first Century" (the 2006 Johan Skytte Prize Lecture), *Scandinavian Political Studies* 2007, pp. 137-174 (137). Koopmans and Veit confirmed Putnam's thesis for Berlin, Germany, see: Koopmans, Ruud and Veit, Susanne, 'Cooperation in Ethnically Diverse Neighborhoods: A Lost-Letter Experiment', *Political Psychology* 2014, pp. 379-400.

107 As exemplary, Bhikhu Parekh writes: "The third important constituent of a global ethics is the principle of respect for difference or plurality". Parekh 2008, p. 226.

108 See: Barry 2001, p. 19.

about the day he took an Iraqi colleague to an American bookstore in New York to show him thousands and thousands of different magazines covering all different fields of interest for the consumer.[109] Individuals in modern societies can choose from a plethora of ideological convictions and can switch during their lifetime. The presence of so many options makes the act of choosing worthy of study itself.

Yet, when it comes to minorities, it is ethnic and religious culture which are highlighted out of many sources of differentiation. The analytical issue at stake is that multiculturalists embrace the fallacious reasoning of the is/ought problem: there *is* religious and cultural pluralism; therefore, there *ought to be* this kind of pluralism. There *is* (descriptive) indeed a plurality of religious cultures within a nation, but that does not logically lead to the multiculturalist doctrine which *prescribes* this plurality.[110] Kymlicka believes that "of course, the whole point of multiculturalism is to normalize diversity",[111] while other multiculturalists invoke cultural pluralism as their founding principle.[112] Multiculturalist thinkers believe it is not enough to merely establish that something is different, but that it is *good* that there is plurality, whatever the content may be. In popular culture we notice that difference should be celebrated; we get told "if we were all the same the world would be a dull place" (imagine those poor monocultural African tribes not mixed with Asian homosexuals and Maori).

The focus on plurality is actually an odd one in itself. The festive embrace of difference often regards cosmopolitan manifestations of culture. One can think of music festivals celebrating African music, enjoying an Indian curry, incorporating sarongs in one's wardrobe. The celebration of difference in this sense is limited to music, food, dress and art but conversely, when members of cultural minorities turn to practices *beyond* what can be "celebrated", multiculturalists call for tolerance (or "an intercultural dialogue"[113], which I consider a form of extended tolerance). An example is the Islamic call for prayer, the 'muezzin' calling from the top of a minaret in neighbourhoods in European cities. This can be quite an intrusive sound, even annoying to some. Yet, multiculturalist thinking warrants people to be tolerant. Thus, when the practice under scrutiny or group reputation turns non-celebratory, it is *respect for diversity* that is required. When a practice performed by a minority is not appreciated by the "cultural hegemony", multiculturalists call out on the *value* the practice has for those practicing it, for the sake of difference and in the name of equality. Multiculturalists lift the status of religious minorities, and single its members

---

109 Ibn Warraq, *Why the West is Best. A Muslim Apostate's Defense of Liberal Democracy*, New York: Encounter Books 2011, p. 36-37. Ibn Warraq is the pen name of a Pakistani born American writer. He uses a pseudonym for safety reasons.

110 See: Barry 2001, p. 22.

111 Kymlicka, Will, "Testing the Liberal Multiculturalist Hypothesis: Normative Theories and Social Science Evidence", *Canadian Journal of Political Science* 2010, pp. 257-271 (265).

112 Higham 1993, p. 205.

113 For instance, Parekh 2008, p. 226.

out for their distinctness. American historian John Higham (1920-2003) finds praising plurality curious: "On the surface, one would think that the goal of equality would not be well served by highlighting or increasing differences among people. At least, we are entitled to some explanation of how an emphasis on differences of endowment will advance equality. To my knowledge none has been suggested by our multiculturalists".[114]

Instead, it would be better if the concept of respecting culture would be replaced entirely by the ideal of keeping and improving good practices, while getting rid of undesirable ones. This would of course require a *standard* of what we consider to be good and what we consider to be bad practices. Unfortunately, the chances of agreeing on or carrying out such a standard are frustrated by the multiculturalist call for non-intervention and respect, often regardless of what that practice entails. Or, as British author Patrick West writes in *The Poverty of Multiculturalism* (2005): "We are commanded to respect all difference and anyone who disagrees shall be shouted down, silenced or slandered a racist. Everyone must be tolerant. And that's an order".[115]

What Patrick West is trying to convey is that there is intolerance towards those who are assumed to be intolerant. Here we enter the realm of *political correctness*. Political correctness is defined as: "agreeing with the idea that people should be careful to not use language or behave in a way that could offend a particular group of people", or "conforming to a belief that language and practices which could offend political sensibilities (as in matters of sex or race) should be eliminated", according to dictionary Merriam Webster.[116] It is considered a contentious term, and generally the label of being politically correct is imposed on people by their (political) opponents.[117]

Refraining from doing or saying anything that another group might find offensive is not new. On a daily basis, throughout every age in the world's history, certain issues have been silenced. Take for instance the Victorians, who were prudish about sex. Or any topic that seemed related to socialism in the 1950s in the United States due to the threat of communism. However, as American sociologist Stan Gaede explains in *When Tolerance is No Virtue* (1993), today's "PC" *has no substance*: it is intolerance itself that should not be tolerated: "Thus, although the politically correct would have a great deal of difficulty agreeing on what constitutes goodness and truth, they have no trouble at all agreeing that

---

114 Higham 1993, p. 213.

115 West, Patrick, *The Poverty of Multiculturalism*, London: Civitas 2005, p. 35.

116 <http://www.merriam-webster.com/dictionary/politically%20correct>. See also: Aufderheide, Patricia (ed.), *Beyond PC. Toward a Politics of Understanding*, Minnesota: Graywolf Press 1992 and Browne, Anthony, *The Retreat of Reason. Political Correctness and the Corruption of the Public Debate in Modern Britain*, London: Civitas 2006.

117 Fairclough, Norman, "Political Correctness': The Politics of Culture and Language", *Discourse & Society* 2003, pp. 17-28 (21).

intolerance itself is wrong. Why? Because no one deserves to be offended".[118] Obviously, this position is logically untenable. As Gaede puts it: "If you are intolerant of someone who is intolerant, then you have necessarily violated your own principle. But if you tolerate those who are intolerant, you keep your principle but sacrifice your responsibility to the principle".[119] Nevertheless, tolerance can be a convenient norm in a society that is characterised by a plurality of norms and behaviour. In fact, tolerance would be redundant in a society where all humans act and believe the same.

But is the definition of tolerance used correctly and consistently? I believe not. There has been a multiculturalist mix-up. Tolerance is not the same as approval. Nor is it indifference; there is an important distinction. For instance, one could not be bothered by a Hare Krisha neighbour. This is not "tolerating" another man's religion; it merely means a person does not have any offsetting thoughts on the topic. As American philosopher Brian Leiter (1963) formulates:

> For there to be a *practice* of toleration, one group must deem another differing group's beliefs or practices "wrong, mistaken, or undesirable" and yet "put up" with them nonetheless. That means that toleration is not at issue in cases where one group is simply *indifferent* to another. I do not "tolerate" my neighbors who are non-White or who are gay, because I am *indifferent* as to the race or sexual orientation of those in my community. "Toleration", as an ideal, can only matter when one group *actively* concerns itself with what the other is doing, believing, or "being".[120]

The act of toleration is thus accompanied by the conviction that some belief or practice is *wrong*. The underlying premise of supporting the idea of tolerance is quite simple: many of the arguments trade on a simple idea: namely, that "[...] *being able to choose what to believe and how to live* [...] makes for a better life. Being told *what you must believe* and *how you must live*, conversely, make lives worse".[121]

Multiculturalism has departed from tolerance. Originally, tolerance dealt with not banning or outlawing a practice. Under multiculturalism, it has become about recognising cultural identity by means of withholding negative judgement. It considers rejection as a

---

118 Gaede, Stan, "*When Tolerance Is No Virtue.* Political Correctness, Multiculturalism & the Future of Truth & Justice", Downers Grove, IL: InterVarsity Press 1993, p. .

119 Gaede 1993, p. 23.

120 Leiter, Brian, "Why Tolerate Religion?", *Constitutional Commentary* 2008, pp. 1-27 (2-3). We can distinguish between state tolerance and tolerance in interpersonal relations, even though the issues are often the same (p. 5).

121 Leiter calls this the "Private Space Argument." Human wellbeing is maximised if (within certain limits) individuals have a "private space" in which they can freely choose what to believe and how to live. See: Leiter 2008, pp. 7-8.

lack of respect, and views this as intolerance. Parekh, for example, assesses whether minority cultures should conform to fundamental liberal values: "This amounts to saying that minority cultures should be respected only of they become liberal, an extreme form of intolerance that shows scant respect for their identity".[122] Not respecting illiberal cultures nor its ensuing identities is perfectly consistent with tolerance, I believe. Under tolerance, it is perfectly possible to not interfere in behaviour, for example, the veiling of women in Islam, yet have an outspoken negative opinion on it: "I agree you have the right to demonstrate this behaviour, yet I advise against it and I hope you will choose otherwise". This is not an act of intolerance, although multiculturalists would label it as such. Intolerance would entail taking steps to ban the practice, such as using violence or introducing legal penalties. Voicing disagreement while allowing a custom to carry on is, in fact, *tolerance*. If one does not disagree with a custom, we have to label non-interference as approval or indifference, which tolerance empathically is not.

Interestingly, toleration also implies a power relationship. As Dutch legal philosopher Paul Cliteur (1955) states: "Tolerance is about putting up with something that people can also refuse to put up with. That means that tolerance always implies the superior power of the tolerant one over the one whose practice is tolerated".[123]

A problem arises when a cultural practice causes harm. It is a classic problem that one's freedom can limit another's. One should think of John Stuart Mill's (1806-1873) famous Harm Principle. Considering both physical force in the form of legal penalties, as well as the moral coercion of public opinion, Mill writes that "the only purpose for which power can be rightfully exercised over any member of a civilized community, against his will, is to prevent harm to others".[124] Toleration should end there where freedom is exerted to effectively cause harm to another individual. Thus, while the idea of tolerance is in essence laudable, it is not the obvious means when a practice is not merely perceived by outsiders as wrong, but also by those individuals undergoing it. Female genital mutilation and forced marriage are examples that illustrate the limits of the desirability of tolerance quite well.

Puzzling is the idea that *in*tolerance is as morally suspect as racism and discrimination. According to a multiculturalist these are the *worst* beliefs and behaviour, more abject than bad cultural practices causing harm to fellow community members. This coheres with a third option when dealing with difference. *Non-judgmentalism* is the natural progression from celebration and tolerance. When members of multiculturalist minorities demonstrate behaviour that is flat out harmful and *dangerous* (in multiculturalist academic literature referred to by the euphemist 'illiberal') to other members, such as honour-based violence,

---

122 Parekh, Bhikhu, 'A varied modern world', pp. 69-75 (72), in: Cohen *et al.* 1999.
123 See: Cliteur, Paul, *Moderne Papoea's – Dilemma's van een Multiculturele Samenleving* (Modern Papuans – Dilemmas of a Multicultural Society), Amsterdam: De Arbeiderspers 2002, p. 138.
124 Mill, John Stuart, *On Liberty*, (1859) Cambridge: Cambridge University Press 2003, p. 13.

multiculturalists turn silent.[125] We must conclude that, apparently, multiculturalists do not consider it their *métier* to answer the question where to draw the line between tolerable and intolerable practices, and what moral and pragmatic standard should be used in deciding.

In his *Multiculturalism. Some Inconvenient Truths* (2010), British scholar Rumy Hasan (1959) points to the multiculturalists' (laudable) goal of fighting racism. That is why, he states, there is a belief that cultural differences are deemed to be respected, and, this unfortunately and erroneously leads to downplaying any problems within a minority culture. The fear is that criticising aspects can accentuate negative stereotyping and "[...] give the green light to further racist slanders and attacks".[126]

Thus, multiculturalists maintain that culture is *good*. When it becomes painfully obvious that culture is not always valued by its members, proponents of the multiculturalist ideology are analytically challenged. Does the tension perhaps exist because multiculturalism by definition makes a fetish of cultures?[127] This idea seems logical; the idea of protecting and thereby perpetuating minority cultures stems from the assumption that the individuals who form the group share that wish. If there is internal dissent, multiculturalists regress into vagueness, and demonstrate the inability to take sides. The best tool multiculturalists tend to use is making general statements about the fact that cultural practices should be in accordance with human rights.

When invited to "pass a verdict" if confronted with a "different" custom, it is not uncommon for multiculturalists to fall prey to *relativism*. Relativism is best defined by listing the following claims taken from American philosopher James Rachels' *The Elements of Moral Philosophy* (2003). It is originally based on the anthropologists' line of approach. First, relativists claim that different societies have different moral codes. Second, that what is right within a society is determined by the moral code of that society. That means that if the moral code of a society dictates that certain actions are correct, then that action *is* right, at least within that society. Third, there is no objective standard we can resort to when judging the moral code of one society as better or worse than another's. Fourth, our own

---

125 Violent family members are a problem cross-culture and religion. However, the specific *planning* of murdering often young women is typical of Islam-rooted communities. Worldwide, 58 per cent of the victims were murdered for being "too Western" and/or for resisting or disobeying cultural and religious expectations. Moreover, major religious and political leaders in developing Muslim countries keep silent and it is mostly Islamic communities that maintain an enforced silence on all matters of religious, cultural, or communal "sensitivity", thereby perpetuating violence. See: Chesler, Phyllis, 'Worldwide Trends in Honor Killings', *Middle East Quarterly* Spring 2010, pp. 3-11.
126 Hasan 2003, p. 104.
127 As Ophelia Benson and Jeremy Stangroom wonder in *Does God Hate Women?* (2009). In order to maintain an overly positive attitude towards culture one must treat a culture as monolithic. "As soon as you admit that cultures have internal dissent and disagreement and nonconformity, the whole idea of protecting or deferring to particular 'cultures' breaks into incoherence". Benson & Stangroom 2009, p. 101.

society's moral code is merely one among many and it has no special status. Fifth, there is no such thing as a "universal truth" in ethics. This means that there are no moral truths that hold true across universally across space and time. Lastly, trying to judge the conduct of other peoples is an act of mere arrogance, an act of "cultural chauvinism". We should therefore adopt an attitude of tolerance when we consider the practices of other cultures.[128] Cultural relativism is tied to *moral* relativism. That can be *descriptive*: "some human beings have fundamentally different moral standards and values". There is also *normative* moral relativism: "For individuals or groups with divergent moral frameworks, when their moral differences cannot be rationally resolved they should not judge the moral behaviour of each other nor act toward each other in such a way as to attempt to bring one side into conformity with the standards of the other".[129] Not good, not bad, but different. This is the category that multiculturalists embrace.

The consequences of accepting the doctrine of cultural relativism is that we can no longer state that the practices of another society are inferior (or superior) to our own. We can also no longer criticise our own culture, as there is no universal standard to judge our practices with. We can only establish the fact that certain practices occur in our society and that not all societies are homogeneous and there is no universal standard to decide what is right and what is wrong. Accordingly differences are good, or should at least be tolerated.

Connected to relativism is post-modernism, an intellectual trend still not abandoned by academics, nor by other intellectual or media elites, and a trend which has seeped through in wide popular convictions. Iranian-Canadian sociology professor Haideh Moghissi (1944), who authored *Feminism and Islamic Fundamentalism: The Limits of Postmodern Analysis* (1999), lists the characteristics of postmodernism. I cite her list in its entirety:

- The disenchantment with the foundation of modern social thought, with Western modernity, and the demystification of scientific objectivity and objective knowledge.
- The emphasis on narratives and the rejection of metanarratives and grand theories.
- Suspicion of classical notions of reason, truth, universal progress, and the rejection of the idea of the existence of a hidden essential meaning and direction in history, with the emphasis, instead on discontinuity, difference and the celebration of the 'local'.
- The concern over representations of the 'Other', both imagined and real, and over the process of marginalization of Others.

---

128 Rachels, James, *The Elements of Moral Philosophy*, New York: McGraw-Hill 2003, pp. 18-19.
129 Miller, Christian, 'Moral Relativism and Moral Psychology', pp. 346-367 (346-347), in: Hales, Steven (ed.), *A Companion to Relativism*, Chicester: Wiley-Blackwell 2011.

- An absorption with language and the study of discourse as ways of thinking and speaking which reflect the distribution of power in society.
- An engagement with questions of sexuality as a historical construct and with sexual diversity and difference.
- A preoccupation with identity and with the notion of identity as a choice not a destiny.
- A mistrust of power.
- An awareness that the way things are and are done is not the only way and that all beliefs and knowledge are cultural constructs, and hence contingent and conversable.[130]

Postmodernism, like cultural relativism, promotes a celebration of cultural difference and rejects an emphasis on universal human rights. Moghissi sees common ground between postmodernists and Islamic fundamentalists. Both share an "[...] unremitting hostility to the social, cultural and political processes of change and knowledge and rationality, originating in the West, known as modernity".[131] Multiculturalists share the postmodern reluctance for cultural change. That is why "differences" have to be "tolerated", so that members from minority groups do not have to succumb to the "imposition" of majority norms and practices. This leads us to the final premise.

6. Minority Cultures Must Not be Criticised by the Dominant Culture which Has the Positive Obligation to Preserve These

If a multiculturalist had the choice between changing harmful minority practices or changing the way these practices are 'perceived', he would choose the latter. One reason for this call for leaving minority cultures intact is the concern that a given community may go *extinct*. This is not a form of genocide, but the idea that a group's distinct ethno-culture over the generations dissipates and disintegrates into mainstream culture. The loss of language, for instance, or intermarriage leads to extinction. In the world's history, many cultures have ceased to exist at a given point. One can think of the Ancient Greek, Romans, Inca's, and Maya's. But even nowadays cultures are going extinct, for instance, the Alyutors (25 members left), the Kamasins (2 members left) and the Kerek (4 members left), all people endangered with assimilation into the Russian population.[132] Their children are more likely to feel in tune with a Russian identity than their grandparents. For multiculturalists who believe minority culture is a defining marker of mental wellbeing, this process of extinction must be stopped. As Cliteur writes:

---

130 Moghissi, Haideh, *Feminism and Islamic Fundamentalism. The Limits of Postmodern Analysis*, London and New York: Zed Books 1999, pp. 50-51.
131 Moghissi 1999, p. 52.
132 <http://en.wikipedia.org/wiki/List_of_extinct_indigenous_peoples_of_Russia>.

Ethnic multiculturalists often complain about cultures vanishing without rendering account of *why* that has happened. Or rather: they suggest the disappearance has something to do with dark machinations such as colonialism, imperialism or its sublimated version: universalism. But is it not possible that cultures vanish because people turn away from them – completely voluntary? Sometimes, humans simply leave an identity behind, like a snake losing its skin. Why should we not accept that as a fact of life?[133]

One could raise the issue that under modernisation and globalisation, members of minority cultures are faced with much more 'change' than members of the majority culture and that this is a difficult psychological process. But change can also be very positive; there are great psychological *advantages* for members of minority cultures changing their culture under the influence of the dominant majority. More freedom, more liberty, more choices, greater wealth, peace, stability and many more of the plusses the West has which caused immigration flows towards the Euro-American culture. Apparently, the monoculture from the "culture of origin" compelled first generation immigrants to *move away in search of change*.

Yet, promoting majority culture is considered oppressive. Haideh Moghissi writes that some scholars are suffering from the "Lawrence of Arabia syndrome", and that they hold on to lower moral expectations when analysing "simpler societies". This leads to a situation where intellectuals rise to defend practices, even when activists and intellectuals are crying out in countries elsewhere. "The condition of 'the Lawrence of Arabia syndrome' leads Western scholars to leap to the defense of any and all aspects of the foreign cultures they study, especially third-world societies, even if this means defending conduct they would never tolerate in their own country and even if it means ignoring or criticising intellectuals from the societies they study who condemn the very things they defend".[134] For instance, in the multicultural debate, multiculturalist intelligentsia in the West craft an image of Muslim women with depicting them as "[...] empowered, militant, and dignified citizens with a firmly integrated sense of self".[135]

Yet, Muslim women in Europe do not always have the "agency" that is projected upon them. Nor always the lack of it either. But what matters here is that multiculturalists use the "agency-argument" to shelve their judgement in order not to take sides. Instead of condemning acts that would never be allowed in the Euro-American culture, multiculturalists focus on the *liberty to choose*. A good example is Parekh's defence of female genital

---

133 Cliteur, Paul, 'Van etnisch naar kosmopolitisch multiculturalistisme' (From ethnic to cosmopolitan Multiculturalism), pp. 61- 76 (73), in: Manen, N.F. van, *De multiculturele samenleving en het recht* (The Multicultural Society and the Law), Nijmegen: Ars Aequi Libri 2002.
134 Moghissi 1999, p. vii.
135 Moghissi 1999, pp. 49-50.

mutilation. Although the UK government criminalised it in 1985, Parekh (who calls it 'clitoridectomy') focuses on those adults freely undergoing it and the benefits it has for these women.[136] He addresses the problem of harmful customs within a community, yet believes that members of the cultural hegemony should not interfere, as culture can be best changed from within, as well as through a process of "intercultural dialogue".[137] The ideal is that a sense of societal belonging is cultivated without the pressure of assimilation, where legitimate cultural differences are protected, plural cultural identities are cherished, and the shared and precious identity of shared citizenship is not weakened.[138]

But regardless of whether membership of a culture is coerced, maintained under pressure or freely chosen, it is very well possible to pass judgement nonetheless. To some, this may be misleading and seem like a wild statement. The point is that the fact that someone does something out of free will by no means implies we should forsake public judgement. Especially not if the debate concerns rites considered unacceptable for members of the majority culture and when members from the minority culture vehemently protest against it. Criticism and rejection is then perfectly warranted.

However, Charles Taylor writes: "[A]ll should enjoy the presumption that their *traditional* culture has value",[139] and "cultures [...] are almost certain to have something that deserves our admiration and respect, even if it is accompanied by much that we have to abhor and reject". That it is better to withhold negative judgement when it comes to objectionable ideas and practices is not explicated by multiculturalists *as such*, though negative judgement logically falls under the header of nonrecognition. Parekh steers in that direction by stating that the basic concern underlying political correctness – which he would like to rename 'political decency' – is *valid*. "It represents a protest against stigmatization, intended or *unintended* humiliation, subtle and crude ways of keeping others in their place, triggering their painful personal and collective memories, and perpetuating inequalities of power and esteem. Forms of expression and modes of address are never politically and culturally innocent".[140]

Importantly, multiculturalist discourse consists of a subset of terminology. This discourse is identified through terms as equality, dignity, respect, recognition, difference, tolerance, agency, inclusion – all good. Insensitive, arrogance, superiority, oppression, racism, discrimination, dominance, supremacy, exclusion – all bad. Even *unintended* humiliation should be carefully avoided in order not to cripple people with self-hatred.

---

136 Among more, benefits which Parekh lists are FGM as regulating women's sexuality and that it allows them to remind them that they are primarily mothers rather than wives. See: Parekh, p. 71, in: Cohen *et al.* 1999.
137 Parekh 2000, pp. 336-337.
138 Parekh 2000, p. 343.
139 Taylor 1994, p. 68. [Italics added]
140 Parekh 2008, p. 55. [italics added]

When it comes to abhorrent practices, this principled intellectual 'laissez-faire' approach is connected to the doctrine of multiculturalism. Rumy Hasan describes a 'soft' form of multiculturalism in the United Kingdom, which started to take shape in the 1980s. Paramount to this 'soft' multiculturalism is not so much legal exceptions or state subsidies, but instead a *non-interventionist* approach on behalf of local and national government.[141]

This has connotations within the doctrine of "live and let live" which is founded upon the notion of recognition of and respect for difference.[142] There is, however, one exception to the 'laissez-faire' approach. That is: multiculturalists condemn judging. That means that if someone condemns a minority practice, a multiculturalist would condemn that condemning. The act of condemning condemnation is not that overt with it usually entailing stating that moral indignation is 'intolerant', even though, as I argued above, moral indignation is constitutive of toleration. This attitude can only be maintained by *not being specific*.[143] That is because the moment a *specific* practice (e.g. full face veiling, ritual slaughter, and radicalisation of youths) needs to be evaluated, a *general* positive attitude is insufficient.

Let us return to *Sealandistan*. In Sealandistan, the two communities are equal in size. If we would alter the case a bit, making the Blueskins, where animals have a better future than the elderly, the hegemonic community. Traditionally, the elderly are fed a lethal pill by their relatives after their 90th birthday, to prevent suffering, although Blueskins – as members of the majority – are free to criticise this custom and it is likely that the tradition will perish in the process of modernisation. This is because change in a hegemonic community is either not considered to have adverse psychological effects, or people are just expected to deal with stress induced by change. On the other hand, the minority Greenskin feast of animal kicking must be respected, so the Blueskin intellectual elite believes. Even moral indignation towards the practice is considered "intolerant". The multiculturalists' fear is, that a national debate on the (de)merits of this monthly happening might cause tension within the nation. Even more, those wanting to address the issue are consistently portrayed as racists, as "not *all* Greenskins celebrate the feast". Even though some Greenskins themselves indeed fiercely oppose the practice – some even dispute that it is a part of their traditional cultural heritage, Blueskin multiculturalist philosophers have embraced the notion that for Greenskins it is important that their minority cultural identity is recognised. Moreover, those few Greenskin public intellectuals criticising the practice have been shunned from the community, and Blueskins therefore do not accept them as noteworthy representatives anymore. They do listen to Greenskin leaders who say that racism and discrimination are the underlying motives for critiquing the lack of animal welfare.

---

141 Hasan, Rumy, *Multiculturalism. Some Inconvenient Truths*, London: Politico's Publishing 2010, pp. 10-11.
142 Hasan 2010, pp. 13-14.
143 See: Waldron 1991, p. 756.

The Parliament of Sealandistan has decided animal welfare laws do not apply to Greenskins and has agreed to subsidise the feast. Some Blueskins actually participate, as they want to celebrate diversity.[144] Nonetheless, for most – non-elite – Blueskins, this 'feast' is unacceptable. Every month, the squares of Sealandistan colour red with animal blood, new generations are continuingly indoctrinated with this horrible custom, and the police has difficulty controlling the protests of animal rights activists demanding that animals be replaced by piñata's. However, the nation continues allowing the feast as Greenskins are considered to need their minority culture for a sense of self-worth and it is believed that their sense of belonging largely depends on the feast. Not intervening in the monthly animal kicking avoids societal tensions, the argument goes. Also, some are worried that abolishing the practice might drive the tradition underground, making it impossible to exert some control on the event at all.

Now we reverse the situation. This time Greenskins make up the dominant majority. Under the influence of modernity, the feast of animal kicking has been altered. Children now dress up as their favourite animal, and no kicking is involved. The Greenskins are proud of their ability to progress morally. Although, it did make some members of the older generation a bit grumpy. They feel Sealandistan was better in the old days, when people did not give up on their traditions under the pressure of something as futile as "animal welfare". They miss the old days, hanging around with family and friends, kicking animals to death in happy harmony. Some are even a bit lonely, reminiscing about the days that were.

Nevertheless, at least they do not have to worry about being slipped a lethal pill after the age of 90, a practice common under the Blueskins. This cultural minority traditionally "takes care" of its elderly in a way that revolts the Greenskins. The Blueskins, however, do not see anything wrong with this practice. They celebrate life passionately, and it helps them to know they will not be left to suffer, old and forgotten. Ninety is a beautiful age. Who would want to be older than that, anyway? Moreover, the funerals are truly festive, with people coming together in beautiful traditional dress, singing old Blueskin songs. Blueskin community leaders state that the '90 Pill'-tradition is an "act of true love". However, not all Blueskins value the practice. Slowly, but surely, modernity is entering the community. More and more, the elderly are coming forward saying they do not want other people deciding for them when to go. Parents and children are learning to make clear arrangements on the basis of mutual consent; still, there is a long way to go. Change takes time, and the (subsidised) community leaders are not willing to give up just yet. In the meantime, Blueskin intellectuals hope to speed up the process of modernity by calling for legal penalties for this "act of murder" of their elderly. The reason being that as it is now, the '90 Pill'-tradition is exempted for murder from the Sealandistan penal code. These

---

144 Some Blueskins even wear traditional Greenskin clothing, which Greenskins think looks a bit silly.

intellectuals are in a double bind: not only are they loathed in their own community, they are also ignored by the Greenskin elite, as the latter see them as obnoxious troublemakers. In addition, the Greenskin politically correct intelligentsia believes that it is important for the wellbeing of the minority of Blueskins to be respected and recognised in their cultural identity, even if that entails tolerating a practice they themselves find revolting. Some even take great pride in not succumbing to the increasing pressure to abolish the '90 Pill'-tradition, and revere their broadmindedness although others are willing to meet the critics halfway, and suggest to up the age to 95. They are concerned that banning the practice entirely might endanger the culture of Blueskins and will cause social tensions. Moreover, the Greenskins believe legislating against the practice is counterproductive, as they think it will frustrate the natural process of letting go of the tradition within the Blueskin community. This debate has been lingering for quite some time. In the meantime, many elderly are put to rest, even if they had many years to go still.

Who is ready to judge? In assessing the situation in Sealandistan, we can now see what this case obviously lacks, which is the universalist position that kicking animals to death for fun or terminating the lives of healthy elderly without consent are practices one should judge as harmful and not to be tolerated. No matter what individuals state is valuable to their sense of identity or communal belonging.

From the doctrine of multiculturalism, however, there are three responses to the feast of animal kicking and the '90 Pill'-tradition: celebration, calling for tolerance, and relativism (non-judgmentalism). This is because multiculturalists conclude from the idea that minority culture is so important to one's identity (which, as I stated above, is not necessarily the case), that minority cultures need to be free from criticism and preserved. Kymlicka states that a larger and political, institutionalised structure is needed to preserve minority culture and protect it against the homogenising forces of the majority culture within a state. Each individual needs to feel a sense of security from the cultural framework(s) from which he makes his choices, he argues.[145]

An alternative to this "intellectual laissez-faire" is provided by John Stuart Mill. In his article 'Mill and the Value of Moral Distress', Jeremy Waldron takes the position that moral distress is actually *positive*, and not a form of harm that Mill would not admit. This means that the feeling of being disturbed by the simple knowledge that lifestyles are practiced or opinions held which are taken to be immoral, is not harmful, but contributes to social progress.[146] Moral distress should thus not be suppressed, but ventilated. Mill's treatise involved, *inter alia*, the question of what the limits of the power that can be legitimately exercised by society over the individual are. But even more so, it was an argument for free

---

145 Kymlicka 1989, p. 169.
146 Waldron, Jeremy, 'Mill and the Value of Moral Distress', *Political Studies* 1987, pp. 410-423 (410).

speech. Mill thought of free speech not merely as an end, but as a means for social and moral progress.

Now, one could easily argue that being disturbed by someone else's lifestyle is something that should be kept private and ignored. Mill, though, was convinced that when widespread moral distress is detectable in the community, then – other than taking it is a ground for interference – that is a positive and healthy sign that the processes of "ethical confrontation" are taking place.[147] Ethical confrontation, as Waldron defines it, is "[...] the open clash between earnestly-held ideals and opinions about the nature and basis of the good life. Ethical confrontation should be understood to include conflicts on all sorts of issues – moral, philosophical, political and religious – and to range from verbal debate on the one hand to the demonstration and flaunting of the substance of rival lifestyles on the other".[148] If there is no ethical confrontation, this would be alarming evidence that we are failing in our task to keep our society progressive. How so? Because, first, it contributes to the emergence of new and better ideas: "[...] brand new ideas do not spring up ready-formed in the minds of their proponents; they emerge as it were phoenix-like from 'the collision of adverse opinions' in the antagonism of open debate and confrontation".[149] The second argument does not relate to ideas themselves, Waldron continues, but to the way in which they are held.

> According to Mill, progress is empty and the truth about the good life not worth pursuing, if the views that result are not held in a lively and committed spirit with a full awareness of their meaning and significance for human life and action. When ideas and lifestyles clash in open debate, each is put on its mettle, and its adherents are required continually to reassert and therefore to re-examine the content and grounds of their views. No view, however popular, can afford to take its pre-eminence for granted in an atmosphere of open controversy; each person will take his view seriously and be made acutely aware in the course of the debate of all its implications for his life and practice. So, if a given creed has anything to offer, ethical confrontation will bring it out; and if it has darker, hidden implications, those too in the course of earnest and committed debate about its desirability.[150]

Moreover, involvement in ethical confrontation, Mill believed, benefited humans both morally and intellectually. That is partly a matter of "[...] the development of a certain sort of open-mindedness – the open-mindedness that results when each man is intellectually

---

147 Waldron 1987, p. 417.
148 Waldron 1987, p. 414.
149 Waldron 1987, p. 415.
150 Ibid.

alert to the possibility of criticism and cares passionately about its adequate rebuttal". The existence of clashing opinions is the only explanation of the progressive character of Western civilisation.

If anything, Waldron submits, these arguments suggest rethink of moral offence and distress. Ethical confrontation stimulates progress and improves people morally and intellectually. However, this is not a painless affair; if one takes its views seriously, it hurts to be contradicted and it distresses to see lifestyles that contradict one's grounds. Colliding opinions naturally disturb people. However, "[i]f nobody is disturbed, distressed, or hurt in this way, that is a sign that ethical confrontation is not taking place, and that in turn, as we have seen, is a sign that the intellectual life and progress of our civilization may be grinding to a halt".[151] To conclude, a progressive person has no interest in avoiding the "distress occasioned by contradiction or the pain and shock of forceful debate".[152]

Unfortunately, a multiculturalist prefers to respect minority culture as a way to avoid causing offence. Members of minorities are fine just the way they are. Voicing critique is expected to cause psychological harm and it is better to accommodate minorities in their cultural needs.

The question then arises when asking how to preserve a minority culture is: culture *at which stage*? Hypothetically, if we would want to preserve an Afghan minority culture in France, we have to ask which version. If we choose the Afghani 1970s, we can leave the burkas, as women wore mini-skirts. If we would like to preserve contemporary Afghan culture, we should subsidise a French Taliban. Preservation in the form of subsidies, but also halting debates on cultural beliefs or practices from the basis of "respecting differences" implies taking a "[…] favoured 'snapshot' version of it, and insist that this version must persist at all costs, in its defined purity, irrespective of the surrounding social, economic, and political circumstances".[153] Members of minority groups are subsequently encouraged, morally, politically and institutionally, to hold on to their traditional culture, regardless of abhorrent practices that comes along.

We should instead acknowledge that tight-knit communities *exert pressure* on individuals *not to integrate within the dominant culture*. One can think of gossip, social control, ostracising, or violence, not excluding murder. As a consequence, being a member of an ethnic or religious cultural minority is not beneficial to the freedom of choosing life options, but a restriction. Cultural groups can thus very well *limit* the ability to "choose life options". Some people leave such suffocating communities. These are people who have been raised into a group culture and decided later in life to choose a lifestyle diverting from the one

---

151 Waldron 1987, pp. 416-417.
152 Waldron 1987, p. 423.
153 Waldron 1991, p. 788.

they were born into. Moreover, many people alter the 'culture' they grew up in, and every generation develops in a slightly different way from the one before.

Besides, it is perfectly possible to respect an individual while questioning and criticising his cultural heritage and wanting him to adopt certain norms, beliefs and practices. In fact, through art, literature, debate, education or mere conversation, people address injustices and promote ideals. If we look back to our history, we notice the phenomenal, unprecedented change in, for instance, technology, medicine, emancipation, literacy, equal access to institutions, and more, in just three generations. If there would have been an influential force imposing cultural stagnation throughout the past 100 years, we would still have census suffrage, common illiteracy, no women in public functions, and moreover, no I-phone, to name just a few elements of the past. We would still believe homosexuality is a punishable sin and that women should be fired from their jobs the moment they are pregnant. Critiquing cultural beliefs and practices is a common everyday exercise. Wanting to improve society (and even being conservative is striving to improve society by stopping progressives) is even the primary goal of education and debate. It is why individuals create medicine, restore buildings, and vote for Parliament. It is why people write and read books, give and go to lectures.

In short, even *if* we were to accept that culture is important for one's identity and that nonrecognition constitutes psychological harm, then *still* it is not a logical conclusion that cultural practices and beliefs should be maintained through respect or tolerance.

CONCLUSION

The multiculturalist moral and political perspective on human life is one that values cultural identity, diversity, tolerance, and authenticity, *regardless* of the level of abhorrence of certain practices. Not recognising minority cultural identity is assumed to cause psychological suffering. It is the multiculturalist belief that culture is good because it is valued by its bearers; that too much focus on what is undesirable threatens the "fact" that minority members need their culture intact, and that too much change is a threat to identity. Communities are expected to provide individuals with an integrated sense of self, even if those communities embrace harmful practices. The focus is always on groups, not on individuals. Changing group culture should come "from within", and "outsiders" should refrain from "imposing" their norms.[154] Instead we are blinded by the positive evaluation of minority culture. At best, there is room for "intercultural dialogue": an invitation to talk in order to integrate cultures. As a consequence, undesirable minority practices are

---

154 See also: Guiora, Amos, *Freedom from Religion: Rights and National Security*, Oxford: Oxford University Press 2013, p. 5.

expected to be voluntarily relinquished without imposing norms, judging and "excluding the Other".

Individuals who wish to loosen their heritage, are guided back by two forces: people from their own community (family members, neighbours, community elders) and multi-culturalists, who maintain that one's background determines identity. To suggest a minority has the moral and legal right to be preserved – by not-judging, subsidising, exempting from laws – and justifying that process by calling on a psychological need to belong to a minority community or 'authenticity', makes no sense. It also implies wanting to preserve a culture that is partly withering away because its members are in the process of relinquishing their heritage voluntarily. Eventually, cultures develop under the influence of globalisation, international trade, consumerism, technology, Hollywood entertainment, internet and mass migration. In short: we live in a world of cultural exchange. And this may be good change, but also change that we should not be happy about. This is for instance the case when immigration brings with it a stark increase in religious fundamentalism that curtails the freedom to choose from life's many options.

In order to address issues connected to a modern multicultural society, identity claims need to be substituted for arguments and ethical confrontation should take place. Instead, multiculturalists have a wrong focus when it comes to passing judgements. The content of a judgement of an idea or practice is deemed offensive for those *not* involved. "Not everyone is pressured into it, people choose freely, not all adhere to these ideas" will be the most often heard objections when debating the limits of tolerance. That is because a multiculturalist is worried that negative critiques are projected upon "the innocent", on those who are not part of the practice, but who are still seen as members of the community. They are considered to suffer from harm from "guilt by association". That is why, when invited to make a moral judgement, a multiculturalist who is not ready to give up on his convictions must resort to non-judgmentalism.

It is not surprising that multiculturalism has received wide criticism nor is it without reason that many political leaders publicly gave up on it. Yet, the reason they did so was not that they thought multiculturalist ideology was internally inconsistent or based on false premises, rather it was *reality* that actually caught on. The question is now how this political ideology of multiculturalism plays out in the real world, outside of Sealandistan. In that real world, in the United Kingdom, there are special religious tribunals where minority members are faced with a sublegal regime. Islamists and multiculturalists publically call for more recognition of these "Sharia councils". Before we look into that, it is important to study the political ideology of the religious leaders behind these councils.

2   Islamic Fundamentalism

Introduction

It is at the cross section of multiculturalism and Islam-related practices that contemporary multiculturalism is seen to be struggling the most. Multiculturalist sensitivities still detract many from studying the underlying foundations of Islamist ideology.[1] Surrounding this is a common belief that it is wrong to focus on Islamic fundamentalism, while there are so many Muslims who do not adhere to that. The idea is that focusing on the negative side is unpleasant for Muslim citizens who want nothing to do with this political Islam. Some go beyond unpleasant, but call this "racist" or "discriminatory", "as if all Muslims are terrorists". *Of course* not all Muslims are fundamentalist. That is not what I wish to convey. In fact, worldwide, it is non-fundamentalist Muslims who suffer most from Islamic fundamentalism. Yet, at the same time, Islamic fundamentalism has become a problem in the West, as well. According to a 2013 poll, about half of European Muslims adhere to fundamentalist notions of Islam: that there is only one interpretation of the Koran, that Muslims should return to the roots of Islam, and that religious obligations are more important than secular laws.[2]

There is a steady body of Islamist thought justifying a parallel legal order, such as expressed in Sharia councils. It is not an accident that 45-73 per cent of European Muslims believe religious laws are more important than secular laws: they are led by the idea that religion is not limited to the private sphere, but that the body of Islamic laws – Sharia –

---

1   "A candid perusal of religion is often rejected as being "merely negative" or motivated by feelings of spite on the part of the researcher. Great pressure is exerted to portray religion only from its most positive side.", Cliteur 2010, p. 80. See also: Bale, Jeffrey, 'Denying the Link between Islamist Ideology and Jihadist Terrorism: "Political Correctness" and the Undermining of Counterterrorism', *Perspectives on Terrorism* 2013, via <http://www.terrorismanalysts.com/pt/index.php/pot/article/view/290/html>.

2   According to a 2013 poll in six European countries (Germany, France, the Netherlands, Belgium, Austria, and Sweden) among 9,000 Turkish and Moroccan immigrants and natives. See: Koopmans, Ruud, 'Religious Fundamentalism and Hostility against Out-groups. A Comparison of Muslims and Christians in Western Europe', *Journal of Ethnic and Migration Studies* 2015, pp. 33-57. That does not mean that all fundamentalist European Muslims are committed to using violence to overthrow secular regimes in favour of a Sharia state. Nonetheless, other studies have shown that the number of people willing to use violence to defend their religion is much smaller than those merely believing a fundamentalist version of Islam, but still is a staggering ten percent. See: 'Schweigen, Fragen, unerwünschtes Lob. Ruud Koopmans über die Reaktionen auf seine Fundamentalismus-Studie', *WZB Mitteilungen* 2014, pp. 53-55 (54). See also: Roex, Ineke, Stiphout, Sjef van, and Tillie, Jean, *Salafisme in Nederland* (Salafism in The Netherlands), Universiteit van Amsterdam, Instituut voor Migratie en Etnische Studies 2010.

supersedes secular political and legal rights and duties.[3] Therefore, this deserves to be studied rather than ignored or downplayed, as multiculturalists tend to do.

For decades now, scholars have been yielding to the Islamists' intellectual seductions.[4] Western scholars deny the punishing features of Islamic practices and traditions and instead emphasise the positive aspects of Islamic culture. However, this is not the best way to show one's solidarity with Muslims around the globe. I wonder why then, given the gripping evidence of the fundamentalists' repressive measures against women, homosexuals, Jews, Christians, atheists, unbelievers and non-fundamentalist Muslims, this subject is usually neglected in academic analyses.[5] Haideh Moghissi guesses why that may be the case: "is this tendency driven by fear of physical violence or 'Orientalist' tendencies? Is it driven by a paralyzing anxiety to be accused of cultural insensitivity? Or is it a postmodern specimen of the attitude to 'exotic' practices and institutions which viewed from afar, are celebrated as 'authentic', 'local' responses to indigenous problems – and excused as inevitable because they 'fit' with the culture?"[6]

Islamic fundamentalism is not something scholars should overlook, especially as immigration and globalisation have led to an expansion of Islamic fundamentalism. It is important therefore to not let "cultural sensitivities" overshadow the fact there currently is increasing competition between Islamic and secular law on Western soil.

This chapter will examine Islamic fundamentalism, which for the purpose of clarity will be equated with the concepts of Islamism and political Islam. Next, in the third chapter, we will see the union of Islamic fundamentalism and multiculturalism in the case study of Sharia councils in the United Kingdom where religious tribunals are allowed to function and high-impact speeches have been made on behalf of accommodation. Moreover, as I will discuss there, several influential religious leaders who founded Britain's first Sharia council have been trained at Egypt's al-Azhar University and Medina University in Saudi Arabia. They have come to Britain to espouse the ideology of Islamic fundamentalism Islam. What is this ideology that multiculturalists prefer to downplay?

SHARIA AS THE SACRED LAW OF ISLAM

German political scientist Bassam Tibi (1944), author of *Political Islam, World Politics and Europe* (2008), *Islamism and Islam* (2012) and *The Sharia State* (2013) uses the terms political Islam, Islamism or religious fundamentalism interchangeably when he describes

---

3   Koopmans 2015.
4   Beautifully formulated by Moghissi 1999, p. viii.
5   See also: Baron, B., 'Tolerable Intolerance?' Silence on Attacks on Women by Fundamentalists', *Contention* 1996, in: Moghissi 1999, pp. 4-6.
6   Moghissi 1999, pp. 6-7.

the political and religious doctrines of radical Muslim thinkers.[7] In order to understand the background of Sharia councils in the United Kingdom, it is essential to comprehend the political ideology that is Islamism.

In his analysis, Tibi makes a distinction between Islam and Islamism.[8] He claims the distinction between Islam and Islamism is crucial for a peaceful co-existence between Muslims and non-Muslims alike stating that "[t]he religious faith of Islam is not an obstacle to peace or a threat to the non-Muslim other. Islamism, on the other hand, creates deep civilizational rifts between Muslims and non-Muslims".[9] The key difference is that Islam, on the one hand, is about faith – for instance, adhering to the five pillars: 1) declaring there is no god except God, and Muhammad is God's Messenger, 2) ritual prayer five times a day, 3) giving a small percentage of one's savings to the poor and needy, 4) fasting and self-control during Ramadan, and 5) pilgrimage to Mecca at least once in a lifetime – if one is able to do so. Islamism, on the other hand, is about political order, a religionised political order, aimed at establishing a unity of state and religion under a system of constitutionally mandated Islamic law.[10] The efforts of Islamic fundamentalists are much more than just a religious movement. In one phrase: Islamic fundamentalism is the political ideology of a Sharia state.[11] British-German Professor of Arabic and Islam Joseph Schacht (1902-1969), the leading Western scholar on Islamic law, described Sharia as the sacred law of Islam, as the epitome of Islamic thought, as the most typical manifestation of the Islamic way of life, "the core and kernel of Islam itself". It consists of an all-encompassing body of religious duties; it is the complete aggregate of the commands of Allah which regulates the lives of all Muslims in every aspect.[12] Broadly speaking, Islam is divided into two religious sects, these being Sunni and Shi'a Muslims. The focus of this book is on

---

7   See also: Bennoune 2013; Tibi, Bassam, 'The Politization of Islam into Islamism in the Context of Global Religious Fundamentalism', *Journal of Middle East and Africa* 2010, pp. 153-170; Cliteur, Paul, 'Female Critics of Islamism', *Feminist Theology* 2011, pp. 154-167; Desai, Meghnad, *Rethinking Islamism: The Ideology of the New Terror*, London/New York: I.B. Taurus 2007; Sifaoui, Mohamed, *Pourquoi l' islamisme séduit-il?*, Paris: Armand Colin 2010; Strindberg, Anders and Wärn, Mats, *Islamism: Religion, radicalisation, and Resistance*, Cambridge: Polity 2011.

8   Many do not make a distinction between Islam and Islamism and believe the fault lies within Islam as such. See, for instance, Sultan, Wafa, *A God Who Hates. The Courageous Woman Who Inflamed the Muslim World Speaks Out Against the Evils of Islam*, New York: St. Martin's Press 2009 and Ali, Ayaan Hirsi, *Heretic. Why Islam Needs a Reformation Now*, New York: Harper Collins 2015. Samuel P. Huntington makes a distinction between Islam and Islamic fundamentalism, yet believes the problem is Islam: "The underlying problem for the West is not Islamic fundamentalism. It is Islam, a different civilization whose people are convinced of the superiority of their culture and are obsessed with the inferiority of their power". (Huntington, Samuel P., *The Clash Of Civilizations and The Remaking of World Order*, New York: Simon and Schuster Paperbacks 1996 (2003), p. 217.

9   Tibi, Bassam, *Islamism and Islam*, New Haven & London: Yale University Press 2012, p. vii.

10 Tibi 2012, pp. 1-3. See also: Tibi, Bassam, *The Shari'a State. Arab Spring and* Democratization, London: Routledge 2013, p. 186.

11 Tibi 2013, p. 95.

12 Schacht 1982, p. 1.

Sunni Islam. It is important to recognise that there are four Sunni schools of law (*madhhab*): the Hanafi, Maliki, Shafi'i and Hanbali school, all of which are identical in approximately 75 per cent of their legal conclusions.[13]

Sharia is foremost a *body of laws* that believers have to adhere to, rather than a source of moral values believers may voluntarily draw inspiration from.

The fundamentalists' goal is to reform society in such a fashion so that it corresponds most towards an idealised past, for which the model can be found in Islamic laws.[14] That means that *Islamic* fundamentalists share the ideal that society must be saved and purified by means of establishing a true *Islamic* society. This is done on the basis of a 'correct' interpretation of divine texts with the earliest states as under Muhammad in the 7th century serving as example.[15]

An examination of Islamic religious sources reveals that Muhammad Ibn Abdullah was born approximately in 570 AD in the Arabian city of Mecca. Supposedly, he received his first revelation from Allah at age 40, when he was visited by archangel Gabriel who channelled Allah's views. These revelations formed the Koran, the holy book of Islam, which

---

13 See: 'Introduction', pp. vii-xii (vii), in: Keller, Nuh Ha Mim, *Reliance of the Traveller: A Classic Manual of Islamic Sacred Law*; 'Umdat al-Salik' by Ahmad ibn Naqib al-Misri (d. 769-1368) in Arabic with Facing English Text, Commentary, and Appendices. Edited and translated by Nuh Ha Mim Keller, Beltsville: Amana 1991. I will refer to Keller throughout this book. This volume of Islamic law is a translation by Nuh Ha Mim Keller of the original Arabic text by Ahmad ibn Naqib al-Misri (d. 1368). Although it is mostly from the Shafi'i school of jurisprudence, the four Sunni schools are identical in approximately 75 percent of their legal conclusions. Also, this is not a text just by this one author, but a collaborative effort – as are most works on Islamic law – by a whole school of research and interpretation in explaining "rules of divine origin". Moreover, during the course of history, sheikhs have updated this collection. It is important to note that before publication of the book in 1991 Keller received a convincing degree of recognition by renowned Islamic scholars who stated Keller "understands the texts of this volume and is qualified to expound it", praised him for his "accuracy and integrity", and that "this translation is superior to anything produced by orientalists". It has been certified by the al-Azhar University in Egypt, which is acknowledged as one of the world's leading centers for training Islamic scholars.
The Hanafi school is the most prevalent one in Muslim-majority societies, with followers in about one-third of them, including: India, Pakistan, Bangladesh, Afghanistan, Central Asia, the Caucasus, the Balkans, Turkey, Parts of Iraq and Egypt. The Maliki school, the second most-dominant school, prevails in countries such as: The Arabian Gulf States (Kuwait, Qatar, Bahrain, Dubai, and Abu Dhabi), East and West African countries (upper Egypt, Sudan, Tunisia, Algeria, Libya, Morocco, Mali, Nigeria, Chad, Niger, Senegal, Mauritania), Syria and Yemen. The Shafi'i school is widespread in countries such as: Indonesia, Malaysia, Singapore, Sri Lanka, Maldives, Palestine, Jordan, Lebanon, Yemen, and East Africa (Somalia, Kenya, Tanzania). The Hanbali, the most conservative school of Islamic jurisprudence, has most of its adherents in Saudi Arabia. The Ja'fari school of thought is the school of jurisprudence of most Shi'a Muslims. The Shafi'i school is considered to be conservative, as well. See: Re-Orienting the Veil, <http://veil.unc.edu/>, by the University of North Carolina in cooperation with the Center for European Studies/European Union Center of Excellence.
14 Moghissi 1999, p. 69.
15 At the most basic level, fundamentalism refers to a mentality towards time; it proposes to go back to "an ideal past, initial conditions" or "golden age". Whether there ever was such an Islamic "golden age" is subject to debate, but for now beside the point. See for someone who doubts there ever was such an era: Ibn Warraq, *Why I Am Not a Muslim*, Amherst: Prometheus 1995.

Muslims take as "God's word". Next to the Koran, the second most important religious source is the Sunna. Together, the Sunna and the Koran make up the key sources which form the basis of Islam. The Sunna however consists of two components. The first is a large body of statements or testimonies about the exemplary conduct of Muhammad and those who accompanied him, his "companions". These statements are known as *hadiths*. They often have a normative character and consist of examples of behaviour in which Muhammad forbade, disapproved, approved or proscribed a certain type of action. These hadiths serve as a vitally important source of Islamic law. Overall, there are six major collections of hadiths in the Sunni Islam. Of that six, the sayings of Muhammea as collected by the Persian Muslim scholar Muhammad al-Bukhari (810-870) have the highest standing. This collection, called *Sahih al-Bukhari*, was put together over 200 years after Muhammad allegedly received Allah's instructions. The Sahih al-Bukhari consists of nine volumes and deals with, *inter alia*, prayer, funerals, tax, pilgrimage, fasting, sales and trade, debt transfer, agriculture, freeing slaves, wills, jihad, marriage, divorce, food and meals, slaughter, dress, good manners, interpretation of dreams, virtues of the Koran, divine will, punishment laws, disbelievers, bathing, menstrual periods, and on how to deal with apostates.[16] Such a source of information is just as important as the Koran for Islamic law.

The Sunna is said to be passed on by Muhammad's companions, generation after generation. With companions are meant those who accompanied him during his quest for power, and their descendants, and through these generations there is a so-called "chain of transmissions" of what Muhammad did and said, and approved and disapproved of. The term *companions* refers to both the generation of men who knew him personally and strove with him to establish Islam and the two generations that succeeded them. There is a hadith quoting Muhammad saying: "The people of my own generation are the best, then those who come after them, and then those of the next generation".[17] All three generations (the sahaba plus one generation) together are known as the *salafiyaah*, or *salaf*, and they are considered to represent Islam in its most pure, undiluted form. Any recorded statement by Muhammad must be able to be traced back through an uninterrupted chain (*isnad*) of reliable transmitters (the salaf) to Muhammad himself. If the chain is weak or unreliable, the hadith is considered to be less fit as a source of Islamic law.

Next to the Koran and the Sunna, there is a third source of Sharia, namely consensus, or *ijma*, which can be reached by the *Umma* (all the world's Muslims, a Muslim nation, transgressing borders, worldwide), but consensus generally refers to the *ulama*. The term *ulama*, also spelled ulema, is used to describe the body of Muslim scholars who are trained in and have studied Islamic disciplines. They are accepted as the arbiters of what laws follow

---

16 Bukhari's full collection of hadiths is available online via <http://www.sahih-bukhari.com/>.
17 Lacey, Robert, *Inside the Kingdom, Kings, Clerics, Modernists, Terrorists, and the Struggle for Saudi Arabia*, New York: Viking 2009, p. 9.

from Sharia. Fourthly and lastly, there is analogical reasoning, or *qiyas*. This is a method for extending rulings to new situations while limiting innovation. For instance, if wine is prohibited because of intoxication clouds the mind which diverts from a proper focus on Allah, then marijuana must also be forbidden.[18] These sources make up Sharia, often comprehensibly categorised in *fiqh* (jurisprudence). There are fiqh books filled with casuistry, written by authoritative scholars, encompassing every aspect of life, from criminal law and administrative law, to not to pluck your eyebrows and how to enter a bathroom. These fiqh books are seen as extremely important 'manuals'.

It is important to note that Islamic law applies the following scale of religious qualifications, ranging from 1) obligatory (*fard* or *wajib*), 2) recommended (*mandub*), 3) permissable (*mubah*), 4) reprehensible (*makruh*), and 5) forbidden (*haram*). Forbidden acts fall under the header of "enormities". An enormity is a shocking, evil, or immoral act, and is defined as "[...] any sin entailing either a threat of punishment in the hereafter explicitly mentioned by the Koran or hadith [...]". A random selection out of hundreds of forbidden acts to illustrate: idolatry, greed, sarcasm towards the poor because of their poverty, wanting the life of this world (more than the next), eating or drinking from a gold or silver vessel, sexual intercourse with a woman during menstruation, tattoos, men imitating like women or vice versa, women visiting graves, not giving surplus water to someone thirsty, looking with lust at a woman who is not one's unmarriageable kin, touching such a woman, or being alone with her, sodomising your wife, cursing a Muslim, suicide, theft, drinking alcohol, showing others the weak points of the Muslims, and not repenting from an enormity.[19]

POLITICAL ISLAM PART I: WAHHABISM

Islam started in the seventh century as a political ideology, to which people were initially invited to submit under leadership of Muhammad. At later stages in Muhammad's conquest, it was violently forced upon those not freely submitting. In the past few centuries, though, the power of Islam had weakened. This changed in the 18th century, again, in the Arabian Peninsula, when 'Wahhabism' developed.

Wahhabism is a puritanical and reactionary ideology based on the theological foundations laid down by Muhammad bin Abd-al-Wahhab (1703-1792). In the 18th-century Arabian Peninsula, the practice of "government" consisted mainly of local and changing tribal or settlement alliances. Ibn Abd-al-Wahhab was constantly rejected by communities for his narrow and uncompromising views, but this changed as he aligned himself with

---

18 MacEoin, Denis and Green, David (eds.), *Sharia Law or 'One Law for All?'*, London: Civitas: Institute for the Study of Civil Society 2009, p. 27.
19 See: Keller 1991, under p.0.0 and w.52.1 (280). Keller lists 442 of such enormities.

Muhammad bin Saud (d. 1765) in 1744. Ibn Saud was an "able and ambitious desert warrior".[20] The pact between them had the goal of establishing a kingdom based on Sharia in an effort to challenge the Ottoman hegemony, where Ibn Abd-al-Wahhab would deliver the spiritual, and Saud the political and military.[21] Ibn Abd-al-Wahhab was strongly influenced by the teachings of earlier mentioned 13/14th-century Hanbali scholar Ibn Taymiyyah, – who epitomises political Islam.

One of Ibn Taymiyyah's focal points was that the act of interpretation of the Koran, called *tafsir*, may not be based on personal opinion. One cannot discover the meaning of Koranic texts on one's own. In *Ibn Taymiyya and His Times* (2010), Walid Saleh informs us that: "[a] string of prophetic traditions that warn against such a practice are produced, all with the aim of showing that no one has the right to expound freely on the Qur'ān. Indeed, Ibn Taymiyyah is categorically against such a method even if it reproduces the true and valid meaning of the Qur'ān!"[22] Making one's own interpretation is thus out of the equation. Well, then, how do believers know what to believe and how to live according to Islamic rules? The ulema, the elite of religious interpreters, is decisive in these matters, and in Saudi Arabia that means that the correct way is to replicate Islam's pious elders, those who had travelled with Muhammad and the two following generations, the *salaf*.[23] The idea of replicating the Salafi Koranic interpretations, as well as copying the lives of the prophet and the salaf, laid the foundation of what is now commonly known as the Salafi Movement, or Salafism.[24] Only with Salafism can Islam counter the pollution and watering down by un-Islamic influences, which has diminished its perfection – that is the idea. Even more arresting is Ibn Taymiyyah's principle that there is a *need* for violence in defence of true Islam. He stated, for example,

> [t]o fight in defense of religion and belief is a collective duty according to consensus; there is no other duty after belief than fighting the enemy who is

---

20   McHale, T.R., 'A Prospect of Saudi Arabia', *International Affairs* 1980, pp. 622-647 (624).

21   El Fadl, Khaled Abou, *Speaking in God's Name. Islamic Law, Authority and Women*, Oxford: OneWorld 2010, p. 73 (note 43) and Desai 2007, p. 43. Although the first state produced by this alliance did not last, it laid the foundations for the existing Saudi state in Arabia and inspired similar activism elsewhere down to the present day, see the lemma "Precolonial reform and experimentation from 1683 to 1818" in the Encyclopedia Britannica Online via <http://www.britannica.com/EBchecked/topic/295765/Islamic-world/26943/Precolonial-reform-and-experimentation-from-1683-to-1818#ref317414>.

22   Saleh, Walid, 'Ibn Taymiyya and the Rise of Radical Hermeneutics: An Analysis of "An Introduction to the Foundation of Quranic Exegesis"', pp. 123-162 (147), in: Ahmed, Shahab and Rapport, Yossef (eds.), *Ibn Taymiyya and His Times*, Oxford University Press 2010.

23   Buttner 2008, p. 65. The sahaba are those who are said to have actually travelled with Muhammad, the salaf include the two generations after the sahaba.

24   Ibid.

corrupting life and the religion. There [are] no preconditions for this duty and the enemy should be fought with one's best abilities.[25]

This fighting should lead Muslims back to the times of the salaf, and is based on an imperial glory of Islamic civilisation and serves as a guideline for the Islamist demand for a return to history.[26]

Ibn Taymiyyah's teachings strongly influenced Ibn Abd-al-Wahhab. In 'Totalitarianism and Radical Islamic Ideologies', Dutch jurist and political philosopher David Suurland (1975) tells us what the consequence is of this Wahhabi take on Islam:

> To Wahhab, Jihad was the ultimate manifestation of Islam, a furnace in which Muslims are melted out, that allows the separation of the bad Muslim from the good one and that grants its fighters instant access to paradise. The Jihad of Wahhab had little to do with the noble notion of inner struggle; instead, it was focused on purifying the world through the murder of the unbelievers, the infidels, the Christians, the Jews and those Muslims who did not conform to his puritanical version of Islam. In the ideal Wahhabi society, the freedom of the believer is reduced to following the instructions of the faith to the letter. Any diversion, dissent or innovation is in their eyes an act of polytheism, or even worse, apostasy, and thus punishable by death.[27]

Since true Islam was the Islam of Muhammad and his companions, any diversion from the Salafi way of life can be judged as an act of disbelief – *kufr*, related to *kufar*, infidels – and thus an act of apostasy, punishable by death. Confirmation of this is, for instance, found in the hadith: "for the Prophet said, 'If somebody (a Muslim) discards his religion, kill him'".[28]

Let us return to the covenant that Wahhab made with Saud in the 18th century. Saud's gain from cooperation was that Wahhab consecrated the Saudi tribe's raids. Instead of rivalling tribes simply being raided for food, women or profit, those raids became "[...]

---

25   Euben, Roxanne Leslie and Zaman, Muhammad Qasim (eds.), *Princeton Readings in Islamist Thought: Texts and Contexts from al-Banna to Bin Laden*, Princeton: Princeton University Press 2009, p. 443.

26   Tibi 2013, p. 104.

27   Suurland, David, 'Totalitarianism and Radical Islamic Ideologies', pp. 257-309 (287-288), in: Labuschagne, Bart and Sonnenschmidt, Reinhard (eds.), *Religion, Politics and Law: Philosophical Reflections on the Sources of Normative Order in Society*, Leiden: Brill 2009.

28   Ali burnt some people and this news reached Ibn 'Abbas, who said, "Had I been in his place I would not have burnt them, as the Prophet said, 'Don't punish (anybody) with Allah's Punishment.' No doubt, I would have killed them, for the Prophet said, 'If somebody (a Muslim) discards his religion, kill him'". Sahih Bukhari, Volume 4, Book 52, number 260.

jihad – a holy war, to promote, by the sword, Islam's triumph over unbelief".[29] In return for religious legitimacy, Ibn Abd-al-Wahhab received military backing for his ideological and religious war. Saud and Wahhab's pact was sealed by the marriage of Saud with Wahhab's daughter – their descendants would eventually become Saudi Arabia's political leaders for generations. As a result of the Saudi-Wahhabi coalition, Saud, and later his descendants, unleashed a campaign of terror in the Arabian Peninsula, and, for the first time in the history of Islam, there was a legitimised violent jihad against fellow Muslims.[30] The Saud clan would wage war for almost 200 years, yet finally managed to capture Mecca, Medina and Jeddah in 1926, a success booked by descendent Abdul Aziz (1876-1953), now known as Ibn Saud. Those physically responsible for the terror campaigns which were to establish the Kingdom, were the *Ikhwan*, a Wahhabi organisation made up of newly Islamised Bedouin who lived by the strictest Wahhabi tenets. The Ikhwan would be the instrument for moulding the new Saudi Wahhabi society.[31] In the 1920s, their brutality led to 400,000 people killed or wounded and over a million people fled the conquered territories.[32] By the 1930s, Wahhabi religious command had subordinated the Saudi population.[33] In 1932, Ibn Saud declared the territory the Kingdom of Saudi Arabia, made himself king, and his family members the "Royal Family".

POLITICAL ISLAM PART II: THE MUSLIM BROTHERHOOD

Islamic reactionaries admired and respected the Saudi Wahhabis, and they served as a source of inspiration in other circles in the Middle East. They were considered "authentic Muslim warriors" who fought off European control. As a reaction to the political and economic decline of the Islamic world in medieval and modern times, a puritan religious movement beyond Saudi Arabia was in the making which strove to purge itself of all non-Islamic influences and which envisioned a return to the earliest pristine days of Islam.

As Wahhabism was unfolding at the Arabian Peninsula, there was a similar ideological development concerning Salafism taking place in Egypt. Take for instance Muhammad Abduh (1849-1905), an Egyptian reactionary theologian and jurist. He explained the backwardness and weakness of Muslims from the fact that they no longer lived by the principles of the salaf. He mentored Muhammad Rashid Rida (1865-1935), and together

---

29 Kepel, Gilles, *The War for Muslim Minds: Islam and the West*, Cambridge, Massachusetts: The Belknap Press of Harvard University Press 2004, p. 159.

30 Suurland 2009, pp. 257-309 (290).

31 Gold, Dore, *Hatred's Kingdom: How Saudi Arabia Supports the New Global Terrorism*, Washington, DC: Regnery Publishers 2003, pp. 44-45.

32 Gold 2003, p. 49.

33 Schwartz, Stephen, '*Shari'a* in Saudi Arabia, Today and Tomorrow', pp. 19-40 (25), in: Marshall (ed.), *Radical Islam's Rules: The Worldwide Spread of Extreme Shari'a Law*, Lanham, Maryland: Rowman & Littlefield Publishers 2005.

they began the Islamic "reform movement" in Cairo.[34] Rida (who is said to have been financially backed by Ibn Saud[35]) was one of the most important people to be influenced by the Salafi doctrine. He also strongly believed that the weakness and political decline in the Islamic world could only be countered by a return to true Islam. Rida's proliferation of Salafism had profound consequences, for it was Rida who mentored Hassan al-Banna (1905-1949). In 1928, Al-Banna founded a new Islamic organisation, "The Muslim Brotherhood", or in Arabic, *Ikhwan al-Muslimum*. The mission of the organisation was (and still is) to establish a pure Islamic society; a Sharia state. The Brotherhood's credo is: "Allah is our objective. The Prophet is our leader, Qur'an is our law, Jihad is our way, Dying in the way of Allah is our highest hope". On this use of the term jihad, Suurland explains: "It should be explained that the concept of jihad has two forms: the first being the large jihad, which is a life-long obligatory struggle against one's inner-evil, and the small jihad, which is actual armed warfare against unbelievers and those who actively oppose Islam. In this credo, Hassan al-Banna is also directly referring to the small jihad".[36]

Al-Banna's views had a strong *political* dimension. Crucial in understanding Islamism is that it is not a religious movement with political consequences. Rather, it is a political movement with religious consequences.[37] It was al-Banna's ambition to create a global Islamic empire with Sharia as global law: "It is a duty incumbent on every Muslim to struggle towards the aim of making every people Muslim and the whole world Islamic, so that the call of the Muezzin can resound in all the corners of the world: God is greatest [Allahu akbar]!"[38]

He complemented the Salafi doctrine with a rhetoric concerning colonialism and the threat of British control, the influence of foreign companies, on blind imitation of the West, on man-made laws that were failing to prevent crime, on educational mismanagement, and in general on intellectual chaos, the loss of moral values, on signs of desperation

---

34 Buttner 2008, p. 65.

35 "There is money in the affair", one of Ibn Saud's advisors confirmed, see: Kramer, Martin, *Islam Assembled: The Advent of the Muslim Congresses*, New York: Columbia University Press 1986, p. 110, in: Gold 2003, p. 91.

36 Suurland quotes Jamal al-Banna, *Al-Jihad*, al-Qahirah: Dar al-Fikr al-Islami 2002, p. 4: "Refer to the verses (4:71-81) in the Noble book to understand how Allah urges the Muslims to remain alert and to acquire experience in warfare, in armies and troops, as individuals, as circumstances may dictate. (...) Notice how Allah associates warfare with prayer and fasting, establishing it as one of the pillars of Islam". The book Al-jihad by Hassan al-Banna was written to prove to his fellow Muslims that the small jihad was an "integral part of Islam". See footnote 65, in: Suurland 2009, p. 280. Although, for the past few decades, the Muslim Brotherhood has been communicating a message of rejecting violence and inter-faith dialogue, Suurland deems it at best unreliable, considering its associates, *inter alia*, Sayyid Qutb; Amin Al-Husseini, chief Mufti of Jerusalem and associate of Adolf Eichmann; Sheikh Ahmad Yaseen, founder of Hamas; Abdullah Yusuf Azzam, influential ideologue and patron of Osama bin Laden; and Ayman al-Zawahiri, second in command and ideologue of Al-Qaeda.

37 See also: Nawaz, Maajid, *Radical*, London: WH Allen 2012, pp. 85-86.

38 Lia, Brynjar, *The Society of the Muslim Brothers in Egypt*, Reading: Ithaca Press 1998, p. 79.

and loss of will. The Muslim Brotherhood's goals were to free the "Islamic homeland" from foreign authority and to establish an Islamic state within that Islamic homeland.[39] Al-Banna envisioned a new kind of society, one that was orderly, serene and authoritarian, one that was based on conformity and obedience in all areas of life. That also meant rolling back any progress in women's rights, crush individuality and getting rid of human differences.[40] To achieve this, the concept of the Umma, a unified Muslim population (the "Islamic nation"), was needed to drown out disputes.[41] This Umma had to be instilled with an unrelenting anger towards evil enemies, and an enthusiasm for both ultra-conservative communitarian obedience and violence and war.[42] The movement grew rapidly; from four branches in 1929 to over half a million active members in Egypt in 1945; in 1948 there were 2000 branches, crossing the border to Palestine, Sudan, Iraq and Syria. In 1948 Hassan al-Banna was assassinated by two unknown gunmen while waiting for a taxi. But that was not the end of the Muslim Brotherhood.

After the assassination, the Muslim Brotherhood welcomed a new member: renowned literary critic, novelist and poet Sayyid Qutb (1906-1966). He would become the Brotherhood's leading ideologue, inspiring members all over the world, even long after he was convicted of plotting the assassination of Egyptian president Nasser and executed by hanging in 1966.[43]

Jahiliyyah

To understand Qutb's ideology better, it is important to know that in addition to the well-known belief that good Muslims go to heaven (a reward), there is also an imperative what good Muslims should work towards *avoiding* here on earth, and that is the idea of *jahiliyyah*.[44] *Jahiliyyah* is the 'Pre-Islamic Period of ignorance'. That is: Islam was revealed

---

39   Tamimi, Azzam, 'Islam and democracy from Tahtawi to Ghannouchi', *Theory, Culture & Society* 2007, pp. 39-58 (48-50).

40   Berman 2010, p. 45. Following the 2011 uprisings against Mubarak in Egypt, the Muslim Brotherhood won the elections in 2012. This instantly led to a social and legal marginalising of women. See: Dyer, Emily, *Marginalising Egyptian Women. The Restriction of Women's Rights under the Muslim Brotherhood*, London: The Henry Jackson Society 2013.

41   Tamimi 2007, p. 49.

42   "[...] the kind of politics that regards terror as a goal in itself, and not just a tactic, and regards death as desirable". In: Berman 2010, p. 45. Berman concludes it is a recognisable political tradition from the 1930s and 1940s: fascism. Al-Banna was an admirer of Adolf Hitler and supported him publicly. He had *Mein Kampf* translated into Arabic in the 1930s. See: Horowitz, David and Spencer, Robert, *Islamophobia. Thought Crime of the Totalitarian Future*, David Horowitz Freedom Center 2011, p. 9. See also: Nawaz 2012, p. 80: "As a political project, Islamism was inspired by the rise of European fascism".

43   Tamimi 2007, pp. 48-50.

44   Gold 2003, p. 91. See on *jahiliyyah* also: Ellian, Afshin, 'The Legal Order of Political Religion', pp. 187-232, in: Molier, Gelijn, Ellian, Afshin and Suurland, David (eds.), *Terrorism, Ideology, Law and Policy*, Dordrecht: Republic of Letters 2011.

to mankind, but mankind turned its back to Islam and degenerated into *jahiliyyah*, roughly translatable as ignorance, and which refers to a state of spiritual darkness.[45] "[I]t signals not only human arrogance, but a transgression against divine authority, the scope of which encompasses both public and private domains of human life as well as both visible and invisible dimensions of the universe".[46] Between 1948 and 1950, Qutb studied in the United States and he was shocked by examples of transgressions signalling *jahiliyyah*. He experienced American moral depravity, in particular as it was manifested in individualism, materialism, racism, the economic system, and open sexuality – at least compared to the more restricted sexual codes of Qutb's own culture.[47] It led him to the conclusion that the world is in moral decline: "[…] humanity is devoid of those vital values which are necessary not only for its healthy development but also for its real progress", he wrote in *Milestones*, his main political work composed when he was in prison.[48]

If mankind were to be saved, it needs to submit (Islam literally means submission) itself to the laws of Islam, or else humanity will regress into a state of *jahiliyyah*. Suurland writes:

> At some point in time, man no longer relied on Allah and his commandments but instead they relied on mankind itself. Man created institutions that were not ordained by Allah and they relied on them. Man created systems of governance such as democracy, which were tyrannical because now some man ruled over others thereby enslaving them. Man-made laws are a particularly malicious form of *jahiliyyah* because what they actually represent is the fact that men trust each other more than they trust Allah. It is blasphemy of the worst sort because it ascribes partners to God. Since God is one, a concept known as *Tawheed*, you cannot worship anything besides him.[49] Certainly not anything man-made. In short, what we today call the modern world, with its institutes, its laws and its secular systems of government, all of which have no basis in Sharia, is a form of tyranny bound to enslave man and keep them from realizing that their true freedom lies in the religion of Allah and submitting to its com-

---

45 There is, for instance, this hadith on *jahiliyyah*: "A man said, "O Allah's Apostle! Shall we be punished for what we did in the PreIslamic Period of ignorance?" The Prophet said, "Whoever does good in Islam will not be punished for what he did in the Pre-Islamic Period of ignorance and whoever does evil in Islam will be punished for his former and later (bad deeds)". See: Sahih Bukhari, Volume 9, Book 84, number 56.

46 Euben & Zaman 2009, p. 30.

47 Suurland 2009, p. 282.

48 Qutb, Sayyid, *Milestones* (1964). Translated in Bostom, Andrew G. (ed.), *The Legacy of Jihad: Islamic Holy War and the Fate of Non-Muslims*, Amherst: Prometheus Books 2005, in: Suurland 2009, p. 283.

49 This also means that doubt about one's religion is out.

mandments. All those who do not submit, oppose. Those who oppose obstruct the freedom of all and are thus inevitably enemies.[50]

In line with Ibn Taymiyya, Salafism, and Wahhabism, all those who 'hinder' Islam are enemies of Islam. Enemies of Islam should be fought (Jihad) until either killed or converted. For Christians or Jews, or any other variant that adheres "to the religion of Abraham", there is the *Dhimmi* status, which is a system of taxation in exchange for protection, as long as they comply with a number of Islamic rules.[51] That means that any political system (or law) that deviates from Sharia, for instance, a system that separates law and religion, is contrary to Islam – which is considered an act of apostasy – and contrary to what is good for mankind. Democracy thus contradicts Islam. American researcher Raymond Ibrahim (1973), author of *The Al Qaeda Reader*, states the view of Islamists: "democracy is a man-made infidel religion, devised to give the right to legislate to the masses – as opposed to Islam, where all legislative rights belong to Allah Most High: He has no partners".[52] Democracy "rebels against" and prevents Allah's Sharia from becoming established law. Moreover, democracy's freedom of religion abolishes apostasy as a crime.[53] Democracy's principle of equality of citizens is considered *blasphemous*, as the Koranic Dhimmi conditions are unacceptable to democratic standards.[54]

Also important, men's dominion over women is legally abolished in a modern liberal democracy. Koranic verse 4:34 reads: "Men have authority over women, for Allah has made the one superior to the other". Yet, in a modern democracy men and women have the same legal status. It is also the issue of sex equality and fundamentalist ideology that make the debate on Sharia councils so heated.

Central to Islamist debate on the role and function of the two sexes is the notion that divinity has intended different functions for men and women, and that these are justified because of fundamental differences in their nature. Denying such differences is considered unjust, and therefore Islamists deal with these differences better than any other religious or social order could, they believe. Islam distinguishes between "equality" (which is affirmed for both sexes) and "identicalness" (which is rejected).[55] Justice is thus found in the recognition of the dissimilarities between men and women, which requires different rights,

---

50 Suurland 2009, pp. 283-284.
51 The Koran reads: "Fight those who do not believe in Allah or in the Last Day and who do not consider unlawful what Allah and His Messenger have made unlawful and who do not adopt the religion of truth from those who were given the Scripture - [fight] until they give the jizyah willingly while they are humbled." (9:29). Jizyah is the taxation for non-Muslims.
52 Ibrahim, Raymond (ed.), *The Al Qaeda Reader: The Essential Texts of Osama Bin Laden's Terrorist Organization*. Portland: Broadway Books 2007, p. 130. See also: Euben and Zaman 2009, p. 30.
53 Also beyond Wahhabism: See: Keller 1991, under o8.1 and o8.4. It is obligatory to ask the apostate to repent and return to Islam, if he does not he should immediately be killed (under o8.2.)
54 Ibrahim 2007, p. 135.
55 Euben & Zaman 2009, pp. 252-253.

duties and punishments for either sex. That the Western world has been seeking equality of rights is considered as not doing justice to the different dispositions of the sexes, as Ayatollah Khomeini's disciple Murtaza Mutahhari (1920) explained in *The Rights of Women in Islam*.[56]

Accepting (legal) equality of the sexes is thus not possible within Islamist doctrine. To Islamists, accepting all this means humanity will regress further into the dark state of *jahiliyyah*. This must be avoided, and that is an eternal struggle which will continue until the religion is purified for God.[57]

SHARIA STATE EXAMPLE I: THEOCRATIC SAUDI ARABIA

In the 1970s and 1980s, the Muslim Brotherhood and Saudi Wahhabi's joined each other and formed a global movement. In exchange for Saudi funds for its global operations in spreading their Islamist message, the Muslim Brotherhood made sure Saudi Arabia was protected against potential adversaries. With this increased protection, Saudi Arabia continued to strengthen its utopia within its boundaries. Let us take a look inside the most 'complete' Sharia state, to see what happens if Islamist principles are the basis of a nation's blueprint, starting with the juridical foundation.

The 1992 Saudi "basic law" consists of 83 articles divided into nine chapters. Article 1 of the first chapter, "General Principles", states: "The Kingdom of Saudi Arabia is a sovereign Arab Islamic State. Its religion is Islam. Its constitution is Almighty God's Book, The Holy Qur'an, and the Sunna (Traditions) of the Prophet (PBUH). Arabic is the language of the Kingdom. The City of Riyadh is the capital". The Koran and the Sunna thus *are* the nation's constitution. On the sources of law the constitution states, in Article 7, that "Government in the Kingdom of Saudi Arabia derives its authority from the Book of God and the Sunna of the Prophet (PBUH), which are the ultimate sources of reference for this Law and the other laws of the State". This is confirmed in Article 8: "Governance in the Kingdom of Saudi Arabia is based on justice, shura (consultation) and equality according to Islamic Sharia". There is a Council of Senior Ulama responsible for fatwas (religious opinion or decision) based on the Koran and Sunna, and the judiciary and the king shall rule solely according to Sharia.[58] In Chapter 3 of the constitution, "The Values of Saudi Society", it

---

56 Euben & Zaman 2009, pp. 261-262.

57 As Qutb wrote in 1964, two years before he was executed. Suurland emphasises that Jihad, according to Qutb, is *explicitly* not fought "because of any threat of aggression against Islamic lands or against the Muslims residing in them. The reason for jihad exists in the nature of its message and in the actual conditions, it finds in human societies, and not merely in the necessity for defence" (Qutb in *Milestones*), Suurland 2009, p. 286.

58 Articles 45, 46, and 55 of the Saudi Basic Law. From: <http://www.saudiembassy.net/about/country-information/laws/The_Basic_Law_Of_Governance.aspx>.

is laid down that: "The family is the nucleus of Saudi Society. Members of the family shall be raised in the Islamic Creed, which demands allegiance and obedience to God, to His Prophet and to the rulers, respect for and obedience to the laws, and love for and pride in the homeland and its glorious history" (article 9). There is no room for disagreement on that, as Articles 11 and 12 inform us of the following Saudi values: "Saudi society is based on full adherence to God's guidance. Members of this society shall cooperate amongst themselves in charity, piety and cohesion" and "Consolidation of the national unity is a duty. The State shall forbid all activities that may lead to division, disorder and partition". Ultimately, the goal of the Saudi state is to "protect the Islamic Creed, apply the Sharia, encourage good and discourage evil, and undertake its duty regarding the Propagation of Islam (Da'wa)" (article 23, Chapter 5, "Rights and Duties"). Finally, the state "shall protect human rights in accordance with the Sharia (article 26). There is no doubt that Saudi Arabia's political system constitutes a theocracy: the state and religion are fully aligned.[59]

The constitution tells us about the state's *formal* criteria, namely a reference to the Koran and Sunna, the two most important sources of Islamic law, or Sharia. But what about the *content*? What are some of the consequences when the Koran and Sunna are applied as basis for a nation's constitution, legislation and enforcement?

First of all, there is no freedom of religion. Wahhabi (Sunni) Islam is the only option, and is mandatory. Any diversion from this can be labelled apostasy or heresy and those found guilty of this crime face the risk of penalties, including flogging and death by execution. The building of churches is prohibited and bibles may not be distributed. Practicing Sufism, a mystical branch within Islam, and possession of Sufi writings is a capital offence. But Shi'a Muslims suffer the worst treatment of Muslims in the kingdom.[60] Floggings, executions, and lifelong sentences are based on the sole charge of heresy. There is no recourse to a fair trial.[61] The Saudi state also incites hatred against Shia Muslims through publications and education.[62] There is thus no formal tolerance of religious diversity; the theocracy does not allow multifaithism or atheism.

Second, no freedom of religion obviously implies no freedom of speech. One example is Raif Badawi, who was arrested for his blog "the Saudi Free Liberals Forum" in 2012. He

---

59   I take P.J. Tierney's definition of theocracy: "It is a political system that organizes people around faith in a deity. Decisions are made and actions taken relative to their common life by seeking a deity's direction, by ascribing authority and power to a deity. Theocracy exists when the origins of government and state power derive their legal authority from a divine source and derive their legitimacy from a deity. The deity and laws attributed to divine source are definitive". Tierney, P.J., *Theocracy: Can Democracy Survive Fundamentalism?* Bloomington: iUniverse 2012, p. 302.

60   Schwartz 2005, p. 29.

61   Take for instance Ahmed Turki al- Sa'ab, a Shi'a leader, who was quoted by the Wall Street Journal about the difficulties Shi'a Muslims face in Saudi Arabia. He was arrested 6 days after publication of this article, and was convicted to 7 years in prison and 1,200 lashes after a security officer and the judge talked amongst each other, while the defendant was denied council. Schwartz 2005, p. 29.

62   Schwartz 2005, p. 31.

wrote on the need for secularism, against the Saudi interpretation of Islam and the lack of freedom: "As soon as a thinker starts to reveal his ideas, you will find hundreds of fatwas that accused him of being an infidel just because he had the courage to discuss some *sacred topics*. I'm really worried that Arab thinkers will migrate in search of fresh air and to escape the sword of the religious authorities".[63] He was arrested and sentenced to 10 years in prison, a thousand lashes and a fine of 1 million Saudi riyals (237.000 euro's).[64] The court ordered the closedown of his website. He is but one example of many who share his fate, as the state does not allow its citizens to work against "consolidation of the national unity", cause division, or not fully adhere to the Saudi interpretation of Sharia.

In general, Amnesty International reports on arbitrary arrest and detention without charge for those who publicly criticise the government, for those who violate religious standards and for Shia religious leaders.[65] Although the Saudi law officially states hearings are public, judges may decide to close the doors, leaving many trials closed to the public. There is also no common right to access the prosecutor's evidence. Moreover, the law and practice discriminates against non-practising Sunni, Shia, or other denominations, foreigners, and women.[66]

Saudi Arabia is also notorious for its criminal punishments, known as *hudud* laws: punishments fixed in the Koran and hadiths for crimes considered to be against the rights of God. Sharia mandates the cutting off of a hand for stealing, a punishment carried out in Saudi Arabia.[67] Flogging is a sentence regularly executed, and the death penalty exists and is carried out – also for acts which are not considered crimes in liberal democracies.

---

63 'A look at the writings of Saudi blogger Raif Badawi – sentenced to 1,000 lashes', *The Guardian* 14 January 2015, via <http://www.theguardian.com/world/2015/jan/14/-sp-saudi-blogger-extracts-raif-badawi>.

64 The thousand lashes are executed in weekly sessions of fifty, as a person would die from receiving a thousand lashes at once. In January 2015, Badawi received the first fifty, but the second session was cancelled, as his medical team stated he was not sufficiently recovered from the first fifty. See: 'Raif Badawi: Saudi blogger is spared public flogging for a second week', *The Independent* 23 January 2015, via <http://www.independent.co.uk/news/world/middle-east/saudi-blogger-raif-badawi-is-spared-public-flogging-for-a-second-week-9997804.html>

65 Saudi Arabia 2013 Human Rights Report; Country Reports on Human Rights Practices for 2013 by the US Department of State, Bureau of Democracy, Human Rights and Labor, p. 10, via <http://www.state.gov/documents/organization/220586.pdf>. Moreover, those arrested are sometimes cut off from all outside contact, including family and legal counsel, so that a person can go 'missing' for long periods. There are reports that government officials torture prisoners. There is, for instance, the case of human rights activist Mekhlef bin Daham al-Shammary, who was detained for 'annoying others' with his online essays that criticised government officials and Saudi religious scholars, as the charge read in the prosecutor's file. He criticised several Saudi religious scholars for focusing on moral issues such as gender mixing in public instead of unemployment, poverty and other societal problems. See: 'Saudi human rights activist in prison for 'annoying others', *The National* 20 July 2010, via <http://www.thenational.ae/news/world/middle-east/saudi-human-rights-activist-in-prison-for-annoying-others>.

66 Saudi Arabia 2013 Human Rights Report.

67 The Prophet said, "The hand should be cut off for stealing something that is worth a quarter of a Dinar or more." Sahih Bukhari, Volume 8, Book 81, number 780.

Capital crimes include adultery, armed robbery, apostasy, drug smuggling, kidnapping, rape, witchcraft and sorcery.[68]

Ibn Warraq, author of *Why I Am Not a Muslim* (1995) and *Why the West is Best. A Muslim Apostate's Defense of Liberal Democracy* (2011) writes on the lack of individual liberties: "In Islam, there is the concept of an individual with legal obligations, but not of the moral person who may freely choose his own path in life. There is no sense of the individual who can make rational decisions and accept moral responsibility for his actions. Ethics is reduced to obeying orders. Under Islam, the limits to the possible contents of your life are set by Allah and his law, while the collective will of the Muslim people is emphasised over any sense of individual rights."[69] This is especially true when living under an Islamic totalitarian regime, where it is hardly possible to escape government influence and the pressure of sticking to religion in theocratic Saudi Arabia. The secret police (*mabahith*) keeps Saudi citizens in check. British historian Robert Lacey (1944), author of *Inside the Kingdom, Kings, Clerics, Modernists, Terrorists, and the Struggle for Saudi Arabia* (2009), writes: "The Mabahith are a department of the Saudi Ministry of the Interior, so vast and pervasive in their watchfulness that secret is scarcely the word for them. They have woven themselves into the very fabric of Saudi life. There is a Mabahith informant praying in every significant Saudi mosque, ready to make a phone call should the imam's sermon get too fiery, nor would any university faculty be complete without its careful listener by the coffee machine".[70]

On the streets, Saudi citizens have to deal with the highly visible *mutaween*; the Saudi religious police who are formally known as the Committee for the Promotion of Virtue and the Prevention of Vice. It is the task of this 'morality police' to roam the streets and enforce Sharia-based laws. This means that prayers need to be done five times a day by everyone (cafes and businesses must thus be closed), women may not smoke, alcohol is obviously forbidden, and women have to be fully covered, which is a way of segregating men and women. A low point, even from the Saudi perspective, was reached in 2002, as the mutaween became world news. They prevented schoolgirls from leaving a burning

---

68 To give an idea of the scope of the amount of death penalties: in May 2013, Amnesty International stated that 47 people had been known to be executed that year so far. But it is feared that the number of executions may actually be higher than declared, as secret and unannounced executions have been reported as well. Apart from executing individuals without a fair trial based on charges for crimes non-Sharia regimes do not recognise (such as adultery and apostasy), the cruelty is staggering. Secret footage available online, for instance, demonstrates five men hanging from a horizontal pole with their heads wrapped in bags. See also: 'Saudi Arabia: Five beheaded and 'crucified' amid 'disturbing' rise in executions', *Amnesty.org* 21 May 2013, via <http://www.amnesty.org/en/news/saudi-arabia-five-beheaded-and-crucified-amid-disturbing-rise exe cutions-2013-05-21>. YouTube has several videos of beheadings by sword, or by kicking oil barrels away from several men's feet who are hanging next to each other on a horizontal rope in the middle of a busy road. There are videos shot from a car window, showing hanging bodies next to a freeway.

69 Ibn Warraq 2011, p. 205. See also: Ibn Warraq 1995.

70 Lacey 2009 (Kindle Locations 1499-1502).

school building in Mecca, because they were not wearing the full face covering headscarves and abayas (the typical Saudi black robes) as required. The religious police beat the girls back into the building, they beat those who were trying to rescue the girls, and prevented firemen from going in. Around 15 girls burned to death and dozens were injured.[71]

Women in general do not fare well under the Saudi Islamic doctrine, to state it euphemistically. It is well known that women are not equal to men in the kingdom.

Take for instance the practice of *purdah* (segregating women from men). It can imply veiling, but also secluding women in private homes through curtains or separating walls, and keeping women prisoners in their own homes.[72] Thus, even in the private sphere, women can be segregated. The full face veil is part of the aim to segregate the sexes in public, in order to avoid *fitna*. The concept of *fitna* is relevant to the study of Islamic fundamentalism and the veiling of women. *Fitna* refers to calamity, sedition, subversion, agitation, disharmony, (sexual) temptation, sin, and seduction.[73] It is not the case that all women are *intimidated* into covering up. A reason why some women freely cover up, is because they believe it will indeed please their creator. Others believe piety brings them power, it gives them a sense of being in control. This was witnessed by Swiss-Iranian Carmen bin Laden (1954), who married the brother of Osama bin Laden and moved to Saudi Arabia. In *Inside the Kingdom. My life in Saudi Arabia* (2004), she writes on how she saw powerless women throw "all their courage" into religion: "I think that it was simpler for them than fighting for their rights as human beings. I think that they believed that if they were strictly religious, then the men – like other women – would respect that. It seemed to work. Religious women did get more respect than the Westernized (women)".[74]

But in general, individual liberties are very much restricted. It is the only country in the world where women are not allowed to drive a car – a woman who broke the ban on driving was sentenced to 10 lashes.[75] Furthermore, women cannot leave the house without a male escort, nor may they leave the country without a male family member's consent. The airport checks the computer system for this consent and notifies the family if their relative intended to travel without permission. Permission is needed for work and seeking medical treatment as well. Daughters may be married off against their will, and a father has the right to seize custody of his children and deny the mother access to her children

---

71 Chesler 2006, p. 189. See also: 'Saudi police 'stopped' fire rescue', *bbc.co.uk* 15 March 2002, via <http://news.bbc.co.uk/2/hi/middle_east/1874471.stm>.

72 See for someone's personal struggle with Afghani purdah: Chesler, Phyllis, *An American Bride in Kabul: A Memoir*, New York: Palgrave Macmillan 2013.

73 Euben & Zaman 2009, p. 113.

74 Bin Ladin, Carmen, *Inside the Kingdom. My life in Saudi Arabia*, New York: Warner Books 2004, in: Chesler 2006, p. 136. Muslim convert Yvonne Ridley embraces Islamic piety: "In Islam, superiority is achieved through piety – not beauty, wealth, power, position or sex". See: Ridley, Yvonne, 'How I Came to Love the Veil', *The Washington Post*, 22 October 2006.

75 She got a royal pardon; see: Eltahawy, Mona, 'Why Do They Hate Us?', *Foreign Policy* 23 April 2012.

for good.[76] In court, one male testimony needs to be countered by two female testimonies. On this, former grand mufti Bin Baz said: "the Prophet (peace be upon him) explained that their shortcoming in reasoning is found in the fact that their memory is weak and that their witness is in need of another woman to corroborate it. Therefore, it is related to non-proficiency in witnessing due to woman's forgetfulness or (that) she may add something in her witnessing".[77]

Women outnumber their male counterparts on universities, but they are stuck while watching men far less qualified control every aspect of their lives. Women are everlastingly minors regardless of their age or education. Child marriage is practised in the country.[78] Islamic family law in general, and not just the Saudi Hanbali school of interpretation, allows women to be married off at a young age – following the example of Muhammad who consummated his marriage with Aisha as she turned 9 years old.[79] The marriage contract consists of two parties, the husband and the woman's male guardian, often her father. Furthermore, women must be obedient wives, of which a man may marry up to four.[80] The family is the nucleus of Saudi society, as Article 9 of the Basic Law reads. That also means that women who are victims of abuse can be forced to return to their abusive father of husband. Women who file complaints run the risk of being sent to prison, rather than a shelter. This was the case for Samar Badawi in 2006, a divorced mother who challenged a complaint of "familial ingratitude" lodged against her by her abusive father. The judge reprimanded her and said he would teach her obedience and flog her himself.[81] Saudi Arabia is also the country where a gang rape survivor was sentenced to jail for agreeing to get into a car with an unrelated male.[82]

The family nucleus also means that all sex outside of marriage is a crime. "Deviant sexual behaviour" is a crime as well. A married man engaging in sodomy or any non-Muslim who commits sodomy with a Muslim can be put to death, lashed or jailed, although homosexuality is said to be "vibrant" in the Kingdom.[83] This should not be mistaken for tolerance. Homosexuality is outlawed and those found guilty are convicted. Sharia prohibits

---

76   Bin Ladin 2005.
77   Schwartz 2005, p. 33.
78   Eltahawy 2012.
79   Muhammad allegedly married his third wife Aisha when she was 6, and consummated the marriage before she reached the age of 10. "Narrated 'Aisha: that the Prophet married her when she was six years old and he consummated his marriage when she was nine years old, and then she remained with him for nine years (i.e. till his passing away)". Sahih Bukhari, Volume 7, Book 62, number 64.
80   Sura 4:3 of the Koran states an explicit endorsement of the practice: "Marry of the women, who seem good to you, two or three or four; and if ye fear that ye cannot do justice to so many then one only".
81   'Abused women battle Saudi injustice', *Financial Times* 14 October 2006, via <http://www.ft.com/intl/cms/s/0/d9ee5a5a-d7b0-11df-b478-00144feabdc0.html#axzz3Q1TFiDV9>.
82   Eltahawy 2012.
83   'The Kingdom in the Closet', *The Atlantic* 1 May 2007, via <http://www.theatlantic.com/magazine/archive/2007/05/the-kingdom-in-the-closet/305774/>

men imitating like women (and vice versa), which also serves as ground for prosecuting homosexuals and transvestites.[84] The official textbook position, what students learn in Saudi Arabia's educational facilities, is that 'Homosexuality is one of the most disgusting sins and greatest crimes [...]. It is a vile perversion that goes against sound nature, and is one of the most corrupting and hideous sins [...]. The punishment for homosexuality is death. Both the active and passive participants are to be killed whether or not they have previously had sexual intercourse in the context of a legal marriage [...]. Some of the companions of the Prophet stated that [the perpetrator] is to be burned with fire. It has also been said that he should be stoned, or thrown from a high place".[85] The *mutaween* is known to raid parties and arrest dozens of men at the same time. This was, for instance, the case on March 10, 2005, when about a hundred men were arrested by the secret police at a private party held in a rented hall in Jeddah. The government-affiliated newspaper Al-Wifaq reported that they were dancing and "behaving like women". Human Rights Watch reported that two weeks later, dozens of them were sentenced to jail and flogging in a closed session in which defence attorneys were excluded.[86]

Lastly, Saudi Arabia formally abolished slavery in 1962. However, considering some migrant workers are denied exit from their employers who make them work pro bono while enduring severe abuse, the factual abolishment of slavery is yet to happen. This might be easier said than done, as slavery is endorsed by Sharia.[87]

Take for instance migrant workers – mostly from East Asia – whom hardly have any protection against abuse. They do not fall under the national labour laws. Through a sponsorship system called *kafala*, employers have the right to withhold wages, making workers work against their will and retain worker's identity documents making it impossible for a large number of workers to exit the country. In 2012, it was reported that thousands of domestic workers were forced to work 15-20 hours a day, 7 days a week, and denied their salaries. "Domestic workers, most of whom are women, frequently endure forced confinement, food deprivation, and severe psychological, physical, and sexual abuse. In December 2010, authorities made no attempts to rescue an Indonesian migrant domestic worker who had worked for 10 years without pay and whose sponsors were "renting" her out to other houses, according to one Saudi woman who informed authorities. In November 2010, authorities in Abha, Southern Saudi Arabia, recovered the body of Kikim Komalasari, a 36-year-old Indonesian domestic worker, bearing signs of extensive

---

84 Enormity number 107, see: Keller 1991.
85 '2008 Update: Saudi Arabia's Curriculum of Intolerance. With Excerpts of Saudi Ministry of Education Textbooks for Islamic Studies', Center for Religious Freedom of Hudson Institute with Gulf Institute 2008, p. 5, via <http://www.hudson.org/content/researchattachments/attachment/656/saudi_textbooks_final.pdf> Center for Religious Freedom of Hudson Institute.
86 'Saudi Arabia: Men 'Behaving Like Women' Face Flogging', *Human Rights Watch* 7 April 2005, via <http://www.hrw.org/news/2005/04/06/saudi-arabia-men-behaving-women-face-flogging>.
87 See, for instance, Ali, Kecia, *Marriage and Slavery in Early Islam*, Cambridge: Harvard University Press 2010.

physical abuse. In September an appeals court overturned a 3-year prison sentence for the employer found guilty of severely assaulting Sumiati Mustapa, her Indonesian domestic worker. In June, the government ordered the beheading of Ruyati Binti Sapubi, an Indonesian domestic worker convicted of murdering her employer who allegedly refused to allow Binti Sapubi to return home. Courts sentenced another Indonesian domestic worker to death for killing her employer after he allegedly tried to rape her", Human Rights Watch stated.[88]

This was a brief impression of life in the Saudi Sharia state, a kingdom founded in 1932 after almost 200 years of immense battle and violent jihad initiated by Ibn Abd-al-Wahhab and Saud. Islamism is a religious political ideology, which comes with indoctrination, a total lack of free speech, persecution of those not belonging, a secret police infiltrating society and a vice squad monitoring people's actions on the streets. It is a totalitarian form of society: "[…] in which all activities are immediately linked to one another, deliberately presented as modalities of a single world; that form in which a system of values predominates absolutely, such that every individual or collective undertaking must necessarily find in it a coefficient of reality; that form in which, lastly, the dominant model exercises a total physical and spiritual constraint on the behavior of private individuals".[89]

It is of course not the first time in world history that political leaders declare the Divine to be the sole guidance for governance. It is also not unique to Sunni Islam – Shia Iran established a theocracy in 1979. But what is new in world history, is that this Islam-based political ideology that should lead to a Sharia state is now vented out by a nation with immense resources and access to people worldwide – more than ever through the Internet and television.[90] As a result of the 1970s covenant between the Egyptian Muslim Brotherhood's version of political Islam and Saudi Wahhabism, Saudi Arabia became one of the biggest worldwide export centres of Islamic fundamentalism.[91] In 2003, Saudi expenses in spreading the Wahhabi doctrine over the world were estimated at 70 billion US dollars in nearly 30 years, mostly for building mosques, religious schools, and Wahhabi religious centres. To mention just two out of many organisations: the Saudi sponsored al-Haramain and the International Islamic Relief Organization founded thousands of mosques, schools, colleges and Islamic centres all over the (non-Islamic) world and sent out over 9,000

88 'World Report 2012: Saudi Arabia', *Human Rights Watch*, via <http://www.hrw.org/world-report-2012/world-report-2012-saudi-arabia> (no date specified).
89 Lefort, Claude and Thompson, John, 'Totalitarianism without Stalin', pp. 52-88 (79), in: Lefort, Claude, *The Political Forms of Modern Society: Bureaucracy, Democracy, Totalitarianism*, Cambridge: Polity 1986. See also: Suurland, David, *Secular, Totalitarian and Islamist Legal-Political Philosophy*, dissertation Leiden University 2011.
90 The Middle East Media Research Institute (MEMRI) provides an English translation for Arabic, Farsi, Urdu-Pashtu and Dari media, but satellites and the internet bring the Islamist message to Muslims worldwide.
91 Gold 2003, p. 101.

preachers. Over 13 million books have been printed. In Indonesia alone, the Relief Organization funded 575 Wahhabi mosques.[92]

To give an idea of the content of Saudi propaganda and indoctrination: in 2005, American research organisation Freedom House reported on the content of Saudi publications used in mosques and Islamic schools in the United States – it is safe to assume the message is the same in every nation. Muslims are instilled with the following ideas and convictions: it is a religious obligation for Muslims to hate Jews and Christians, and they are warned against befriending, imitating or helping "infidels" in any way. (In fact, Wahhabis and other Islamists – such as Al Qaeda's current leader Ayman al-Zawahiri (1951) – divide individuals between good Muslims (who deserve loyalty) and "infidels" (who deserve enmity). This loyalty versus enmity-doctrine – the *"al-wala' wa al-bara"*-doctrine is an important part of political Islam.[93])

Freedom House further reports that Nazi-like hatred for Jews is preached and the Protocols of the Elders of Zion – an anti-Semitic hoax document originating from Russia in 1903 which describes a Jewish plan for global domination – is taken as a historically valid source.[94] Moreover, it is the right thing to hold contempt for America, as it is ruled by civil law, rather than by totalitarian Wahhabi-style Islamic law. As long as the United

---

92 Kaplan, David E., Monica Ekman, and Latif, Aamir, "The Saudi Connection How Billions in Oil Money Spawned A Global Terror Network; Karachi", *US News & World Report* 135.21 2003, p. 18. In 2004, the FBI blocked the assets of the al-Haramain Foundation after it found that it was directly funding Al Qaeda. 'Saudi Publications on Hate Ideology Invade American Mosques', Center for Religious Freedom, New York: Freedom House 2005, p. 4.

93 Koranic verses supporting this are, *inter alia*, 2:191 "Slay the unbelievers wherever you find them", 3:28 "Muslims must not take the infidels as friends", 3:85 "Any religion other than Islam is not acceptable", 5:33 "Maim and crucify the infidels if they criticise Islam", 8:12 "Terrorize and behead those who believe in scriptures other the Quran", 8:60 "Muslims must muster all weapons to terrorize the infidels", 8:65 "The unbelievers are stupid; urge the Muslims to fight them", 9:5 "When opportunity arises kill the infidels wherever you find them", 9:30 "The Jews and Christians are perverts, fight them", 9:123 "Make war on the infidels living in your neighborhood", 22:19 "Punish the unbelievers with garments of fire, hooked iron rods, boiling water, melt their skin and bellies, 47:4 "Do not hanker for peace with the infidels; behead them when you catch". List compiled by Engin, Serkan, 'Why We Must Ban Islam', *The Conservative Papers* 23 March 2015, via <http://conservativepapers.com/news/2015/03/23/why-we-must-ban-islam/#.VRD-mfmsWT8>. See also: Bale 2013, under note 39 and Ibrahim 2007, pp. 63-115.

94 To give an impression of The Protocols of the Elders of Zion; Sergyei Nilus' epilogue to the 1905 Edition of the Protocols reads: "According to the records of secret Jewish Zionism, Solomon and other Jewish learned men already, in 929 B.C., thought out a scheme in theory for a peaceful conquest of the whole universe by Zion. As history developed, this scheme was worked out in detail and completed by men who were subsequently initiated in this question. These learned men decided by peaceful means to conquer the world for Zion with the slyness of the Symbolic Snake, whose head was to represent those who have been initiated into the plans of the Jewish administration, and the body of the Snake to represent the Jewish people - the administration was always kept secret, EVEN FROM THE JEWISH NATION ITSELF [sic]. As this Snake penetrated into the hearts of the nations which it encountered it undermined and devoured all the non-Jewish power of these States. It is foretold that the Snake has still to finish its work, strictly adhering to the designed plan, until the course which it has to run is closed by the return of its head to Zion and until, by this means, the Snake has completed its round of Europe and has encircled it - and until, by dint of enchaining Europe, it has encompassed the whole world."

States is ruled by infidels, citizenship should be avoided, and instead Muslims should work towards the creation of an Islamic state. On a Muslim who is "guilty" of extramarital sex or homosexuality, it is said that it is lawful to "spill his blood and to take his money". Regarding other non-Wahhabi Muslims, the Saudi state instructs to condemn those as infidels, especially those who preach tolerance or engage in genuine interfaith dialogue. Sufi and Shiite Muslims are viciously condemned, and those who leave Islam "should be killed". Women should be segregated from men, veiled and may not work in certain jobs or divert from their assigned roles (subordinate wife, primarily care provider).[95]

This proselytising is having a wild effect, and is a serious threat to world peace and stability worldwide. The globe is witnessing an intricate network of well-financed Islamist groups, who use severe brutality in combination with a multibillion dollar proselytising campaign as means to reach their goal of a Sharia state, and will not stop until that goal has been reached.[96]

SHARIA STATE EXAMPLE II: ISLAMISATION IN MALAYSIA

But terror is not the only way to establish a Sharia state. An example of how a nation can intrinsically change for the worst is Malaysia. I take it as an example of how a nation Islamised in a short period of time from a top-down, organised approach.[97] This is, besides terror, another way of achieving the way in which citizens subject themselves to the ever-growing demands of Sharia. Some say Malaysia is "moderate" when it comes to Islam. But also in a "moderate" form, political Islam is detrimental to citizens. This case shows how certain repressive elements of Islamism work in practice, and that the ideal and practice of equal rights is incompatible with an Islamist politico-religious framework. Malaysia is not unique though: what is described here is comparable to the situation in all nations that are confronted with a high degree of Islamisation.

Ethnic Malaysian Muslims account for over half the population of 28 million people. In 1958, Prime Minister Tunku Abdul Rahman (1903-1990) stated that Malaysia is not an

---

95 'Saudi Publications on Hate Ideology Invade American Mosques', Center for Religious Freedom, New York: Freedom House 2005, p. 13.

96 According to the Global Terrorism Index 2014, there has been a five-fold increase in the number of people killed by terrorism since 2000. Before 2000, nationalist separatist organisations were the biggest drivers of terrorism, but religion as a driving ideology for terrorism has dramatically increased. Two-thirds of terrorist casualties (around 18.000) were claimed by IS, Boko Haram, the Taliban and al Qacda. Contrary to public opinion, poverty and many other economic factors are found to have little or no explanatory power. 'The Global Terrorism Index 2014' report by The Institute for Economics and Peace (IEP), pp. 3-4, via <http://www.visionofhumanity.org/sites/default/files/Global%20Terrorism%20Index%20Report%202014_0.pdf>

97 See on the top-down approach also: Suurland 2011, p. 361.

Islamic State and that Islam is merely its official religion. He said: "There is no way we should have an Islamic State here [...] we cannot force the non-Malays and non-Muslims to follow our way of life. Our slogan 'live and let live' must be maintained because it is the only practical solution in a multi-racial society like ours".[98] Unfortunately that spirit was not there to stay. In 2008, Marina Mahathir, daughter of former Prime Minister Mahatmir bin Mohamad, stated:

> Malaysia used to have the best legislation protecting the rights of Muslim women in the world. And now we've gone backwards slowly. The 13 states are all allowed to make their own laws in this area and therefore you get variations [...] We have this dual system between Muslim and non-Muslim women, we are living under a different system – what you in the West call Sharia law. So we are living under a kind of apartheid not based on skin colour but religion.[99]

There was no Ikhwan or Boko Haram-styled violent jihad, but an Islamist political effort aimed at Islamising the nation from the early 1980s onwards. First, in 1982, the Malaysian government instituted procedures and government agencies that had as primary goal to ensure that economic, social and community state projects were in line with Islamic teachings. Second, the authority of the *ulama* – the religious elite of scholars at the top of the hierarchy and the arbiters of Sharia – was centralised. There were 100 ulama in the Department for Islamic Development in 1982, and over 700 in the Ministry of Education. This has played a huge role normalising and disseminating Islamic extremism amongst Malaysian Muslims. At the same time, a federal-level Technical Sharia and Civil Law Committee was established, which transformed Islamic law into a systematised and bureaucratised Islamic judicial and legal system.

Presently, the Malaysian "Islamisation agenda" is no different from Islamist movements in the Arab region, nor is it unique for Malaysia. The primary Islamist state goal is to be the guardian of a moral code set by Islamic law, or Sharia, based mainly on the Koran, the Sunna and legal interpretation by the ulama. As guardian of an Islamic moral code, the Islamisation of Malaysia – as everywhere in the world – is overwhelmingly occupied with regulating family laws such as polygamy, divorce, custody and inheritance, and to issues as veiling, and gender relations (often in the form of sex segregation). A second component is the imposition of laws concerning Islamic criminal punishment. Generally, the effects of this Islamisation for women have been negative and restrictive. For instance, instead of expecting men to assert self-control or socialise them into that, the solution to women's

---

98 Riddell, Peter, 'Islamisation and Partial Shari'a in Malaysia', pp. 135-160 (137), in: Marshall (ed.) 2005.
99 Lichter, Ida, *Muslim Women Reformers. Inspiring Voices Against Oppression*, Amherst: Prometheus Books 2009, pp. 240-241.

safety is veiling women's bodies, to seclude them from men other than their kin, regulating their role as mothers (caretakers and service-providers for male family members' needs), and making sure they are obedient (including always sexually available) wives.[100]

A Muslim wife must be obedient and must not commit *nushuz* (rebellion of the wife against her husband's authority).[101] Koranic verse 4:34 reads:

> Men are the protectors and maintainers of women, because Allah has given the one more (strength) than the other, and because they support them from their means. Therefore, the righteous women are devoutly obedient, and guard in (the husband's) absence what Allah would have them guard. As to those women on whose part ye fear disloyalty and ill-conduct, admonish them (first), (next), refuse to share their beds, (and last) chastise them (lightly); but if they return to obedience, seek not against them means (of annoyance); for Allah is Most High, Great (above you all).[102]

There is also this hadith: "The Prophet said, 'If a woman spends the night deserting her husband's bed (does not sleep with him), then the angels send their curses on her till she comes back (to her husband)'".[103] Sexual availability is a wife's marital obligation under Sharia: "It is obligatory for a woman to let her husband have sex with her immediately when: 1) he asks her; 2) at home (home being the place where he is currently staying, even if being lent to him or rented); 3) she can physically endure it'; [...]". If a woman *shows signs* of 'rebelliousness' (e.g. "when she answers him coldly when she used to do so politely, or he asks her to come to bed and she refuses", the husband "warns in words", but if she *commits* 'rebelliousness' he "[...] may hit her, but not in a way that injures her, meaning he may not (A: bruise her,) break bones, wound her, or cause blood to flow".[104] The idea that women are inferior, and subordinate to men, and second class citizens is characteristic of Islamic fundamentalism. Men are expected to take the responsibility of protecting women and providing her with her basic needs – life, morality and chastity.[105]

The key principle of religious family law in general is to define and regulate membership of the community. Women, clearly, are vital to the transmission of collective identity, and

---

100 Othman, Norani, 'Muslim Women and the Challenge of Islamic Fundamentalism/Extremism: An Overview of Southeast Asian Muslim Women's Struggle for Human Rights and Gender Equality', *Women's Studies International Forum* 2006, pp. 339-353 (344-345).

101 Othman 2006, p. 342.

102 *The Holy Qur'an*, translated by Abdullah Yusuf Ali, Worldsworth Editions Limited 2000. See on an overview of exegesis on this sura: Chaudhry, Ayesha, *Domestic Violence and the Islamic Tradition*, Oxford: Oxford University Press 2013.

103 See: Sahih Bukhari, Volume 7, Book 62, number 122.

104 Keller 1991, m5.1 and m10.12.

105 Othman 2006, p. 342.

their reproductive function and their assigned role of primary caretaker are exerted to control communal membership.

What is particular for Islam though is that the necessity of restricting women's liberties and discouraging independence is based on idea of *fitna*, which I have mentioned before. Also mentioned in the previous section was the concept of *jahiliyyah*, the opposite of utopian Islam, which refers to a state of severe moral decline, a spiritual darkness, and which must be avoided by adhering to a fundamentalist interpretation of Islamic law. Fitna is a comparable concept. Through the eyes of Islamic fundamentalists, women are a constant source of fitna – sexual temptation leading to social disorder, moving towards catastrophe. 'Uncontrolled' and uncovered women are taken as the cause of moral decadence and other social problems. Women thus need to be removed (through veiling, segregation or seclusion) from the public sphere.[106] It thus does not come as a surprise that the first category of individuals that Islamists target, are women. Preventing sexual aggression and assault becomes solely a woman's responsibility – the idea is that, if a woman is not properly covered, she should not be surprised if a man cannot contain himself. What is problematic is that this makes what is perceived as the lack of proper veiling a justification for sexual assault.[107]

The more Islamisation, the more women's status, rights and body come under heavy regulation. This too happened in Malaysia. In the late 1970s and through the 1980s, all Islamic reactionary movements pushed for head covering and a loose long body covering type of dress. Norani Othman, Professor of Sociology in Malaysia and founding member of "Sisters of Islam" (an organisation that challenges extremism), states: "The mere insistence of the hijab on women by many traditionalizing ulama and militant or activist Islamists challenges the moral autonomy of the individual and reduces the personal independence of Muslim females".[108] Let alone when dress codes are formally regulated, as is the case in some parts of Malaysia. In the north of Malaysia, Islamisation has led to fines for headscarves that do not cover enough, and lipstick and high heels have been banned. New laws segregated the sexes at public events, and even separate payment counters in supermarkets. Couples sitting too closely together on park benches are fined.[109] It was proposed to ban women from jobs with night shifts, such as the police force and hospitals, as to not disrupt family life.

---

106 See also: 'Council of Islamic Ideology declares women's existence anti-Islamic', *Pakistan Today* 15 March 2014, via <http://www.pakistantoday.com.pk/2014/03/15/comment/coucil-of-islamic-ideology-declares-womens-existence-anti-islamic/>.
107 For instance, there was the Chief Mufti of Australia who said in response to a gang rape: "If she was in her room, in her home, in her Hijab (headscarf), no problem would have occurred". See: 'Five Reasons To Ban the Burqa', *Frontpage Mag* 11 July 2011, via <http://www.frontpagemag.com/2011/dgreenfield/five-reasons-to-ban-the-burqa/>.
108 Othman 2006, p. 342.
109 Lichter 2009, p. 240.

Some Muslim women feel compelled to cover themselves. They may so out of a sense of retaining a 'lost' cultural identity – an identity under siege due to Western influences, at least, that is the message. In fact, it is a vital part of the Islamisation agenda to spread the belief that the 'ideal' identity of an Islamic woman must be 'recovered'. This idea is espoused by both male as female Islamists.[110]

The pressure to conform to formalised Islamic laws increased tremendously over the past decades. In 2009, a Malay was sentenced to public caning for drinking a beer in public, as alcohol is forbidden under Islamic law.[111] In 2010, three women were caned after been found guilty of extra-marital sex. In fact, the fatwas nowadays are so invasive and micro-managing people, that an e-fatwa website is now available for citizens. The list with over 1,500 rulings includes a ban on Halloween, Valentine's Day, Botox, yoga, black metal music, and wagyu beef, as the cows are supposedly occasionally fed beer.[112] Moreover, the organiser of a dog-petting event received death threats as Muslims are not supposed to touch "unclean" animals. In October 2014, the state of Kelantan began enforcing a law that allows Muslim men to be imprisoned up to a year for missing Friday prayers three times in a row. The Shi'a denomination is outlawed.[113] Bibles have been confiscated since 1981, as the government fears they may be used for proselytising. Up until 2014 Christians were even forbidden to use the word "Allah" for their Christian god. The Christian minority is concerned for its safety, as churches are firebombed.[114] The civil courts consider apostasy claims the sole preserve of Sharia courts, where apostasy is considered a crime.[115] Kassim Ahmad (1933), a Malaysian intellectual who stated that Muslims only need the Koran, not the hadiths, who questions the headscarf for women, and described Muhammad

---

110 Othman 2006, p. 343.

111 Under public pressure the sentence was converted to community work.

112 'Moderate Malaysia has so many fatwas there's a website to keep track of them', *Global Post* 5 January 2015, via <http://www.globalpost.com/dispatch/news/regions/asia-pacific/141222/moderate-malaysia-has-so-many-fatwas-there-s-website-keep->.

113 'Growing Islamic fundamentalism seen pushing Malays to quit country', *Malay Mail Online* 30 October 2014, via <http://www.themalaymailonline.com/malaysia/article/growing-islamic-fundamentalism-seen-pushing-malays-to-quit-country#sthash.TD5Jb1f0.dpuf>.

114 See: 'Rise of strict Islam exposes tensions in Malaysia', *bbb.co.uk* 26 August 2011, via <http://www.bbc.co.uk/news/world-radio-and-tv-14649841>. The government's National Council for Islamic Religious Affairs deemed the word Allah a sacred word specific only to the religion and followers of Islam. The highest court rejected this fatwa (religious ruling) in 2014. Malaysia's E-Fatwa portal states: "The 82nd Muzakarah (Conference) of the Fatwa Committee of the National Council for Islamic Religious Affairs Malaysia held on 5th-7th May 2008 has discussed the Issue on the Claim of the Christians to Use the Word Allah. The Conference decided that the word Allah is a sacred word specific only to the religion and followers of Islam and it cannot be used or made to be similar with religions other than Islam. As such, it is the duty of Muslims to protect it with the best manner and if there existed any elements of abasement or abuse of the word, it must be curbed according to the provisions of the laws as stipulated in the Federal Constitution". Via Malaysia's E-Fatwa website: <http://www.e-fatwa.gov.my/fatwa-kebangsaan/isu-tuntutan-penganut-kristian-terhadap-penggunaan-kalimah-allah>.

115 Cumper, Peter, 'Multiculturalism, Human Rights and the Accommodation of Sharia Law', *Human Rights Law Review* 2014, pp. 31–57 (44).

as "just a messenger of Allah", is prosecuted by the government.[116] For the past 15 years, (educated and high-skilled) Malay are increasingly emigrating from the country in order to escape Islamic fundamentalism.[117]

Tolerance and pluralism are not values which are welcome in this version of Islam, and tolerance and pluralism are actively suppressed by the ulama, the minority religious elite. But, one may wonder, if this is not what Malaysians want, then where is the protest? There hardly is any. People do not dare to speak up against the tide of Islamisation for fear of reprisals; documentary maker Norhayati Kaprawi said about contemporary Malaysian society: "It's full of fear. If you don't follow the mainstream you will be lynched."[118] Othman explains that open debate on religion is hardly present in Malaysian society. That is because, as Othman as a citizen of Malaysia herself believes, few Malaysians have the courage to express critical views. Most have been socialised into accepting what the ulama prescribes, and individuals are ashamed of their ignorance about Islam. Also, elected politicians are held back by an inner constraint to come across as anti-Islam if they – even merely appear to – question the validity of any decision set out in Sharia-based law proposals. Moreover, politicians use Islam to gain political currency, and lastly, in the absence of an open democratic process and debate, the all-invasive Islamic laws and fatwas are imposed on Muslims without their knowledge and consent. Islamisation takes place in a shroud of secrecy, fear and ignorance and it intensively pervades the lives of Malaysians. "This abdication of civil courage and responsibility by both Muslims and Malaysian citizens of other faiths and religious affiliations has encouraged the fostering of an incipient Islamic theocracy in Malaysia and the authoritarian rule of a minority in matters of Islam", Othman concludes.[119]

In a Sharia state, citizens do not have the right to challenge the Sharia rules that are enforced upon them.[120] Policing free speech, either through legislation or intimidation, is thus vital in establishing and maintaining a Sharia state. It is not without reason that the most authoritarian Sharia state in the world, Saudi Arabia, denies its citizens freedom of speech and freedom of belief. In a Sharia state, religious minorities are unwelcome and the basic notion of equal rights is ignored. Individual rights and moral independence are subordinated to fulfilling religious duties as a member of the collective Umma.

---

116 'I will fight Islamic authorities till the end, vows Kassim Ahmad', *The Malaysian Insider* 18 January 2015, <http://www.themalaysianinsider.com/malaysia/article/i-will-fight-islamic-authorities-till-the-end-vows-kassim-ahmad>.

117 'Growing Islamic fundamentalism seen pushing Malays to quit country', *Malay Mail Online* 30 October 2014, via <http://www.themalaymailonline.com/malaysia/article/growing-islamic-fundamentalism-seen-pushing-malays-to-quit-country#sthash.TD5Jb1f0.dpuf>.

118 'Rise of strict Islam exposes tensions in Malaysia', *bbb.co.uk* 26 August 2011, via <http://www.bbc.co.uk/news/world-radio-and-tv-14649841>.

119 Othman 2006, pp. 346-347.

120 Tibi 2013, p. 182.

THE ORGANISATION OF ISLAMIC COOPERATION AND THE CAIRO DECLARATION

Malaysia is but one of many examples of nations that have Islamised under the influence of Saudi funds. There are many more nations that have come to present themselves as Islamic nations. In 1969, Saudi Arabia initiated the foundation of the Organisation of Islamic Conference (later changed to *Cooperation*), the OIC. It is the only intergovernmental organisation based on a shared religion, and is one of the largest intergovernmental organisations with 57 Member States in 2011.[121] Those 57 Member States – regardless of theological, social, cultural diversity among them – share a commitment to Islamic values and Sharia.

The OIC incorporates not only Hanbali Saudi Wahhabism, but also Maliki, Hanafi, Shafi'i (all Sunni) schools of thought, and Shia Islam. Yet, the idea of a unified Umma of an estimated 1.6 billion Muslims around the world is strong: "[t]he Organization is the collective voice of the Muslim world and ensuring [sic] to safeguard and protect the interests of the Muslim world in the spirit of promoting international peace and harmony among various people of the world."[122] In the 1972 Charter, the OIC affirms its support for the rights of people conform the UN Charter and international law.[123] The plural form of people is also uses in the preamble of the Universal Declaration of Human Rights. But in the Universal Declaration of Human Rights there is also a reference to "all members of the human family", whereas the OIC limits itself to Muslims, and more specifically, the *group* of Muslims in the form of the Umma as the legal subject, not the individual. Further-more, as an organisation founded on the shared religion of Islam, the OIC sets out, *inter alia*:

> [...] "To disseminate, promote and preserve the Islamic teachings and values based on moderation and tolerance, promote Islamic culture and safeguard Islamic heritage";
>
> "To protect and defend the true image of Islam, to combat defamation of Islam and encourage dialogue among civilisations and religions";
>
> "To promote and to protect human rights and fundamental freedoms including the rights of women, children, youth, elderly and people with special needs as well as the preservation of Islamic family values";
>
> "To safeguard the rights, dignity and religious and cultural identity of Muslim communities and minorities in non-Member States".

---

121 Or, to be precise, 56 nation-states and the Palestinian Authority.

122 'About OIC', via <http://www.oic-oci.org/oicv2/page/?p_id=52&p_ref=26&lan=en>.

123 "7. To reaffirm its support for the rights of peoples as stipulated in the UN Charter and international law", Charter of the Organisation of Islamic Cooperation, via <http://www.oic-oci.org/english/charter/OIC%20Char-ter-new-en.pdf>.

The OIC Charter is clear on its goals: Islam is a religion and a culture and must be protected and promoted on behalf of all Muslims in the world. Moreover, nations with an Islamic foundation should unite to achieve this on a global, political, level. In line with the UN Charter's Article 102 ("Every treaty and every international agreement entered into by any Member of the United Nations after the present Charter comes into force shall as soon as possible be registered with the Secretariat and published by it"), the OIC Charter is registered as a treaty and has thus become a recognised international legal instrument. In 1975, 6 years after its establishment, the OIC is granted the status of "Permanent Observer", which allows the OIC to participate as observers in sessions, in the work of the General Assembly and holds a permanent office at the UN Headquarters in New York.[124]

The most obvious motivation for the establishment of the OIC dates back to the postwar 1940s. It stems from the dissatisfaction of the leaders of Islamic countries with the universal, secular and individualist character of the Universal Declaration of Human Rights, established by the United Nations in 1948.[125] Eleanor Roosevelt (1884-1962), who chaired the drafting committee of the Universal Declaration, wrote in her memoirs that Saudi king Ibn Saud (1876-1953) believed that the content of the Declaration was not consonant with the Koran.[126]

Especially Articles 16 and 18 of the Universal Declaration of Human Rights prove to be difficult for the representatives of countries with a predominantly Muslim population. Article 16 concerns equal rights within the setting of marriage:

> Men and women of full age, without any limitation due to race, nationality or religion, have the right to marry and to found a family. They are entitled to equal rights as to marriage, during marriage and at its dissolution.

This article contains many aspects which do not align with Sharia. For instance, Muslims may not enter marriage with non-Muslims, especially women may not, and women do not have the same rights as men when it comes to dissolving the marriage under Sharia. When it comes to divorce, a husband can unilaterally – without permission of his wife – do so by pronouncing the *talaq*. For women, on the other hand, asking her husband for a divorce "when she has not suffered any harm from him", is considered an 'enormity'. As mentioned previously, an enormity is a shocking, evil, or immoral act, and is defined as

---

124 Following the adoption of Resolution 3369 on October 10, 1975 by the 30th UN General Assembly. Other organisations with Permanent Observer status include the European Union, the African Union, the League of Arab States and the International Criminal Court.

125 Laes, Willy, *Mensenrechten in de Verenigde Naties. Een verhaal over manipulatie, censuur en hypocrisie* (Human Rights in the United Nations. A story on manipulation, censorship and hypocrisy), Antwerpen: Garant 2011, p. 155.

126 Roosevelt, Eleanor, *The Autobiography of Eleanor Roosevelt*, London: Hutchinson 1962, p. 253, in: Laes 2011, p. 116.

"[…] any sin entailing either a threat of punishment in the hereafter explicitly mentioned by the Koran or hadith [...]."[127]

Under great lobby efforts of the OIC, the provision of spousal equality in the International Covenant on Civil and Political Rights of 1966 – in a way the successor of the Universal Declaration of Human Rights – has been slimmed down to Article 23 (4):

> States Parties to the present Covenant *shall take appropriate steps* to ensure equality of rights and responsibilities of spouses as to marriage, during marriage and at its dissolution.

The equal rights of spouses have turned into a mere effort on behalf of states, rather than asserting an inherent right to equality. And even more striking, the original ban on restricting marriages on the basis of race, nationality or religion has been edited out of the 1966 International Covenant on Civil and Political Rights.[128]

The same process happened with Article 18 of the Universal Declaration of Human Rights. That provision grants individuals the right *to change* religion or belief, as changing one's religion is an important part of religious freedom. Article 8 of the 1948 Universal Declaration of Human Rights reads:

> Everyone has the right to freedom of thought, conscience and religion; this right includes freedom *to change* his religion or belief, and freedom, either alone or in community with others and in public or private, to manifest his religion or belief in teaching, practice, worship and observance.

Already at the onset of the deliberations on the content of this provision, several Islamic Member States protested.[129] The dominant idea is that 1) a Muslim is *born* a Muslim, 2) this cannot be denounced and 3) if denounced that constitutes a crime in the form of apostasy. Islamic laws are clear: "When a person who has reached puberty and is sane voluntarily apostatizes from Islam, he deserves to be killed." And: "There is no indemnity for killing an apostate."[130] Thus, again under influence by the OIC, the right to change one's religion is deleted from the 1966 International Covenant on Civil and Political Rights, and replaced by the right to "have" or to "adopt" a religion or belief. It now reads:

---

127 Keller 1991, under p.0.0 and w.52.1 (280).
128 Laes 2011, pp. 124-126.
129 For instance, Saudi Arabia, Egypt, Iraq, Syria, Afghanistan and Pakistan protested.
130 Keller 1991, under o8.1 and o8.4. It is obligatory to ask the apostate to repent and return to Islam, if he does not, he should immediately be killed (under o8.2.)

article 18 (1) Everyone shall have the right to freedom of thought, conscience and religion. This right shall include freedom *to have or to adopt* a religion or belief of his choice, and freedom, either individually or in community with others and in public or private, to manifest his religion or belief in worship, observance, practice and teaching.[131]

For Saudi Arabia, both the Universal Declaration of Human Rights and the International Covenant on Civil and Political Rights are deemed incompatible with Sharia, and it ratified neither.[132]

Leaving the OIC without a Declaration of Rights with international standing, the need arose for a legal document which did reflect the Koran and Sunna properly. Therefore, in 1990, the OIC presented the Cairo Declaration on Human Rights in Islam. The Cairo Declaration is intended as an Islamic alternative to the Universal Declaration of Human Rights, since the universal rights system as espoused by the United Nations is considered too secular and Western and should be changed to accommodate Islamic culture and religious values.[133] The Cairo Declaration is the outcome of years of preparation and debate among Member States and now reflects the shared values of Shia, Sunni, and thus Hanbali, Maliki, Hanafi and Shafi'i, and all hybrid forms of Islamic thought. The Declaration is explicitly not secular and not universal. The preamble states:

The Member States of the Organisation of the Islamic Conference,

Reaffirming the civilizing and historical role of the Islamic Umma which God made the best nation that has given mankind a universal and well-balanced civilization in which harmony is established between this life and the hereafter and knowledge is combined with faith; and the role that this Umma should play to guide a humanity confused by competing trends and ideologies and to provide solutions to the chronic problems of this materialistic civilization. [...]

Believing that fundamental rights and universal freedoms in Islam are an integral part of the Islamic religion and that no one as a matter of principle has the right to suspend them in whole or in part or violate or ignore them in as much as they are binding divine commandments, which are contained in the

---

131 See on the political process: Laes 2011.

132 See also: Abiad, Nisrine, *Sharia, Muslim States and International Human Rights Treaty Obligations: A Comparative Study*, London: British Institute of International and Comparative Law 2008, pp. 60-65.

133 In 1997, the representative of Iran and other OIC Members expressed these views, Kofi Annan rejected this stance, stating that human rights were universal, see: Mayer, Ann Elizabeth, *Islam and Human Rights: Tradition and Politics*, Boulder, Colorado: Westview Press 2007, p. 32.

Revealed Books of God and were sent through the last of His Prophets to complete the preceding divine messages thereby making their observance an act of worship and their neglect or violation an abominable sin, and accordingly every person is individually responsible – and the Umma collectively responsible – for their safeguard.[134]

The 25 articles of human rights and duties that follow the preamble all fit within the boundaries of Sharia.[135] All human beings are equal in terms of *human dignity* – as opposed to equality in terms of rights – and united by submission to God, and true faith is taken as guarantee for enhancing human dignity up to a level of human perfection (article 1). The rights that ensue from the Divine are also curtailed by it. Take for instance the right to life: "it is prohibited to take away life *except for a Shari'ah prescribed reason*" (article 2 (a)). Or the right to enjoy safety from bodily harm, which may not be breached "without a Sharia-prescribed reason" (article 2 (d)).[136] Although *prima facie* formulated as a right to life and bodily integrity, it actually legitimises Sharia-based corporal punishments, including the death penalty. The fifth article on marital rights states that men and women have the right to marriage, and that there shall be no restrictions based on race, colour or nationality. This provision omits the right to dissolve the marriage nor includes the right to marry someone with another religion. Article 6 states that "woman is equal to man in *human dignity*".

Equal dignity should not be confused with equal rights, as Associate Professor of Legal Studies Ann Elizabeth Mayer tells us. In *Islam and Human Rights* (2007), she writes: "Given the evasiveness typically found in the wording of Islamic human rights schemes, one is alerted to the fact that the failure to stipulate equality in "rights" is not accidental and that the equality in "dignity" and "obligations" is not intended to signify equality in "rights"."[137] The Parties to the Declaration were consciously avoiding legal equality of the sexes or between people of religion other than Islam.[138] The same can be observed in Article 7, which grants both parents rights with regard to their children "in accordance with the tenets of the Shari'ah"; this factually means no equality between the sexes regarding parental

---

134 The Cairo Declaration on Human Rights in Islam (1990), available via <http://www.oic-oci.org/english/article/human.htm>.

135 All the rights and freedoms stipulated in this Declaration are subject to the Islamic Shari'ah (article 24); The Islamic Shari'ah is the only source of reference for the explanation or clarification of any of the articles of this Declaration (article 25).

136 Article 2 (a): Life is a God-given gift and the right to life is guaranteed to every human being. It is the duty of individuals, societies and states to protect this right from any violation, and it is prohibited to take away life except for a Shari'ah prescribed reason. And 2 (d): Safety from bodily harm is a guaranteed right. It is the duty of the state to safeguard it, and it is prohibited to breach it without a Sharia-prescribed reason.

137 Mayer 2007, p. 102.

138 Bielefeldt, Heiner, 'Muslim Voices in the Human Rights Debate', *Human Rights Quarterly* 1995, pp. 587-617 (603-606).

rights. Furthermore, there are certain provisions on work, education, medical and social care, and criminal law ("as provided for in the Shari'ah"). Lastly, I want to bring attention to the right to express one's opinion "freely in such a manner as would not be contrary to the principles of Sharia'ah" (article 22 (a)).[139] Article 22 includes a prohibition on violating the sanctity of 'the prophets' and on undermining moral and ethical values that may weaken faith in society.[140] This provision of the Cairo Declaration makes critical reflections and public debate on the legitimacy of Islam and Sharia, as well as questioning the validity of Islamic ideas and practices, unlawful.

What may we expect from the Cairo Declaration? What is its legal status? For example, does it create positive (the duty to secure the effective enjoyment of a right) or negative (the duty to abstain from rights violations) obligations for OIC Member States? No, it does not. Mayer states that the "awkward" hybrid model of Western constitutions and internal law, one the one hand, and Islamic elements and concepts, on the other, are puzzling from the perspective of Islamic law. This is because generally, rules that are established outside the system of Islamic methods and criteria are considered irrelevant by Islamic scholars. Still, from a positive perspective, one could see the Cairo Declaration as a step forward, as Islamic culture is merging with the universal human rights standard, albeit superficially. Conversely, a pessimist could argue that the deficiencies of this Islamic version of human rights is holding back the realisation of *universal* human rights. "Since Islamisation pressures seem to continue, a skeptic might predict that any models that give governments grounds for claiming that they have an Islamic warrant for denying the rights afforded under international law could be exploited to impede the cause of human rights", Mayer writes.[141] What will ultimately prove to be the case is subject to speculation. Having said that, it is clear from the formulations of the Cairo provisions that Sharia is invoked to *limit* the scope of rights awarded. Moreover, if the Cairo Declaration had been intended to actually reflect

---

139 Also, "Everyone shall have the right to advocate what is right, and propagate what is good, and warn against what is wrong and evil according to the norms of Islamic Shari'ah" (article 22 (b)); "Information is a vital necessity to society. It may not be exploited or misused in such a way as may violate sanctities and the dignity of Prophets, undermine moral and ethical values or disintegrate, corrupt or harm society or weaken its faith" (article 22 (c)), and "It is not permitted to arouse nationalistic or doctrinal hatred or to do anything that may be an incitement to any form or racial discrimination".

140 Articles 19 and 20 on freedom to express opinions in the International Covenant on Civil and Political Rights read: 19(1). Everyone shall have the right to hold opinions without interference. 2. Everyone shall have the right to freedom of expression; this right shall include freedom to seek, receive and impart information and ideas of all kinds, regardless of frontiers, either orally, in writing or in print, in the form of art, or through any other media of his choice. 3. The exercise of the rights provided for in paragraph 2 of this article carries with it special duties and responsibilities. It may therefore be subject to certain restrictions, but these shall only be such as are provided by law and are necessary: (a) For respect of the rights or reputations of others; (b) For the protection of national security or of public order (ordre public), or of public health or morals. Article 20: 1. Any propaganda for war shall be prohibited by law. 2. Any advocacy of national, racial or religious hatred that constitutes incitement to discrimination, hostility or violence shall be prohibited by law.

141 Mayer 2007, pp. 194-195.

the scope of liberties that *all humans* enjoy under the universal human rights system, there had not been a desire to create an alternative for Muslims.

More importantly, the OIC and its Cairo Declaration prove the point that *despite enormous diversity* among Muslims, Islamic doctrines, and political systems employed by OIC Member States, there is the *general acceptance* that Sharia does and should restrict universal and equal rights. That means that men and women do not have equal rights, it means that Muslims enjoy a better legal (and moral) position than Jews, Christians, Hindus, atheists and other non-Muslims. It means that "cruel and unusual" punishments are legitimised. Despite diversity, the Koran and Sunna allow for interpretations which enable fundamentalist Muslims to legitimise inequality in rights and unfair practices. The fact that Article 22 of the Cairo Declaration prohibits debate (everyone has the right to express opinions freely as long as it does not contravene Sharia principles) seals off the possibility of satirising, questioning, contextualising, doubting, researching or reforming. That means that those outside and inside the Muslim world who voice their opinion against the idea that Sharia should set the norm for freedom and protection, are considered guilty of a crime.

ISLAMOPHOBIA

In order to stifle debate and to suppress criticism of Islam, the Organisation of Islamic Cooperation has been lobbying at the UN, EU and Western parliaments to outlaw "Islamophobia". The OIC launched the Islamophobia Observatory, a watchdog organisation based in Jeddah, Saudi Arabia, in 2007. Since 2008, it has published annual reports on Islamophobia. In the first report, it is stated that:

> One of the major challenges of today's world is the issue of Islamophobia. In recent years, this phenomenon has assumed serious proportions and has become a major cause of concern for the Muslim world. As a result of this rising trend, Muslims, in the West in particular, are being stereotyped, profiled, and subjected to different forms of discriminatory treatment. The most sacred symbols of Islam are being defiled and denigrated in an insulting, offensive, and contemptuous manner to incite hatred and unrest in society. While Islam, as the religion of peace and tolerance, affirms moderation and balance and rejects all forms of extremism and terrorism, the proponents of Islamophobia continue their campaign in defaming Islam and Muslims.[142]

---

142 '1st Oic Observatory Report On Islamophobia May 2007 To May 2008', p. 2, via <http://www.oic-oci.org/uploads/file/Islamphobia/islamphobia_rep_may_07_08.pdf>. The term had been circulating for decades, but was popularised by the British Runnymede Trust, which published a report titled "Islamophobia:

There is material that shows that the term was created by Islamists to create an atmosphere of victimisation, where Muslims are continuously portrayed as victims suffering from hatred, discrimination and negative stereotyping. Although I do not think that Muslim citizens in the West are exonerated from factual discrimination and negativity, I do want to draw attention to the fact that Islamists – supported by many Western elites – established a theme of victimhood which, allegedly, is both caused by critical debate and would be resolved by ending criticism of Islamic and Islamist practices and ideas.[143]

Take for instance Abdur-Rahman Muhammad, an American who was once an Islamist militant. He was present when Islamist members of the International Institute for Islamic Thought, a Muslim Brotherhood front organisation in the United States, convened and decided to propagate this term for political purposes. Muhammad now works to combat Islamic extremism. On Islamophobia, he writes: "This loathsome term is nothing more than a thought-terminating cliché conceived in the bowels of Muslim think tanks for the purpose of beating down critics".[144] Indian-American journalist Asra Nomani (1965), author of *Standing Alone: An American Woman's Struggle for the Soul of Islam*, writes on the "bullying" of the informal honour brigade (the "ghairat brigade") that operates alongside the official OIC channels. The ghairat brigade, partly funded and supported by the OIC, makes personal visits to silence people and uses the internet to consequently label critics as "Islamophobes". There is also a wide community of unorganised people who take up the role of blasphemy police. Whenever someone publicly speaks up against Islam or Islamism, such as Nomani, a consorted effort is made to silence debate on extremist ideology in order to protect the image of Islam. The consequences of the "Islamophobia" meme are huge. Nomani writes:

> Bullying this intense really works. Observant members of the flock are culturally conditioned to avoid shaming Islam, so publicly citing them for that sin often

---

a challenge for us all" in 1997. Therein Islamophobia is defined as an unfounded hostility towards Muslims, and therefore fear or dislike of all or most Muslims. British Runnymede Trust, 'Islamophobia: A Challenge For Us All', *Commission on British Muslims and Islamophobia* (1997), <http://www.runnymede-trust.org/uploads/publications/pdfs/islamophobia.pdf>.

143 Landes, Richard, 'From Useful Idiot to Useful Infidel. Meditations on the Folly of 21st-Century "Intellectuals"', *Terrorism and Political Violence* 2013, pp. 621-634 and Benn, Piers, 'On Islamophobia-phobia', *New Humanist* 2002 via <https://newhumanist.org.uk/524>. Benn contends that: "Many who fear the rise of Islamophobia veer away from critical analysis of Islamic claims and practices, perhaps for fear of what they might find. They denounce critical scrutiny of Islam as somehow impolite, or ignorant of the religion's true nature. This is not intellectually or morally healthy".

144 Berlinski, Claire, 'Moderate Muslim Watch: How the Term "Islamophobia" Got Shoved Down Your Throat', *Ricochet* 24 November 2010 via <https://ricochet.com/archives/moderate-muslim-watch-how-the-term-islamophobia-got-shoved-down-your-throat/> and Muhammad, Abdur-Rahman, 'Whether or not Ground Zero mosque is built, U.S. Muslims have access to the American Dream.' *The Investigative Project on Terrorism*, 5 September 2010, via <http://www.investigativeproject.org/2164/whether-or-not-ground-zero-mosque-is-built-us>.

has the desired effect. Non-Muslims, meanwhile, are wary of being labelled "Islamophobic" bigots. So attacks against both groups succeed in quashing civil discourse. They cause governments, writers and experts to walk on eggshells, avoiding important discussion.[145]

Not only *de facto* are individuals discouraged to keep silent on Islamism. Also *de iure*. The OIC, as the largest voting bloc in the United Nations, resorts to legal instruments – e.g. by means of resolutions – to establish what would in effect be global blasphemy law.[146]

POLITICAL ISLAM PART III: THE MIDDLE WAY TO ESTABLISHING A SHARIA STATE IN EUROPE

There is no question that a debate on the future of Islam is taking place everywhere in the Muslim world as well as in the West. Unfortunately, the most dominant voice of Islam is that which comes from the Islamists, who force their take on Islam either through violent jihad, as the murder of the Charlie Hebdo cartoonists proves once more, or spread the message alongside an Islamisation agenda through a non-violent jihad, often accompanied by intimidating those who use their freedom of speech to push back the Islamist movement. This is a problem worldwide.[147]

Qutb, for a long time the Muslim Brotherhood's most foremost ideologue, made it unmistakably clear that the design of the world order is what is most important. Aforementioned German political scientist Bassam Tibi quotes Qutb on his central tenet: "The *dar al-Islam*/territory of Islam is the place where this *Shari'a* is implemented". For this implementation,

---

145 Nomani, Asra, 'Meet the honor brigade, an organised campaign to silence debate on Islam', *Washington Post* 16 January 2015, via <http://www.washingtonpost.com/opinions/meet-the-honor-brigade-an-organised-campaign-to-silence-critics-of-islam/2015/01/16/0b002e5a-9aaf-11e4-a7ee-526210d665b4_story.html>.

146 See, for instance, Herrenberg, Tom, 'Denouncing Divinity: Blasphemy, Human Rights, and the Struggle of Political Leaders to defend Freedom of Speech in the case of *Innocence of Muslims*', *Ancilla Iuris* 2015, pp. 1-19.

147 Al Qaeda, for instance, published in its magazine *Inspire* a list of people who are "Wanted: Dead or Alive for Crimes Against Islam". The emphasis, however, should be on "Dead" as it is phrased in the caption: "Yes We Can: A Bullet A Day Keeps the Infidel Away". The list includes Ayaan Hirsi Ali, Geert Wilders, and cartoonists, including the murdered chief editor of Charlie Hebdo, Stéphane Charbonnier. See: Bennet, Dashiel, 'Look Who's on Al Qaeda's Most-Wanted List', *The Wire* 1 March, 2013, via <http://www.thewire.com/global/2013/03/al-qaeda-most-wanted-list/62673/>. Other victims of intimidation are listed in Murray, Douglas and Verwey, Johan Pieter, 'Victims of Intimidation. Freedom of Speech within Europe's Muslim Communities', The Centre for Social Cohesion 2008. See also: Ellian, Afshin and Molier, Gelijn (eds.), *Freedom of Speech Under Attack*, The Hague: Eleven International Publishing 2015. On Muslim victims of intimidation and murder by Islamists see: Bennoune 2013.

Muslims need to fight for an 'Islamic world revolution' to establish *hakimiyyat Allah*/Allah's rule in a *shari'a* state, not only in the world of Islam, but also in the world at large. In pursuit of this, it is 'prescribed to Muslims to fight *jihad* to establish God's rule on the globe to save humanity'. This salvation occurs on the grounds of *shari'a*, viewed 'as universal law for the entire world'.[148]

But Qutb's method to bringing Islamism to the world has been updated by someone who is currently the world's principal ideologue of the Muslim Brotherhood: Egyptian-born Yusuf al-Qaradawi (1926). This leading figure is now based in Qatar, he has published multiple books and has an immense following via his website Islam Online and the television program "Shariah and Life" on Al Jazeera – estimated at 60 million viewers. Qaradawi is also founder and president of the Dublin-based European Council for Fatwa and Research (ECFR) and is connected to the Oxford Centre for Islamic Studies of Oxford University, although he is now banned from entering the United Kingdom (and the United States). The ECFR is a board of Islamic scholars who are part of the network of the international Muslim Brotherhood. Several volumes of fatwas have been published under its authority, mainly focused on conformity to Sharia for Muslims in Europe.[149]

To sum up, there are *grosso modo* three ways to subject people to a regime of political Islam: by means of terror, as happened in what we now know as Saudi Arabia and is happening now by, *inter alia*, Al Qaeda, Islamic State and Boko Haram.[150] Secondly, compliance to a Sharia state can be accomplished by means of a top-down political take-over (at whatever pace), as happened in Iran and is now taking place in Malaysia. Thirdly, it can be slowly effectuated in a bottom-up fashion. This is the method of Qaradawi's Middle Way, as I will now explain.

In the 1960s, Qaradawi was commissioned by Egypt's al-Azhar University to write a manual of how Muslims in the West should live by Islamic tenets. The book, *The Lawful and Prohibited in Islam*, has roughly 70 editions in Arabic and has been translated in many languages, including English, German and French. In 1990, he issued an important manifest titled "Priorities of the Islamic Movement in the Coming Phase". The most significant message Qaradawi has is that the conquest of the West should not be by "the sword or

---

148 Tibi 2013, p. 185. See also: Fatah, Tarek. *Chasing A Mirage: The Tragic Illusion Of An Islamic State*, Mississauga, Ontario: Wiley & Sons Canada 2008, p. 275-276.
149 Polanz, Carsten, 'The Legal Theory for Muslim Minorities and the Islamic Dream of Conquering the West', *Islam and Christianity* 2/2012, pp. 18-28 (19).
150 Other than "regional" terrorism (which is about autonomy for an ethnic group within a sovereign state) or "leftist" terrorism (such as animal rights terror or the RAF, which is related to specific aims), Islamist terrorism directed towards the west is about weakening western powers and instilling fear (a hadith on instilling fear is: "We will cast terror into the hearts of unbelievers on account of their associating with Allah that for which He sent down no authority. Their abode is the Fire and wretched is the dwelling-place of the evildoers", 3:151 al-Bukhari). It is also about establishing a Sharia state. All citizens are potential targets. See: Ellian 2011, pp. 187, 219.

armies, but by preaching and ideology".[151] Other than fundamentalists who accept the method of violent jihad, the Muslim Brotherhood adopted a new method that Qaradawi unfolds in his works. Since the 1990s, this new doctrine is referred to as *wassatiyya*: a sort of "middle way" between violent extremism and secularism.[152] I have to emphasise that this new doctrine is not a diversion from the goal of establishing a global Sharia state, but it is a new *method* for achieving this. Whereas Jihadi Salafist, for instance, openly call for jihad or, refuse to participate as Western citizens and reject the West as "Land of Kufr", the new Islamists adopt a more pragmatic way for getting Sharia to dominate every realm of human activity and thought in the West.[153]

Wassatiyya prefers the use of *dawa*. Dawa (literally making an invitation or issuing a summons) is the act of non-violent proselytising, of dialogue ("inviting non-Muslims to Islam"). An important part of Middle Way Islamism is that obligations and restrictions for Muslims following from Sharia – ranging from not being allowed to work at a restaurant where alcohol is served to the duty to fight violent jihad in order to spread Islam – may be *temporarily* set aside in order not to alarm non-Muslim Europeans while working towards a Sharia state.[154] Once established, all suspensions are rescinded.

Qaradawi is not the only proponent of this method and ideology. Another well-known one is Tariq Ramadan (1962), who is Professor of Islamic Studies at Oxford University as well as at universities in Qatar, Morocco and Malaysia. He is the grandson of Hassan al-Banna, founder of the Muslim Brotherhood. Although this in itself is not something that can be held against him, Ramadan is known to ally with the Brotherhood and its goals. Together with Qaradawi, who he extolls, Ramadan is seen as one of the primary developers of this uniquely European concept of Islamic dawa.[155]

Qaradawi promotes this *fiqh-al-aqalliyyat*, or, jurisprudence for Muslim minorities. He believes the Islamist movement plays a vital role in creating separated Muslim commu-

---

151 Qaradawi stated more than once that "Islam will return to Europe as a conqueror and victor after being expelled from it twice … the conquest this time will not be by the sword but by preaching and ideology". See: "Leading Sunni Sheikh Yousef Al-Qaradhawi and Other Sheikhs Herald the Coming Conquest of Rome", MEMRI Special Dispatch Series No. 447, 6 December 2002, via <http://www.memri.org/bin/articles.cgi?Area=sd&ID=SP44702>. See also: Brown, Eric, 'After the Ramadan Affair: New Trends in Islamism in the West', *Current Trends in Islamist Ideology* 2005, pp. 7-29 (9).

152 Vidino, Lorenzo, 'Aims and Methods of Europe's Muslim Brotherhood', *Current Trends in Islamist Ideology* November 2006, via <http://www.hudson.org/research/9776-aims-and-methods-of-europe-s-muslim-brotherhood>.

153 Brown, Eric, 'After the Ramadan affair: New trends in Islamism in the West', *Current Trends in Islamist Ideology* 2005, pp. 7-29 (8).

154 As Qaradawi states: "Necessities make what is forbidden permissible". See: 'Sheikh Qaradawi's First Interview with Onislam.net', *OnIslam.net* 18 October 2010, via <http://www.onislam.net/english/shariah/contemporary-issues-interviews-reviews-and-events/449388-sheikh-qaradawis-first-interview-with-onislam-net.html?Events=>.

155 Wiedl, Nina, 'Dawa and the Islamist Revival in the West', *Current Trends in Islamist Ideology* 2009. See also: Phillips, Melanie, *Londonistan. How Britain Created a terror State Within*, London: Gibson Square 2012, p. 262.

nities in the West. As one of the middle way's key proponents he warns Muslims in the West against the "melting" of Muslims and their identity into the large non-Muslim majority. Yet, he sees it as an opportunity as well: as most expatriated Muslims experience a sense of disorientation in the West, they prove to be ideal recipients for the movement's propaganda. Italian scholar Lorenzo Vidino, author of *The New Muslim Brotherhood in the West* (2010), unfolds Qaradawi's modus operandi for achieving global Sharia domination. He "[…] openly calls for the creation of a separate society for Muslims within the West. While he highlights the importance of keeping open a dialogue with non-Muslims, he advocates the establishment of Muslim communities with "their own religious, educational and recreational establishments". He urges his fellow revivalists to try "to have your small society within the larger society" and "your own 'Muslim ghetto'."[156]

This ghettoisation is part of a wider strategy of the "middle way" towards establishing a Sharia state. This strategy includes seven stages through which Muslim minorities in the West should go, according to Qaradawi. Firstly, Muslims should become *aware* of their Muslim identity. This should *awaken* in the second stage. Stages three and four regard the spreading of the movement and the forming of groups. In the fifth stage, mosques should be constructed and Islamic schools and organisations need to be founded, which Qaradawi views as manifestations of a parallel society. In stage six, the non-Muslim majority becomes used to Islam as a permanent and visible presence. Finally, Muslims use their inner self-assurance to interact with the majority of the host society and begin propagating their faith and values. In this seventh stage Muslims should gain access to key positions in all areas, such as media, politics, economics, sociology and medicine. The purpose is that these "awakened" Muslims seek to adapt Western science as well as concepts of human and civil rights to Islam.[157]

This step-by-step implementation of Sharia in the West is preferred over the introduction of a Sharia state by means of violent jihad. One of the theological justifications of not using violent jihad is that when Muhammad was spreading Islam and he and his followers were the minority in the Arabian Peninsula, no violence was used. It was at a later stage, when Muhammad had formed a majority of Muslims, he began to use severe violence to force Islam upon others.[158]

---

156 Vidino, Lorenzo, 'Aims and Methods of Europe's Muslim Brotherhood', *Current Trends in Islamist Ideology* November 2006, via <http://www.hudson.org/research/9776-aims-and-methods-of-europe-s-muslim-brotherhood>. See also: Schirrmacher, Christine, 'Sharia Judges, Parallel Legal System, Justices of the Peace – A Commentary to Joachim Wagner's "Outlaw" Judges: The Threat Posed by Islamic Parallel Jurisprudence to the Rule of Law"', *Islam und christlicher Glaube* 2012, pp. 35-40.

157 Polanz 2012, pp. 26.

158 Radical preacher Haitham al-Haddad, who obtained a PhD at the University of London (SOAS) on the topic of Muslim Minorities in the West, stated that "The jihad was allowed also through stages and then the final stage is to fight everyone until they establish the law of Allah. The first stage after migrating to Medina the Prophet was allowed, allowed to fight those who fought against him. Then the Prophet was commanded to fight those who fought against him. Then the Prophet, and that is the final stage as Ibn Qayyim said, and

Although the goal is thus the same, Qaradawi prefers this "middle way" strategy so not to scare people off. Part of that strategy is the pragmatic decision to use "dawa language" that avoids negative associations for Western audiences, such as not mentioning the desire of establishing an Islamic state, by describing Islam as a "religion of peace and tolerance", focussing on jihad as an "inner struggle", describing Sharia as a "just order" that guarantees social justice, by emphasising that Sharia is a "set of values" rather than a body of laws, or labelling the headscarf as an expression of female liberation rather than a religious obligation.[159]

The Islamic construct of *taqiyya* legitimises this kind of double speak. At the risk of conveying some sort of a "conspiracy message", I do believe it is important to discuss this concept. *Taqiyya* is described variously as "precautionary dissimulation", "religiously-sanctioned deception", "lying" or "deception" and "keeping one's convictions secret" and "tactical dissimulation" or "holy deception". Early Islamic texts read: "*Al Taqiyya* is with the tongue only; not the heart. A believer can make any statement as long as the "heart is comfortable […]"; "God gave the believers freedom of movement by *takiyya*; therefore conceal thyself […]"; "*Takiyya* is a cloak for the believer: he who has no religion has no *takiyya*, associate your opponents only outwardly and oppose them inwardly".[160] In short, Muslims have holy permission to deceive "infidels".[161] Previously mentioned Middle Way Islamist Tariq Ramadan has been accused this form of "doublespeak". French researcher Caroline Fourest (1975) analysed 15 of his books, 1,500 pages of interviews and circa a hundred recordings and concluded that Ramadan is the political heir of his grandfather Hassan al-Banna as he repeats the discourse that al-Banna had at the beginning of the 20th century in Egypt. She argues that he has one message for his Muslim followers and something else entirely different to his Western audience.[162] This is part of the Islamist strategy

---

this I think all scholars agree on this, the Prophet were commanded to fight everyone until they established the law of Allah." See: 'Haitham al-Haddad', *The Islamic far-right in Britain*, via <http://tifrib.com/haitham-al-haddad/>.

159 Polanz 2012, p. 26 and Wiedl 2009.

160 Campbell, Andrew, "Taqiyya: How Islamic Extremists Deceive the West", *National Observer* 2005, pp. 11-23 (12).

161 For instance, in Koran 3:28 and 40:28. Ibrahim, Raymond, 'How Taqiyya Alters Islam's Rules of War. Defeating Jihadist Terrorism', *Middle East Quarterly* 2010, pp. 3-13, via <https://www.meforum.org/2538/taqiyya-islam-rules-of-war>.

162 Fourest, Caroline, *Brother Tariq: The Doublespeak of Tariq Ramadan*, New York: Encounter Books 2008. For examples, see also: Dankowitz, Aluma, 'Tariq Ramadan – Reformist or Islamist?', The Middle East Media Research Institute (MEMRI) Inquiry & Analysis Series Report No. 266, 17 February 2006: "In a November 2003 interview with the Paris Arabic-language radio [Beur FM], Tariq Ramadan said: 'There is a reformist rationalist stream, and there is a Salafi stream that is trying to remain faithful to the foundations [of the religion]. I belong to the [latter] stream. That is, there are a number of principles that I consider to be basic, and that, as a Muslim, I cannot deny'... However, during a February 2004 UNESCO conference, when [author and French Muslim cleric] Ghaleb bin Sheikh, who belongs to the reformist liberal stream, attacked him, he said: 'I am not a Salafi. A Salafi is someone who clings to the written word [*harfi*] and I am not like that.'"

to openly breach with Sharia principles in order to work towards the implementation and acceptance of Sharia.

The presence of Muslims in the West is deemed "a great benefit" for the global Islamist movement. The idea is that if Muslims in Europe create an Islamic environment for Muslim immigrants and European converts and influence the social and political climate favourably towards Islam and the Umma, this will inspire Western leaders to pressure Muslim rulers on Muslim countries to be more accommodating to the Islamic movement in those countries.[163] For this to work, Muslim minorities need a tailored version of Islamic law. One method of achieving this is through the establishment of Sharia councils, as we shall see in the upcoming chapter.

CONCLUSION

The focus of this chapter has been on the worst version of Islamic fundamentalism. I am aware there is a plethora of varieties in theory and practice. At the same time I am confident that the core is as I have described it. The core of Islamic fundamentalism is a theologically justified political goal of saving and purifying society by means of establishing a Sharia state in which the Umma is unified. This Sharia state can be achieved by means of terror, by a political takeover, or by a bottom-up approach. It is this last version that is most prevalent in Europe under leadership of Islamists.

In the 1970s and 1980s, Wahhabi Saudi Islam and the Egyptian Muslim Brotherhood made a pact to exert Islamist influence in the West. In just a few decades, the Muslim Brotherhood and its affiliates have succeeded in building a vast network of media outlets, think tanks, educational centres and Sharia councils in Europe. Moreover, Sharia-patrolled ghettoes have also become part of society.[164] It is part of the "Islamic movement" Qaradawi calls for, by which he means "organised, collective work, undertaken by the people, to restore Islam to the leadership of society", as he wrote in the introduction of his "Priorities of the Islamic Movement in the Coming Phase". And although the "dialogue" can be one of openly demonstrating allegiance to democracy, religious freedom and equality, between Muslims and non-Muslims, and between men and women, it is very clear that those are constructs and practices that are actually firmly rejected by Islamists.

From the examples of Saudi Arabia and Malaysia, we know what Islamisation of society holds in store for its citizens. This poses a problem because research about European Muslims reveals a strong link between religious fundamentalism and a high level of "out-

---

163 Wiedl 2009.
164 See: Vidino, Lorenzo, 'Hisba in Europe? Assessing a murky phenomenon', *European Foundation for Democracy* 2013, via <http://www.europeandemocracy.org/images/stories/Media/Hisba/Hisba_in_ Europe.pdf>.

group hostility". That means that a sizeable number of fundamentalist Muslims are intolerant towards those who do not share their foundations, significantly more than fundamentalist Christians do. About half of Euro-Muslims believe the West is out to destroy Islam, do not want homosexuals as friends, and believe Jews cannot be trusted.[165] This is not "un-Islamic" as has become clear from studying Islamic fundamentalism and is all the more problematic since this fundamentalism in Europe is increasingly gaining ground among European Muslims. This means that knowledge and awareness on this topic is now more than ever required and an adequate response is needed.

The next chapter is a study on Sharia councils. In *Your Fatwa Does Not Apply Here: Untold Stories from the Fight Against Muslim Fundamentalism* (2013), Bennoune does not want to conflate a wide range of ideologies and movements, but does find there are significant commonalities among the fundamentalists. "They believe in the imposition of "God's law", something called *the* Sharia – their version of it rather than others' – on Muslims everywhere, and in the creation of what they deem to be Islamic states or disciplined diasporic communities ruled by these laws".[166] This brings us to the rights and duties of Muslims in Europe, where privately run Sharia councils have been erected that provide religious law in action for diasporic Islamic communities. In the West, such a minority Muslim legal order is mostly manifest in the United Kingdom.

---

165 According to a 2013 poll in 6 European countries (Germany, France, the Netherlands, Belgium, Austria and Sweden) among 9,000 Turkish and Moroccan immigrants and natives. See: Koopmans 2015, pp. 33-57.
166 Bennoune 2013, pp. 14-15.

3   When Multiculturalism and Islamic Fundamentalism Coincide: Sharia Councils in the United Kingdom

Introduction

Sixteenth-century French political philosopher Jean Bodin (1530-1596) conceptualised the modern sovereign state as having the exclusive right to make laws and execute them within its territory.[1] Nowadays, due to immigration and increasing influence of Islamist doctrines, Sharia is competing as a body of laws within national borders. Almost half of British Muslim young adults prefers Sharia over democratic and secular law while, at the same time, multiculturalists are publicly polishing the image of Islamic laws and advocating for the "right" to resort to those.[2]

This takes Taylorian identity politics (also known as "politics of difference") a step further. Whereas Charles Taylor made the case that minorities had to be recognised for their difference which included the right to be *exempted* from certain universal legal obligations, new multiculturalism creates space for Muslims to have their "own" religious laws as an *additional* body of laws functioning within a state's borders.

That means that representatives of the multiculturalist ideology must have a positive view of Sharia as a basis of a legal system. That raises the question: how *do* multiculturalists view Sharia? Answering that question obviously involves a degree of generalisation. There are, however, some points that are commonly present, which I will illustrate with speeches held by then principal leader of the Church of England, the Archbishop of Canterbury Rowan Williams (1950) and Baron Phillips of Worth Matravers (1938), who was the first Lord Chief Justice of England and Wales to be head of the English judiciary when that function was transferred from the Lord Chancellor in 2006.

In 2008, Williams advocated the integration of parts of Sharia in a speech that caused a major controversy. A few months later, he was backed by Phillips, who asserted that "[t]here is no reason why principles of Sharia Law, or any other religious code should not be the basis for mediation or other forms of alternative dispute resolution".[3]

---

1   Bodin 1992.
2   '40 percent of young UK Muslims want sharia law', Poll by UK think tank Policy Exchange 31 January 2007, via <www.wnd.com/2007/01/39942/>.
3   Phillips, Nicholas, 'Equality before the Law', in: Ahdar & Aroney 2010, pp. 309-318. A video of the speech can be found online via <http://news.bbc.co.uk/2/hi/uk_news/7488960.stm>.

Interestingly, resulting from a series of conventions signed by Turkey and Greece dating back to 1881, a Muslim minority in the Grecian province of Western Thrace depends on Sharia for decisions on family law disputes. Approximately 100,000 Greek citizens live under Islamic law. Greek courts also enforce decisions made by religious authorities.[4] In fact, the Canadian province Ontario used to allow private parties to solve legal matters on the basis of Sharia law through means of enforceable arbitration, as pressed for by Islamic fundamentalists.[5] Under great pressure from women's rights groups and liberal Muslim organisations, Ontario revised several provisions of the Ontario Family Statute Law Amendment Act 2009, so that now any decision made by a third party in arbitration or other proceedings has no legal effect, unless the award is exclusively in accordance with the law of Ontario or of another Canadian jurisdiction.[6] Now the United Kingdom is experiencing a similar debate.[7] The outcome is important: it matters whether the state maintains a doctrine of 'one law for all', or defers to Islamic fundamentalists.

Then Prime Minister Gordon Brown (1951) stated that it "is very clear that British laws must be based on British values and that religious law, while respecting other cultures, should be subservient to British criminal and civil law".[8] David Cameron (1966) rejected any expansion of Sharia law in the United Kingdom, and said it would undermine society, alienate other communities, and that allowing two laws to work side by side would be dangerous, adding: "All citizens are equal before the law". [9]

This Archbishop's speech sparked mass controversy as he made the point that it should be possible for individuals to choose jurisdiction when settling private legal matters, including the option to have matters settled under Sharia law. One may wonder why it is important to look so deeply into speeches which were vehemently rejected. The reason I have chosen to do so nonetheless is because I believe the multiculturalist thought that runs behind it is, in fact, widely shared across Europe's elite. This particular thought of

---

4 Tsaoussi, Aspasia and Zervogianni, Eleni, 'Multiculturalism and Family Law: The Case of *Greek Muslims*', pp. 209-239, in: Boele-Woelki, Katharina and Sverdrup, Tone (eds.), *European Challenges In Contemporary Family Law*, Antwerp: Intersentia 2011.

5 Fatah 2008.

6 See on the Ontario debate, *inter alia*, William, Arsani, 'An Unjust Doctrine of Civil Arbitration: Sharia councils in Canada and England', *Stanford Journal of International Relations* 2010, pp. 40-47; Fatah 2008, and Brown, Alexandra, 'Constructions of Islam in the Context of Religious Arbitration: A Consideration of the "Shari'ah Debate" in Ontario, Canada', *Journal of Muslim Minority Affairs* 2010, pp. 343-356.

7 The United Kingdom consists of three legal jurisdictions: England and Wales, Scotland and Northern Ireland. All three have their own legal systems. The legal aspects of this discussion are mainly of importance in England and Wales, as in the strict sense, there is no 'British law'.

8 'Sharia law not welcome here, says PM Brown', *Birmingham Post*, 9 February 2008.

9 The Archbishop's position was even questioned by his colleagues. 'Cameron steps into Sharia law row', *news.bbc.co.uk*, 26 February 2008. See also: 'Williams 'shocked' at Sharia row', *news.bbc.co.uk*, 8 February 2008 and 'Sharia law row: Archbishop is in shock as he faces demands to quit and criticism from Lord Carey', *London Evening Standard*, 7 February 2008. 'The Church should have the guts to sack the Archbishop...and pick a man who truly treasures British values', *Daily Mail*, 11 February 2008. For a compilation of reactions, see: 'Reaction in quotes: Sharia law row', *news.bbc.co.uk*, 8 February 2008.

respecting and accommodating minority legal systems in Europe is not as vehemently rejected as it seems. In academia there is a trend to endorse Sharia councils. Likewise, the most senior judge at the time felt he needed to defend Williams.

In his defence of Williams, Lord Chief Justice Phillips stated that under the Arbitration Act 1996, private parties had already been able to employ Sharia law in the context of family disputes.[10] Similar to modern and secular legal systems, Islamic family law consists of rules regarding marriage, divorce, inheritance, property division and child custody. Both Williams and Phillips did have a case in point that it was already perfectly possible to have certain matters settled under Sharia, albeit not under the Arbitration Act.

In the United Kingdom, Islamic family law is institutionalised in the form of Sharia councils, which falsely operate under the flag of mediation and arbitration, as I will argue. There have been publicly known Sharia councils in the United Kingdom since 1982, when sheikhs Sayyid Mutawalli ad-Darsh (1930-1997) and Suhaib Hasan (1942) founded the first one. "The Islamic Sharia Council" has not been hindered by the government. In fact, it is a registered charity.[11] It is an umbrella organisation consisting of around a dozen Sharia councils. Other well-known Sharia councils are the Muslim Arbitration Tribunal, which has several departments and the Sharia council hosted by the Birmingham Central Mosque. Estimates run from about ten councils to 85 – with many councils functioning outside the limelight, for instance, out of mosques and from websites.[12]

This chapter is a case study about these Sharia councils in the United Kingdom.[13] The aim is not only to provide factual information about these councils, but also, by describing the councils' Islamist ideological foundations and practices, to challenge some of the assumptions in multiculturalist discourse. Moreover, what is the relationship between multiculturalism and the accommodation of Islamic fundamentalism?

This undertaking consists of several subtasks. First, I explain what multiculturalists understand to be Sharia and the relationship between multiculturalism and Islamic fundamentalism. Second, I describe the Islamist background of Britain's most known and influential Sharia council. Third, I give insight in the practice of Sharia councils. Fourth, having covered that basis, I challenge the wishful thinking that consists of the intention to combine Sharia councils with human rights. Fifth, I discuss Sharia councils compared to rabbinical courts. Sixth, the Arbitration and Mediation Services (Equality) Bill is dis-

---

10   Ahdar & Aroney 2010, p. 317.
11   <http://www.islamic-sharia.org/aboutus/>.
12   The number 85 comes from MacEoin & Green 2009. From interviews conducted with Islamic judges, the estimate comes at about ten, namely those in Wembley, Ealing, two in Manchester, Dewsbury, Bradford, Birmingham, Nuneaton, and London. Chief crown prosecutor Nazir Afzal estimates the number of councils at 90 (telephone interview 11 July 2013).
13   Earlier, I wrote on this topic: Zee, Machteld, 'Five Options for the Relationship between the State and Sharia Councils: Untangling the Debate on Sharia Councils and Women's Rights in the United Kingdom', *Journal of Religion & Society* 2015, pp. 1-18.

cussed, which aims to restrict the remit of Sharia councils. Lastly, I will discuss several secular alternatives to these councils.

DISTINGUISHING POSITIONS IN THE DEBATE

Let us start by identifying positions in this "Sharia council debate". Firstly, there are those denouncing the idea that "it should be possible to choose to have matters settled under Sharia", such as Brown and Cameron. Generally, the idea of endorsing Sharia for British Muslims is not a popular one, to say the least. At the same time, however, and this is particularly important for those with legislative powers, they did not introduce state measures to *counter* Sharia councils. Thus, morally and publicly rejected, but factually and legally unhindered. Condemned, but "laissez-faire". We label this as *tolerance*.

Secondly, there are those who are *intolerant* towards Sharia Councils. Examples include the non-governmental organisations One Law for All, Sharia Watch UK, Women Living Under Muslim Laws, IKWRO (Iranian and Kurdish Women's Rights Organisation, the Lawyer's Secular Society, Southall Black Sisters, and member of the House of Lords, Baroness Caroline Cox, who initiated a bill curtailing the extent to which Sharia councils can operate in the United Kingdom. There is also an active campaign by Muslims against Sharia. Take for instance Shaaz Mahboob, at that time, Vice Chair of British Muslims for Secular Democracy, who stated that "[t]here have been no calls from members of the British Muslim communities demanding the introduction of Sharia as a parallel justice system". He believes that the assumption by the Lord Chief Justice that Sharia law could become a successful alternative form of alternative dispute resolution will only result in further alienating and segregating members of the Muslim communities from the rest of society. Labour MP Khalid Mahmood said: "I, along with the vast majority of UK Muslims, oppose any such move to introduce Sharia law here".[14] Many of the NGOs who run campaigns against Sharia are led by individuals with Islamic roots.

Thirdly, there are those representing traditional and conservative readings of Islam, including Islamists arguing in favour of Sharia councils in the United Kingdom. For instance, the members of the board of the Islamic Sharia Council make their case for more Sharia in the West. Then there are Muslim citizens who subscribe to these views. A 2006 poll suggested that forty per cent of British Muslims supported "there being areas in Britain which are pre-dominantly Muslim and in which Sharia law is introduced".[15] An additional polling agency confirmed these results: 40 per cent of Muslims aged between 16 and 24, compared to 17 per cent of those over 55, said they would prefer to live under Sharia law

---

14 'Backlash over call for Sharia', *Birmingham Mail* 8 February 2008.
15 '40 percent of British Muslims want Sharia Law', ICM poll 20 February 2006, via <ukpollingreport.co.uk/blog/archives/146>.

in the United Kingdom.[16] A year later, another polling agency asked respondents to score this position: "If I could choose, I would prefer to live in Britain under Sharia law rather than British law". For older generations, there was broad consensus that Sharia was unsuited to the United Kingdom: 75 per cent of those over 55 preferred British law, yet this figure dropped as ages went down: 75 per cent of 45-54 year-olds, 63 per cent of 35-44 year-olds, 52 per cent of 25-34 year-olds, and only 50 per cent of 16-24 year-olds.[17]

Fourthly, there are academics from mostly a legal and/or an anthropological background and high-profile European or North American officials or figures "who seem genuinely concerned about the integration of Muslim communities in their respective countries, and consider the move inevitable for any "successful" integration of Muslims", as Yemeni-Swiss Associate Professor Elham Manea (1966) describes.[18] I put these under the banner of multiculturalism.

However well-intended, these multiculturalists do not support those Muslims advocating *against* more Sharia in the United Kingdom. In contrast, they publicly advocate accommodation of Sharia in the United Kingdom; Williams and Phillips being the best examples of high-profile officials who are leading the debate. Whether that is by opening up debate about the possibilities, or stating there is no reason why the Arbitration Act should not accommodate it. Both intellectuals base their conviction on the idea that the combination of Muslim identity, a pluralist society and religious freedoms warrants accommodation of Sharia. The argument is that more latitude should be given to minorities to resort to "their own" religious laws. The multiculturalist assumption is that being a member of a Muslim minority signifies a setback compared to "indigenous" Britons. Legal universalism,

---

16   '40 percent of young UK Muslims want sharia law', Poll by UK think tank Policy Exchange 31 January 2007, via <www.wnd.com/2007/01/39942/>.

17   See: Mirza, Munira *et al.*, *Living Apart Together: British Muslims and the Paradox of Multiculturalism*, London: Policy Exchange, 2007, p. 46, in: 'Sharia Law or One Law for All, p. 12. another poll conducted by the Centre for Islamic Pluralism, which has found that a majority, estimated at a minimum of 65 percent, 'brusquely repudiated the imposition of sharia in Britain'. 'Our survey shows British Muslims don't want sharia', *The Spectator*, 12 July, 2008. The Centre for Islamic Pluralism is an American think tank, which aim it is to 'Foster, develop, defend, protect, and further mobilize moderate American Muslims in their progress toward integration as an equal and respected religious community in the American interfaith environment', see: <www.islamicpluralism.org>.

18   Manea, Elham, 'Introducing Sharia in Western Legal Systems. When States Legally Sanction Discrimination, *Qantara.de* 19 March 2012, via <http://en.qantara.de/content/introducing-sharia-in-western-legal-systems-when-states-legally-sanction-discrimination>. See, for instance, these volumes which contain essays by scholars who are generally positive towards some form of accommodation of Sharia: Ahdar & Aroney 2010; Berger, Maurits (ed.), *Applying Shari'a in the West. Facts, Fears and the Future of Islamic Rules on Family Relations in the West*, Leiden: Leiden University Press 2013 and Griffith-Jones, Robin (ed.), *Islam and English Law. Rights, Responsibilities and the Place of* Shari'a, Cambridge: Cambridge University Press 2013. See also: Berger, Maurits, 'Juist blokkeren van shariaraad is dom' (Actually, blocking a Sharia council is stupid), NRC Handelsblad 15 June 2012 and 'Sharia council: same pitch, same rules', Webmagazine Maastricht University 30 October 2012, via <http://webmagazine.maastrichtuniversity.nl/index.php/research/society/item/357-sharia-council-same-pitch-same-rules>.

the same laws for everyone, is considered discriminatory. Access to Islamic legal institutions is considered emancipatory and just.

This "new" multiculturalism, as American Associate Professor of Law Michael Helfand labels it, focuses on the idea that the state needs to recognise that religious communities are independent legal orders with their own sets of rules and practices. Thus, even beyond recognition of minority cultures and not criticising minority ideas and practices, new multiculturalism adds the need of *legal* autonomy to groups. The idea is that "[c]ultures and religions play a freedom-enhancing role by embedding shared values and interests into a series of rules and obligations. And, by building institutions to govern and maintain these rules, cultures and religions create communities that promote the core values shared by their membership". Helfand believes that if the state grants autonomy and self-gover-nance to minority communities, this can expand the scope of liberty enjoyed by the group members.[19] British professor of Law Maleiha Malik also stands favourable towards accommodating Muslim legal norms. She writes that law can be used as a strategy for the "accommodation of difference". In this sense, law and legal institutions have become more important as tools for the "politics of recognition". Even beyond individual disputes, the law and its institutions are the basis to sustain a sense of community. When it comes to the integration of Muslims, she contends, "it is important that law and legal institutions do not distort or misrecognise the value of religious norms and practices for those Muslims for whom they have significance". If the law does neglect "[...] important features of an individual's personal identity – e.g. as Muslims – this will cause harm to their sense of personal autonomy and self-respect".[20]

In advocating on behalf of Sharia councils, it means that multiculturalism now includes the idea that having an Islamic faith is such a vital marker for individuals' lives, that it is justified to have an additional legal system recognised apart from the standing system of law. That also means that multiculturalists who support this idea probably have a positive view towards Sharia.

MULTICULTURALISTS' VIEW OF SHARIA

What is that view? To start: according to a multiculturalist, Sharia is not what I have pre-sented it to be in the previous chapter. Sharia is obviously not seen as the driving force of adherents of a fundamentalist ideology. The sacred law of Islam is not considered "an all-embracing body of religious duties, the totality of Allah's commands that regulate the life

---

19 Helfand, Michael, 'Religious Arbitration and the New Multiculturalism: Negotiating Conflicting Legal Orders', *New York University Law Review* 2011, pp. 1231-1305 (1274-1275).

20 Malik, Maleiha, 'Muslim Legal Norms and the Integration of European Muslims', EUI Working Paper 2009/29, via <http://cadmus.eui.eu/bitstream/handle/1814/11653/RSCAS?sequence=1>.

of every Muslim in all aspects", as noted Arabist Joseph Schacht wrote in *An Introduction to Islamic Law* in 1964.[21] It is *not* considered as the aggregate of binding instructions following from Islamic sources such as the Koran and hadiths which function as "a totalizing force that inspires and regulates all aspects of public and private life" as Sociology Professor Haideh Moghissi did state.[22]

Moreover, the following is not seen as "true" representations of Islam – although adherents themselves vehemently disagree – Wahhabism, Salafism, Islamism, the regimes of Saudi Arabia and Iran, the Muslim Brotherhood, Al Qaeda (The Base), the Egyptian Islamic Jihad, Hizb ut-Tahrir (Liberation Party), Jamaat-e-Islami (Assembly of Islam), the Taliban (The Students), Al-Shabaab (the Youth), Hamas (Enthusiasm), Islamic State and Boko Haram (Western education is forbidden).

In addition, the following is not "true" Sharia as multiculturalists see it: Tariq Ramadan's and Yusuf al-Qaradawi's Middle Way Islamist method to turn Europe into a Sharia state, no freedom to leave Islam as apostasy is a capital crime, intolerance towards other religions and atheism, no freedom of speech, denouncing democracy as a man-made infidel concept, brutal punishments following from *hudud* laws, no freedom for women to walk around with their heads uncovered, unequal inheritance settlements for men and women, child marriage, forced marriage, the duty of (sexual) obedience for women to their spouses, no equal right to divorce for men and women, homosexuality as a crime, slavery, polygamy, Nazi-like Jew-hatred, violent jihad, vigilantism, segregation of the sexes, taqiyya, or promoting ghettoisation for diasporic Muslims.[23] All this is considered a *deviance* from what Sharia "really" is.

Well, what does it deviate from, one may ask? What *do* multiculturalists consider an accurate representation of Sharia? When studying multiculturalist thought, what Sharia is considered to "really" be, either 1) remains (intentionally or unintentionally) vague, 2)

---

21   Schacht 1982, p. 1.
22   Moghissi 1999, pp. 69-70.
23   Professor of International Law Dominic McGoldrick states that the following rules or practices would clearly be problematic in terms of the European Convention of Human Rights: severe punishments for crimes- death penalty executions or limb amputations; stoning or imprisoning women for adultery; the criminalisation of sexual activities outside of marriage and for homosexual or lesbian activities; nonrecognition of the transgendered; certain rules concerning marriage and polygamy, even with more modern legislative and administrative limitations and restrictions on it that make polygamy difficult; honour killings or attacks; Talaq, i.e. unilateral divorce by men, without the consent of the wife, even with more modern legislative and administrative limitations and restrictions on it; allowing women divorce with their husband's consent but only upon the basis of foregoing financial benefits; child custody only for fathers; lack of succession rights for women, illegitimate children and female children; penalties for apostasy; and the absence of adoption. See: McGoldrick, Dominic, 'Accommodating Muslims in Europe: From Adopting Sharia Law to Religiously Based Opt Outs from Generally Applicable Laws', *Human Rights Law Review* 2009, pp. 603-645 (621-622).

is unaddressed and/or 3) is simply *not* as I have described it, but is considered "far more complex" than that.[24]

To analyse the multiculturalists' view of Sharia, I will now cite parts of the speeches and highlight some of what I consider the most important.

Former Archbishop Rowan Williams proposed rethink of the nature of universal British law in the light of Islamic law and Islamic identity. He wondered what degree of accommodation the law of the land can and should give to minority communities with their own strongly entrenched legal and moral codes. He encouraged listeners to consider "a scheme in which individuals retain the liberty to choose the jurisdiction under which they will seek to resolve certain carefully specified matters. [...] This may include aspects of marital law, the regulation of financial transactions and authorised structures of mediation and conflict resolution – the main areas that have been in question where supplementary jurisdictions have been tried". He stated that accommodating Sharia law to a certain extent was *unavoidable*. Moreover, it was nothing *new*: "as a matter of fact certain provisions of Sharia are already recognised in our society and under our law; so it's not as if we're bringing in an alien and rival system".[25]

He aimed to dispel "one or two myths" about Sharia: "And what most people think they know of *Sharia* is that it is repressive towards women and wedded to archaic and brutal physical punishments; just a few days ago, it was reported that a 'forced marriage' involving a young woman with learning difficulties had been 'sanctioned under *Sharia* law' – the kind of story that, in its assumption that we all 'really' know what is involved in the practice of *Sharia*, powerfully reinforces the image of – at best – a pre-modern system in which human rights have no role."

The problem here, according to Williams, is not that Sharia is repressive towards women; that it encompasses brutal punishments; or that forced marriage is sanctioned under Sharia. The problem is that these practices *reinforce a negative image* of Sharia, an image of "a pre-modern system in which human rights have no role".

It also becomes clear that Williams thinks that the "assumption that we all 'really' know what is involved in the practice of *Sharia*" is unfounded. Pinpointing what Sharia is in a coherent and accessible manner (as I have tried to do by providing a historical account of the roots of (political) Islam, and by systematising its sources, its implications and its

---

24 For example, in the beginning of his lecture Williams states: "This lecture will not attempt a detailed discussion of the nature of sharia, which would be far beyond my competence; my aim is only, as I have said, to tease out some of the broader issues around the rights of religious groups within a secular state, with a few thoughts about what might be entailed in crafting a just and constructive relationship between Islamic law and the statutory law of the United Kingdom.".

25 'In full: Rowan Williams interview' 11 February 2008, via <http://news.bbc.co.uk/2/hi/uk_news/7239283.stm>.

practical consequences) is something at times considered by some scholars as *essentialist*.[26] To a multiculturalist it is a mistake to "reduce" Sharia to a smaller set of characteristics, especially if this set has a negative connotation. Rather, multiculturalists point out the large variety of (the practice of) Sharia and the impossibility of generalisation. Thus, stating that Sharia is (merely) about repression of women, brutal punishments and forced marriage is considered a misrepresentation.

But, what *is* a correct representation in the eyes of multiculturalists then? That is the following.

Sharia is considered to consist of "*Universal* principles: as any Muslim commentator will insist, what is in view is the eternal and absolute will of God for the universe and for its human inhabitants in particular; but also something that has to be 'actualised', not a ready-made system. [...] there is no single code that can be identified as 'the' *Sharia*". And "[t]hus, in contrast to what is sometimes assumed, we do not simply have a standoff between two rival legal systems when we discuss Islamic and British law. [...] To recognise *sharia* is to recognise a *method* of jurisprudence governed by revealed texts rather than a single system."

Moreover, as Williams quoted another Islamic scholar, "[...] that an excessively narrow understanding sharia as simply codified rules can have the effect of actually undermining the universal claims of the Qur'an" [sic]. Williams expressed expectations regarding the flexibility of Sharia in itself, as it is a body of universal principles which are open for interpretation.[27] He stated: "[...] far from being a monolithic system of detailed enactments, *Sharia* designates primarily – to quote Ramadan again – 'the expression of the universal principles of Islam [and] the framework and the thinking that makes for their actualisation in human history'".

---

26   Otto, Jan Michiel, 'The compatibility of Shari'a with the Rule of Law. Fundamentalist Conflict: Between Civilisations? Within Civilisations? Or between Scholars?', pp. 137-154 (141-142), in: Groen, Adriaan in 't et al. (eds.), *Knowledge in Ferment, Dilemmas in Science, Scholarship and Society*, Leiden: Leiden University Press 2007. Maleiha Malik states: "An essentialist approach fails to recognise the diversity that can exist within a social group". (Malik 2009, p. 4.) Essentialism is a term that is sometimes used in a derogatory way, especially when it comes to the multicultural debate. Generally, essentialism may refer to the attribution of a set of immutable features to entities (such as groups, cultures, or religions) which are considered necessary to establish its identity and function. See: Cartwright, Richard, 'Some Remarks on Essentialism', *The Journal of Philosophy* 1968, pp. 615-626.

27   He referred to the opening of the doors of *ijtihad*, which is independent interpretation of Islamic sources. Even though there are many theorists who argue that Sharia is open for interpretation up to the level where it becomes a body of thought in line with secular notions regarding freedom and equality, it is questionable whether this will happen in an effective manner – especially as fundamentalists are very well organised and well-funded. See on *ijtihad* also: Manji, Irshad, "Operation Ijtihad", pp. 158-187, in: *The Trouble with Islam. A Muslim's Call for Reform in her Faith*, New York: St. Martin's Press, and An-Na'im, Abdullahi, *Islam and the Secular State: Negotiating the Future of Shari'a*, Cambridge, Massachusetts: Harvard University Press 2008.

Rather than a body of restrictions and obligations, Middle Way Islamists and multiculturalists portray Sharia as a source of *universal* principles and values. "Universal", he asserts, so apparently, there are Islamic principles that are valid for everyone, everywhere, at any time, and Sharia provides us with a framework and method to uncover these.[28] And: "But while such universal claims are not open for renegotiation, they also assume the voluntary consent or submission of the believer, the free decision to be and to continue a member of the *umma*". Lastly, "*Sharia is not, in that sense, intrinsically to do with any demand for Muslim dominance over non-Muslims*".

As mentioned before, the British did not appreciate Williams' speech. A few months later, then Lord Chief Justice Phillips offered support during his speech entitled 'Equality Before the Law' at the East London Muslim Centre in 2008. Phillips, too, believed that Sharia is generally falsely and negatively portrayed.

> It has become clear to me that there is a widespread misunderstanding in this country as to the nature of Shari'a law. Shari'a consists of a set of principles governing the way that one should live one's life in accordance with the will of God. These principles are based on the Qu'ran, as revealed to Muhammad and interpreted by Islamic scholars. These principles have much in common with other religions. They do not include forced marriage or the repression of women. Compliance with them requires a high level of personal conduct, including abstinence from alcohol. I understand that it is not the case that for a Muslim to lead his or her life in accordance with these principles will be in conflict with the requirements of the law in this country. What would be in conflict with the law would be to impose certain sanctions for failure to comply with Shari'a principles. Part of the misconception about Sharia is the belief that Shari'a is only about mandating sanctions such as flogging, stoning, the cutting off hands or death for those who fail to comply with the law. And the view of many of Shari'a law is coloured by violent extremists who invoke it, perversely, to justify terrorist atrocities such as suicide bombing, which I understand to be in conflict with Shari'a principles. There can be no question of such sanctions being applied to or by any Muslim who lives within this jurisdiction.

Phillips was convinced that the principles of Sharia simply do not include terrorism, the repression of women and forced marriage, the latter described by Williams as something

---

28 Stressing the universality of Islamic principles is rather remarkable coming a) from the head of the *Anglican church* b) on behalf of *minorities* – for, if Islamic principles are for everyone and everywhere, there is no need for the suffix "Islamic" and the entire human race can submit to them (which is obviously the purpose of Islamists in the first place).

to do with custom and culture rather than directly binding enactments by religious authority.[29] Rather than simply stating unacceptable parts of Sharia are un-Islamic, like Phillips did, Williams analysed "neuralgic questions of the status of women and converts" in more depth.

The former Archbishop stated that recognition of the authority of a communal religious court, especially with regard to family law, could have the effect of reinforcing repressive elements, with particularly serious consequences for the role and liberties of women: a Sharia council could, in effect, actually *deprive* individuals of rights and liberties. Therefore, he said, "no 'supplementary' jurisdiction could have the power to deny access to the rights granted to other citizens or punish its members for claiming those rights", And: "citizenship in a secular society should not necessitate the abandoning of religious discipline, any more than religious discipline should deprive one of access to liberties secured by the law of the land". To labour this point, he suggested thinking in terms of what professor of Law, Political Science, and Global Affairs Ayelet Shachar, author of *Multilevel Jurisdictions: Cultural Differences and Women's Rights* (2001), calls "transformative accommodation". She argues that it is institutionally feasible for the state to simultaneously respect deep cultural differences and to protect the rights of vulnerable group members, in particular women.[30]

The issue is that in reality women's rights are not secured in an alternative Islamic jurisdiction. That is one of the main reasons that Williams' speech caused such uproar. Under pressure, four days after his speech, Williams dropped his call for Sharia to apply to marital law, and instead pointed to "sensitive" questions about the status and liberties of women.[31] Yet, Phillips stated that

---

29 See on Imams and child marriages in the UK, for instance: 'Britain's Underage Muslim Marriage Epidemic' Gatestone Institute 15 October 2013, via <http://www.gatestoneinstitute.org/4017/uk-muslim-underage-marriage> and 'The British child brides: Muslim mosque leaders agree to marry girl of 12… so long as parents don't tell anyone' *Dailymail.co.uk* 9 September 2012, via <http://www.dailymail.co.uk/news/article-2200555/The-British-child-brides-Muslim-mosque-leaders-agree-marry-girl-12--long-parents-dont-tell-anyone.html>.

30 Shachar, Ayelet, *Multicultural Jurisdictions: Cultural Differences and Women's Rights*, Cambridge: Cambridge University Press 2001, pp. 4-5. See also: Shachar, Ayelet, 'Privatizing Diversity: A Cautionary Tale from Religious Arbitration in Family Law, *Theoretical Inquiries in Law* 2008, pp. 572-607 (302): "Counter-intuitively, the qualified recognition of the religious tribunal by the secular state may ultimately offer an effective, non-coercive encouragement of egalitarian and reformist change from within the religious tradition itself. The state system, too, is transformed from strict separation to regulated interaction. In this way, the 'multi-layered' or intersectionist identity of the individuals involved may be fostered. This approach also discourages an underworld of unregulated religious tribunals and offers a path to transcend the either/or choice between culture and rights, family and state, citizenship and islands of 'privatized diversity'." How this should be realised remains vague and unaddressed. See for another contribution that calls for the accommodation of religious law in combination with upholding individual rights, while remaining vague on how this should be done: Malik, Maleiha, *Minority Legal Orders in the UK. Minorities, Pluralism and the Law*, London: The British Academy 2012.

31 'Happy clappy Rowan repents in Sharia storm', *Daily Mail* 12 February 2008.

[i]t was not very radical to advocate embracing Shari'a law in the context of family disputes, for example, and our system already goes a long way towards accommodating the Archbishop's suggestion. It is possible in this country for those who are entering into a contractual agreement to agree that the agreement shall be governed by a law other than English law. Those who, in this country, are in dispute as to their respective rights are free to subject that dispute to the mediation of a chosen person, or to agree that the dispute shall be resolved by a chosen arbitrator or arbitrators.

Summing up. Both Williams and Phillips said that they did not want to suggest that there be parallel systems of law. At the same time, Williams asserted that the purpose of the lecture was to share "a few thoughts about what might be entailed in crafting a just and constructive relationship between Islamic law and the statutory law of the United Kingdom". He questioned "our commitment to legal monopoly" and analysed the conditions under which a "supplementary jurisdiction" would be acceptable. Phillips stressed that religious minorities may be exempted from certain laws. Likewise, he suggested, having to live under a singular jurisdiction which is the product of a Judeo-Christian culture while having a dual identity as both Muslim and British citizen is unfair, because it constitutes inequality compared to indigenous Britons. That is all the more the case, as both Phillips and Williams reason, because Jewish courts have long existed in Britain.

They do not support the introduction of Sharia that embodies corporal punishments. Williams also makes it clear that "an increased legal recognition of communal religious identities" may not have a detrimental effect on the status of women. That aside, they argue that for British Muslims it would be unsatisfactory and problematic to live as citizens under the rule of uniform law. For proponents of accommodation of Islamic family law it seems – morally and principally – plain *wrong* not to grant, at least to a certain extent, juridical autonomy to Islamic judges (*qadis*) and Muslims seeking Islamic legal solutions. The moral justification lies in the equal treatment of all religions, and, the reasoning goes, because British Muslims are not free to live under their own laws, as institutionalised by their own courts, they are not treated equally.[32]

The focus is on religious *family law*. "There needs to be access to recognised authority acting for a religious group: there is already, of course, an Islamic Shari'a Council, much in demand for rulings on marital questions in the United Kingdom; and if we were to see more latitude given in law to rights and scruples rooted in religious identity, we should

---

32 See also: Budziszewski, J., 'Natural Law, Democracy, and Shari'a', pp. 181-206 (183), in: Ahdar & Aroney 2010.

need a much enhanced and quite sophisticated version of such a body, with increased resource and a high degree of community recognition [...]."[33]

Up until this point we can summarise the claims by the former Archbishop and Lord Chief Justice as follows:

– Sharia is unfortunately and erroneously portrayed as something that should be denounced, namely as a single body of laws merely concerning the repression of women and cruel and unusual punishments.

– It *actually* is a body of thought that inspires Muslims in the form of certain universal principles. These universal principles are tremendously important for believers, who choose freely to be part of a community whose members are unified under this set of principles.

– Therefore, rather than making Muslims merely adhere to a uniform set of British laws, we should accommodate parts of Islamic law – mainly financial and family law – in the name of equality, especially because Jewish courts are allowed to function as well.

– On one condition: that this supplementary jurisdiction may not be repressive towards women.

What these universal principles are and what it practically means to accommodate Sharia remains unaddressed.[34] Both multiculturalist speeches lack an answer to the question *how* Sharia family law should be accommodated and what such an accommodation would involve. For instance, would it require new laws? What would such laws look like? Should the benefits of Sharia be incorporated in educational programs? Should the United Kingdom maintain formal ties with al-Azhar University for Sharia instructions? Should state courts accept Sharia when parties want to? Should Sharia councils be publicly funded? Should Islamic judges receive government-supervised training? Should barristers be educated in religious laws? A marble court house in the Temple area for an official British Sharia council? Or should we merely not think too critically of Sharia councils?

Moreover, what would it *practically* mean for men to have Islamic family law accommodated? For women? For children? What *specific* problems would be addressed by accommodation of Islamic family law? What solutions would it bring about? Are there benefits other than "recognising Muslim identity"? How – specifically – are the rights of women protected in councils based on a body of thought that is grounded in the belief that justice is found in the recognition of dissimilarities between men and women? Dissimilarities requiring different rights, duties and punishments for either sex? On the basis of which "universal principles" are disputes to be settled? In short, how can we assess multi-

---

33   Ahdar & Aroney 2010, pp. 297.
34   On the two speeches, British scholar John Bowen stated: "These two addresses conveyed an authoritative stamp of approval, but did not clarify what it means to 'recognise sharia'." See: Bowen, John, 'How Could English Courts recognise Shariah?', *University of St. Thomas Law Journal* 2009-10, pp. 411-435 (411).

culturalist proposals to consider "a scheme in which individuals retain the liberty to choose the jurisdiction under which they will seek to resolve certain carefully specified matters", if it is so vague?

Perhaps it is unfair to hammer on the lack of functional content, as Williams merely suggested looking at the possibilities of accommodation "with a clearer eye, not imagine we know exactly what we mean by Sharia, and not just associate it with what we read about Saudi Arabia or whatever".[35] Yet, I do not think it is unfair. I actually believe it is specifically important to point out the generally vague and optimistic character of these multiculturalist contributions to the Sharia debate. It is specifically important to draw attention to the fact that what multiculturalists envision for society regarding the accommodation of Sharia remains (intentionally or unintentionally) vague, is unaddressed and/or is focused on stating what Sharia is not, viz. the content of a fundamentalist ideology. It is vitally important because multiculturalist thought of this kind *creates space for the manifestation of Islamic fundamentalism*.[36] Multiculturalism emphasises the "moral right" to have an identity recognised, an identity that differs from the dominant culture. Multiculturalists want to rid Sharia of its negative components and promote pondering over the possibilities of accommodating the remaining part. But what is that? What does that mean? This generally uncritical and positive attitude is benefiting Islamism.

THE RELATIONSHIP BETWEEN MULTICULTURALISM AND ISLAMIC FUNDAMENTALISM

The NGO Women Living Under Muslim Laws (WLUML) is represented in over 70 countries and provides information about codified and uncodified Islamic laws. It aims to strengthen women's individual and collective effort in search of equality and their rights.[37] In secular states, WLUML is active against the increasing demands that Islamic laws be recognised. It also purports to challenge the idea that there is a "homogenous Muslim world". In 2006, 2 years before the former Archbishop and Lord Chief Justice made their contribution to more Sharia in Britain, WLUML published a report: "Recognising the Un-recognised: Inter-Country Cases and Muslim Marriages & Divorces in Britain". The report's authors lament the call for formal recognition of Muslim family law

---

35 He stated this in an interview with the BBC that same day of the lecture: 'Archbishop on Radio 4 World at One - UK law needs to find accommodation with religious law codes', 7 February 2008, via <http://rowan-williams.archbishopofcanterbury.org/articles.php/707/archbishop-on-radio-4-uk-law-needs-to-find-accommodation-with-religious-law-codes>.

36 See also: David S. Pearl, who contends that conflict between Islamic law and English law is avoided, *inter alia*, by a tolerant attitude which "[…] has allowed space for the unofficial development of new hybrid rules". In: Pearl, David S., *Islamic Family Law and Its Reception by the Courts in England*, Cambridge: Islamic Legal Studies Program, Harvard Law School 2000, p. 4.

37 "About WLUML", via <http://www.wluml.org/node/5408>.

in the United Kingdom. Interestingly, they find that those demanding it are unclear about what it *precisely* is that they want to see recognised. The report gives various reasons why the precise content of the demands is unclear.

Firstly, given the diversity within the Muslim community, it would be unlikely that consensus could be reached about the content of a specific demand of Islamic family law. If efforts to that end were to be made public "[…] that would embarrassingly explode the myth that there has always been a monolithic way of 'being Muslim'". Secondly, what WLUML calls "politicized elements in the community" (Islamists) are well aware that the state would never support formal recognition of separate laws. The report concludes that

> […] given the above two factors, it is far more powerful to continue to make vague demands for recognition as this prevents open public debate both within the community and beyond on specificities while also giving those who make such demands the possibility of claiming for themselves the right to represent the community and its needs *vis á vis* British civil law. Indeed, it is in the best interests of the Shariah councils, for example, that Muslim family laws in Britain remain unregulated and uncodified because this then requires constant reference to the Shariah councils for interpretation.[38]

The lack of functional concreteness on behalf of multiculturalists is particularly relevant to establish. Both multiculturalists and religious fundamentalists place religion as a core unifier of individuals within a community. Both Islamists and multiculturalists want Muslims to be able to live under Sharia. Multiculturalists and Islamists do differ regarding the *extent* to which that should be (made) possible. But both make the case that that is what is needed by Muslims – and a sizeable part of the Muslim population agrees. What it is that Islamists want is clear: a Sharia state for a unified Umma, although they may well coach this in terms which are easier to stomach, as Qaradawi also believes works best. As I wrote in the previous chapter, it is a pragmatic decision to use "dawa language" that avoids negative associations for Western audiences. This also involves a language that avoids specifying the actual implications of introducing more Sharia.

In the 1990s, the European Council for Fatwa and Research (presided over by Qaradawi) published several fatwas about Islamic family law. They urged European Muslims to demand official recognition of Islam from European governments, including the right to apply Sharia in cases of marriage, divorce and inheritance. In a later fatwa, it was repeated that as far as family law was concerned, European Muslims must deal with Muslim judges.[39]

---

38 'Recognising the Un-recognised: Inter-Country Cases and Muslim Marriages & Divorces in Britain', Women Living Under Muslim Laws 2006, p. 81.
39 See: Riccardi, Letizia, 'Women at Crossroads between UK Legislation and Sharia Law', *Journal of Law and Social Sciences* 2014, pp. 86-91 (86); see also: Caeiro, Alexandre and Gräf, Bettine, 'The European Council

This Middle Way Islamist approach to guide Muslims towards Sharia compliance in Europe is supported by multiculturalists that publically state that Muslim minorities have the "right" to have private matters settled by their "own" religious laws.

That multiculturalism, when aimed at accommodating Muslim family laws, aids Islamism is true in the wide sense, but in this specific case Williams and Phillips actually benefit Islamists in a practical way, too. Consider this: in his speech, Williams quotes Tariq Ramadan. To the Western audience, Ramadan presents Sharia as a set of values and principles, a message that is somewhat more easily digestible than the version I have offered in the previous chapter. He writes that Sharia is primarily a question of values: justice, equality, freedom.[40] Yet, in his books and cassettes, available in radical Islamist bookstores, he praises the teachings of his grandfather Hassan al-Banna, the founder of the Muslim Brotherhood, and firmly supports Qaradawi.[41] That Williams draws on Ramadan's work to make a case for more Sharia in the United Kingdom, and subscribes to Islamist double-speak that Sharia is not a body of laws but a set of principles is another indication that multiculturalism gives Islamic fundamentalism oxygen.

The same can be said of Phillips, who states that Muslims living in Britain "are well represented by a variety of groups and individuals, including the Muslim Council of Britain, whose aims include the fostering of better community relations and working for the good of society as a whole". The Muslim Council of Britain is an umbrella organisation that comprises branches of the Muslim Brotherhood and is connected to Jamaat-e-Islami (one of the most influential Islamist organisations).[42] Its founder and (up to 2006) secretary-general, Iqbal Sacranie, is a leading British Islamist.[43] Like Ramadan, Sacranie uses the strategy of "dawa language". He has spoken of the importance of "championing justice and promoting tolerance through constructive engagement with society as a whole [...]". On the other hand, he has also said of author Salman Rushdie "[d]eath, perhaps, is a bit too easy for him. His mind must be tormented for the rest of his life unless he asks for forgiveness to Almighty Allah". Sacranie has called for legislation criminalising any defamation of Muhammad's character, as it is forbidden under Sharia.[44] He has supported Qaradawi, labelled Israel "a Nazi state" and compared Hamas suicide bombers to Mandela and Gandhi, stating all are freedom fighters.[45]

---

for Fatwa and Research and Yusuf al-Qaradawi', pp. 119-121 (120), in: Peter, Frank and Ortega, Rafael (eds.), *Islamic Movements of Europe*, London: I.B. Tauris 2014.

40 Ramadan, Tariq, 'Following *shari'a* in the West', pp. 245-255 (247), in: Griffith-Jones, 2013.

41 Phillips 2012, p. 262.

42 Vidino, Lorenzo, *The New Muslim Brotherhood in the West*, New York: Columbia University Press 2010.

43 See: 'Rushdie in hiding after Ayatollah's death threat', *The Guardian* 18 February 1989, via <http://www.theguardian.com/books/1989/feb/18/fiction.salmanrushdie>.

44 'Just How Moderate is Iqbal Sacranie?', *MCBWatch* 4 August 2005, via <http://mcb-watch.blogspot.co.uk/2005/08/just-how-moderate-is-iqbal-sacranie.html>.

45 Phillips 2012, p. 153.

Other leading figures of the Muslim Council of Britain, such as the former Deputy Secretary General of the MCB, Daud Abdullah, have demonstrated their fundamentalist tendencies. A notable example surrounded the career of singer Deepika Thathaal. Thathaal, artist name Deeyah Khan, walks in a burka in her music video. She then takes her burka off to reveal herself in bikini. Consequently, she was threatened, spat on and was even once pepper sprayed during her performances. At that time, Thathaal could not walk around in Britain without the constant presence of bodyguards. Daud Abdullah released a statement saying: "Many Muslim women do perform to audiences of other women at weddings, for example, because the sexes are strictly segregated. Those performers enjoy a good career. It's when women perform for wider, mixed audiences that differences of opinion emerge [...] These objections are based on the Islamic view that women should not draw unnecessary attention to themselves, because of the impact this will have on a male audience. The moral framework of Islam has already been laid down and women should not push beyond its boundaries for the sake of commercial gain".[46] This part of the Islamist "moral framework" is emphasised by the Muslim Council of Britain, yet ignored by Phillips, who instead gives his public support of the Muslim Council of Britain as well as of parts of Sharia for British Muslims. It is this combination of Islamic fundamentalists and multiculturalist elites that makes endorsement of Sharia effective.

Multiculturalists do not want a Sharia state, but what they do want is mostly limited to emphasising a communal need for shared values and rejecting what is deemed a "too negative" focus on Sharia. Williams stated that we should look at the possibilities of accommodating Sharia "with a clearer eye". Also, we are not to imagine we know exactly what is meant by Sharia. But *who* may not imagine knowing exactly what is meant by Sharia? Multiculturalists? Legal universalists? Or Islamists? May Islamists imagine they know what they mean by Sharia? This question is particularly interesting in combination with Williams' remark that we should "not just associate it with what we read about Saudi Arabia or whatever". Let us see if the claims made by the former senior cleric and most senior judge are justifiable in the light of Sharia councils in the United Kingdom.

Behind the Islamic Sharia Council

In his lecture, Williams specifically devoted attention to the London-based "Islamic Shariah Council". He said: "[t]here needs to be access to recognised authority acting for a religious group: there is already, of course, an Islamic Shari'a Council, much in demand for rulings on marital questions in the United Kingdom; and if we were to see more latitude given in

---

46   Murray & Verwey 2008, pp. 85-89.

law to rights and scruples rooted in religious identity, we should need a much enhanced and quite sophisticated version of such a body, with increased resource and a high degree of community recognition [...]." This is the most concrete suggestion he has to offer. This Sharia council needs to be sophisticated and awarded greater resources and recognition. May we associate it with what we read about Saudi Arabia?

"The Islamic Sharia Council" is based in Leyton, East London, and is the most "professional" and well-known body. It was the focus of BBC's *Panorama* documentary 'Secrets of Britain's Sharia Councils' in 2013. It is located in a terraced house with wheelchair access, a reception, and has a website with downloadable forms. It was founded in 1982, when representatives of ten Islamic centres decided to establish "The Islamic Shari'a Council" as "a quasi-Islamic Court".[47] On its website, it says: "The objective of the Council was not just to guide the Muslims in matters of their religion and to issue fatwas when needed, but also to create a bench of ulama' who would function as Qadis (Islamic judges, MZ) in matters such as matrimonial disputes that were referred to them. The creation of the ISC was thus a manifestation of the will of the Muslim community and a reflection of their collective desire to manage their personal affairs. The concept of the Council was the brainchild of the late Sayyid Mutawalli ad-Darsh (who was Imam at Regent's Park Mosque at the time) and Dr Suhaib Hasan (who is the Secretary of the ISC at the moment)".[48]

This initiative of founding "a quasi-Islamic court" was an enterprise by Islamic fundamentalists, rather than for instance by individuals who sought to help Muslims with spiritual advice. It was the full intention to create a "semi-legal system".

On his personal website, Suhaib Hasan explains why he was one of the founders of the Islamic Sharia Council. He writes: "Is this community not permitted to arrange its personal affairs itself? What about issues of personal law, such as religious marriage, religious divorce, inheritance and endowments? According to the Fiqhi perspective and to historical realities, it is perfectly natural for religious minorities to wish to arrange such issues within their own communities."[49]

---

47 <http://www.islamic-sharia.org/aboutus/>.
48 <http://www.islamic-sharia.org/history-of-isc/>.
49 He quotes jurisprudence from the four Sunni schools of thought to substantiate this position. From the Hanafi school of law, for instance, Hasan quotes "[...] if there is no Sultan nor someone to deputise him, as in the cases of Muslim cities such as Cordoba where non-Muslims had taken control, it is incumbent upon the Muslims to agree upon someone from among them who can be appointed as ruler, and who can then appoint a Qadi [...]." Or, from Maliki law: "Wherever there is no Sultan or there is an unjust Sultan who does not care about the limits laid down by Allah, then the trustworthy and the people of knowledge stand there in the place of the Sultan." The Shafi'i school has a similar point of view: "If the time is devoid of an Imam or a Sultan who has powers to run the affairs (of the country), then all matters are referred to the scholars. It then becomes incumbent upon the people, to whichever class they belong, to refer back to their scholars and to abide by their judgement in all matters. If they do that, they are guided to the right path. They will be the scholars and the rulers. [...]." Lastly, from Hanbali law, most prevalent in Saudi Arabia, Suhaib Hasan quotes: "If a town loses its Qadi, the people should appoint someone as a Qadi for themselves. His orders and rulings are binding as long as there is no Imam to rule over them." See: Hasan, Suhaib,

"The establishment of such a religious body is not unique to the Muslim community", Hasan continues on his blog. "The Jewish minority in Britain has been present for over 350 years and has set up the Beth Din for a similar purpose. Other religious minorities such as the Sikhs and Hindus have also established alternative dispute resolution services for their respective communities".[50]

That is indeed correct, and, like multiculturalists, the Islamic fundamentalists of the Islamic Sharia Council focus on the Muslim community as a collective with special needs. The fact that Jewish Batei Din, rabbinical courts, exist too, is an argument often put forward by both multiculturalists and Islamists. It would be a matter of unequal treatment of Muslims if they were not allowed to have their private legal institutions, so the argument goes.

There is certainly a degree of overlap between religious family law institutions – as will be further discussed below. There are indeed fundamentalist, or orthodox, Jewish councils. There are, however, significant similarities and differences between rabbinical and Islamic councils. One essential difference is that the representatives of the Islamic Sharia Council support, promote and activate the political ideology of Islamic fundamentalism. This means that beyond imposing Islamic family law on Muslims (which would be undesirable enough), the Sharia Council that Williams wants to accommodate consists of individuals who wish to turn the United Kingdom into a Sharia state and impose Islamic law on all citizens. I will discuss three individuals to support this claim: the late Sayyid Mutawalli ad-Darsh (founder of the Islamic Sharia Council, qadi and first president), Suhaib Hasan (Founder, qadi and secretary) and Haitham al-Haddad (qadi and treasurer).

Firstly, there is the founder of the Islamic Sharia Council, Egyptian-born Shaykh Sayyid Mutawalli ad-Darsh (1930-1997). In 1970, he was the rector of al-Azhar University, Egypt's fundamentalist hotbed, and he introduced a plan to launch international dawa.[51] This took ad-Darsh to London as the imam of Regent's Park Mosque. As I wrote in the previous chapter, it was in the 1970s and 80s that the Muslim Brotherhood went global, backed by Saudi funding.

Supported by the Egyptian government, ad-Darsh publicly pushed for official recognition of as much Islamic family law as possible in the United Kingdom from the mid-70s onwards. His views were fundamentalist. For instance, he did not want to agree on specifying a minimum age for marriage,[52] nor was he willing to accept the legitimacy of marriage

---

'Muslim family law in Britain. A paper submitted to the international family law conference on 14 may 2014 at the University of Islamabad', 20 May 2014, via <http://sheikhsuhaibhasan.blogspot.co.uk/2014/05/muslim-family-law-in-britain.html>.

50   Ibid.

51   'Kweekschool van het kalifaat' (Breeding Ground for the Caliphate), *NRC Handelsblad* 28 March 2015.

52   Ad-Darsh on child marriage: "There is no minimum age. The *wali*, guardian, of the children, male or female, has the right to conduct a marriage agreement on their behalf, as long as there is an interest for both parties". In: Wiegers, Gerard, 'Dr. Sayyid Mutawalli ad-Darsh's Fatwas for Muslims in Great Britain: The Voice of

between a Muslim woman and a non-Muslim man. In 1982, he founded the first Sharia council and became a columnist and broadcaster, widely influencing the next generation of Muslims.

In 1992, he participated in a *fiqh* seminar themed "Muslims in the West" in France. It was hosted by the *Union des Organisations Islamiques de France*, which is closely connected to the International Muslim Brotherhood. He spoke alongside a variety of scholars, many from Saudi Arabia. Other participants included the late Syrian Muslim Brotherhood leader Abd al-Fattah Abu Ghudda, the late Lebanese and French Muslim Brotherhood leader Faisal Mawlawi, and present international Muslim Brotherhood leader Yusuf al-Qaradawi. It was this meeting that laid the foundation for *fiqh-al-aqalliyyat*, jurisprudence for Muslim minorities in the West, the Middle Way towards a Sharia state. Many participants were to join the board of the European Council for Fatwa and Research (founded in 1997), currently presided over by Qaradawi.[53]

In the mid-90s, ad-Darsh was one of the first to use the internet to promote Islamism. In an interview 2 years before his death, he stated that he fully sympathised with the ideas of the international Muslim Brotherhood.[54]

In the present day, Shaykh Maulana Abu Sayeed is qadi and president. He stated that there clearly is not such a thing as rape in marriage, as sex is part of marriage. He said the "aggression" of reporting the husband to the police was greater than the "minor aggression" of forcing a woman to have sexual intercourse against her will. Sayeed argued that many married women who alleged rape were lying, because rape is a ground for divorce. "Why it is happening in this society is because they have got this idea of so-called equality, equal rights".[55]

The second figure I would like to highlight is the other founder of the Islamic Sharia Council, the earlier mentioned Shaykh Suhaib Hasan (1942). On his personal blog, Hasan shares some childhood memories from his home in the state of Malairkotla, India. In his own words, it was a childhood fully devoted to Jamaat-e-Islami – next to the Muslim Brotherhood, one of the first and most influential Islamist organisations.[56] Hasan's father had joined right after it was founded in 1941, and actively preached on its behalf. "No exaggeration if I say that I have been brought up in the lap of Jamaat", Hasan writes. One of his most pressing childhood memories "was the day when our whole house witnessed a lot of sadness and gloom. That was the day when the papers brought the news of the

---

Official Islam?', pp. 178-191 (188), in: Maclean, Gerald, (ed.), *Britain and the Muslim World*, Cambridge: Cambridge Scholars Press 2011.

53 Who is now banned from entering the United Kingdom (as well as the United States), see: 'Controversial Muslim cleric banned from Britain', *The Guardian* 7 February 2008.

54 Wiegers 2011, pp. 178-191.

55 'Rape in marriage is no crime says cleric', *Daily Express* 15 October 2010, via <http://www.express.co.uk/news/uk/205474/Rape-in-marriage-is-no-crime-says-cleric>.

56 Roy, Olivier, *The Failure of Political Islam*, Cambridge: Harvard University Press 1994, p. 35.

hanging of a great scholar, an Islamic activist, Abdul Qadir Audah, a leader of the Muslim Brotherhood in Egypt".[57]

After his childhood, Hasan studied in Saudi Arabia and worked in East Africa before moving to Britain in the 1960s.[58] Now he is secretary and judge of the Islamic Sharia Council, spokesman of Sharia law for the Muslim Council of Britain, and member of the board of Qaradawi's European Council for Fatwa and Research.

On his blog, Hasan states he wants a "limited semi-legal system in issues of personal law" based on Sharia for British Muslims. He publicly argues that Britain would greatly benefit from integrating aspects of family law into the nation's civil code. Like Williams and Phillips, he wants to address the "great misunderstanding" of the issue of Sharia in the West. "Whenever people associate the word 'sharia' with Muslims, they think it is flogging and stoning to death and cutting off the hand". He says it is out of the question that penal law would be introduced in the United Kingdom, as "[o]nly a Muslim government that believes in Islam is going to implement it".[59] Nevertheless, he advises Britain to adopt Sharia criminal law, so called hudood, also spelled hudud, laws:

> If sharia law is implemented, then you can turn this country into a haven of peace because once a thief's hand is cut off nobody is going to steal. Once, just only once, if an adulterer is stoned nobody is going to commit this crime at all. There would be no rapists at all. We want to offer it to the British society. If they accept it, it is for their good and if they don't accept it they'll need more and more prisons.[60]

The documentary Undercover Mosque, though, showed him preaching at a sermon, saying that the Caliphate will have "political dominance" in Britain, establishing "the chopping of the hands of the thieves, the flogging of the adulterers and flogging of the drunkards", and waging "jihad against the non-Muslims".[61] Hasan also "reveals the Jewish conspiracy"

---

57   Hasan, Suhaib, 'My Memoirs: Early Days of My Life, Part 1', 27 January 2015, via <http://sheikhsuhaib-hasan.blogspot.co.uk/2015/01/my-memoirs-early-days-of-my-life-part-1.html>.

58   'Sharia law UK: Mail on Sunday gets exclusive access to a British Muslim court', Daily Mail Online 4 July 2009, via <http://www.dailymail.co.uk/news/article-1197478/Sharia-law-UK--How-Islam-dispensing-justice-side-British-courts.html#ixzz3ZMpBmrBz>.

59   'We want to offer sharia law to Britain', the Telegraph 20 January 2008, via <http://www.tele-graph.co.uk/news/uknews/1576066/We-want-to-offer-sharia-law-to-Britain.html>.

60   'Divorce: Sharia Style', Channel 4 Documentary, via: <https://www.youtube.com/watch?v=OB34_zrB2to>

61   'Dispatches - Undercover Mosque', Channel 4 Documentary, via <https://vimeo.com/19598947>. See also: 'Why we should oppose Islamic Sharia councils in Britain', Liberal Conspiracy 16 August 2013, via <http://liberalconspiracy.org/2013/08/16/why-we-should-oppose-islamic-sharia-courts-in-britain/>.

on YouTube by telling viewers about The Protocols of the Elders of Zion, a hoax document about Jewish world domination that Islamists take very seriously.[62]

Thirdly, there is Shaykh Haitham al-Haddad (date of birth unknown). He agrees with Hasan on Sharia punishments, stating that "it is a 'must' for all Muslims to establish hudood punishments", including for apostates and adulteresses. Born in Saudi Arabia, al-Haddad is now qadi and treasurer at the Islamic Sharia Council. He is also president of the British Muslim Research and Development Foundation. He obtained a PhD at the University of London (SOAS) on the topic of Fiqh for Muslim Minorities in the West and often gives lectures at universities – although sometimes he is denied because of his views. Before obtaining a PhD, he studied in Saudi Arabia, where he was a student of the Grand Mufti, the Hanbali scholar Abdul Aziz bin Abdullah bin Baz (1910-1999).[63] It should not come as a surprise that al-Haddad brought Saudi views to Britain.

He believes that "Muslims should prevent [non-Muslims] from ruling any country with a law other than the shari'ah and Muslims should rule the entire planet with this Islamic law, and should this lead to fighting the People of the Book, Allah said: "And fight them until there is no more Fitnah (disbelief and worshipping of others along with Allah) and (all and every kind of) worship is for Allah (alone)". For him, the ultimate aim of all Muslims is to see Islam governing the whole world. The "Islamic Republic of Britain" will only be possible if Muslims use the current political system to their advantage".[64] Besides wanting to establish an Islamic theocracy in the United Kingdom in general, he also believes that it is forbidden to join Christians in celebrating any of their festivals; that women enjoy their husbands being superior to them and should obey them; that female genital mutilation (or, as he euphemistically puts it, "circumcision") is recommended as it is a "virtue" or an "honour" for women and is better for the husband; that those found guilty of engaging in extra-marital sex should be punished in the "harshest manner possible" – stoning to death; and that a husband should not be questioned why he hits his wife. On setting a minimum age for girls to be married off, he said that "Islamic law has no minimum age". "Thirteen, fourteen?" asked an audience member. Al-Haddad replied "the earlier is the better, but you have to be careful of the legal issues".[65]

Moreover, he considers homosexuality a "crime against humanity" and "Jews are the 'descendants of apes and pigs' and the 'armies of the devil'" – and pointed to the Protocols

---

62 'Senior UK Imam Suhaib Hasan reveals "Jewish Conspiracy"', 16 December 2013, via <https://www.youtube.com/watch?v=XGIjh47kP3w>.

63 "He has studied the Islamic sciences for over 20 years under the tutelage of renowned scholars such as the late Grand Mufti of Saudi Arabia as well as the retired Head of the Kingdom's Higher Judiciary Council". 'Author Archives: Shaikh (Dr) Haitham Al-Haddad' at <http://www.islam21c.com/author/shaikhhaithamal-haddad/>.

64 'Haitham al-Haddad', *The Islamic far-right in Britain*, via <http://tifrib.com/haitham-al-haddad/>.

65 'Shaikh Haitham Al Haddad 'The family' Talk at Masjid Umar R.A. Part 2', YouTube clip, published on 15 May 2012, via <http://youtu.be/fST0Vmyim44?t=12m56s>.

of the Elders of Zion.[66] On Salman Rushdie, who al-Haddad beliefs deserves capital punishment, he said in a Friday sermon: "And this reminds us, o Servants of Allah, of the stories of those who compose heretical writings, that you cannot tolerate esoteric interpretation, you rule on their apostasy and desertion of the religion [...] in the West they are known as creative writers, and are considered as amongst the most innocent, but to us they are apostates, and their blood is halal".[67] On the separation between religion and the state, he said: "There is a conflict between these two sets of values. Muslims believe our values are best. The non-Islamic British believe theirs are better. But at the end of the day, understand this: Muslims are never going to give up certain principles, even if they are in conflict. That is a fact".[68]

It should be clear that the individuals driving the largest and most well-known Sharia council in the United Kingdom do not view Sharia as a set of general principles. They take the specific laws and instructions as seriously as one possibly can. They fully adhere to, and are activists on behalf of, Islamism. Their political and religious ideology to turn the United Kingdom into a Sharia state is clear, and so are their ties to Saudi Arabia and the international Muslim Brotherhood. And they know what they are talking about, coming from al-Azhar in Egypt and studying under the Grand Mufti of Saudi Arabia. Their aim of spreading Sharia is not limited to the United Kingdom. In 2012, Al-Haddad expressed his wish to have a formally recognised Sharia council in the Netherlands, as well.[69]

These are the individuals behind the London-based Sharia council that former Archbishop Williams would like to see accommodated and awarded greater resources and recognition. Both multiculturalists and Islamists encourage Muslims to go down the path of Islamic fundamentalism. Multiculturalists may not know exactly what is meant by Sharia, but Islamists surely do. The latter are confident they are working towards official recognition of Islamic law. A statement on the Islamic Sharia Council's website reads: "Though the Council is not yet legally recognised by the authorities in the United Kingdom, the fact that it is already established, and is gradually gaining ground among the Muslim community, and the satisfaction attained by those who seek its ruling, are all preparatory steps towards the final goal of gaining the confidence of the host community in the soundness of the Islamic legal system and the help and insight they could gain from it.

---

66 'Haitham al-Haddad', *The Islamic far-right in Britain*, via <http://tifrib.com/haitham-al-haddad/>.

67 'More Wisdom of Haitham Al Haddad', 4 February 2012, via <http://hurryupharry.org/2012/02/04/more-wisdom-of-haitham-al-haddad/>.

68 'Sharia law UK: Mail on Sunday gets exclusive access to a British Muslim court', *Daily Mail Online* 4 July 2009.

69 Shaykh Al-Haddad advocates the establishment of a Sharia council in the Netherlands as "it is the duty of the Dutch government to take care of its citizens"; see: 'Pleidooi voor sharia-raad' (Plea for a Sharia council), *nos.nl* 11 June 2012, via <http://nos.nl/artikel/382618-pleidooi-voor-shariaraad.html>.

The experience gained by the scholars taking part in its procedures make them more pre-pared for the eventuality of recognition for Islamic law" [sic].[70]

Williams and Phillips and other "new multiculturalists" may not subscribe to Islamist goals, but they are furthering them. They masquerade Sharia by making it fuzzy and elusive. They cleanse it from objectionable aspects and state it should be accommodated but just not the parts that are at odds with British laws, and remain vague on how that should be done and what that means. They create space by emphasising the need for Sharia by Muslims and by reprimanding those who do publicly speak out against it.

Having said all this, it could still be possible that the board members of the Islamic Sharia Council have been ventilating their *private* Islamist opinions and actually perform their duties quite well as Islamic judges. It is possible that they are perfectly able to operate within the boundaries of the human rights standards that Britain seeks to uphold. Let us turn to the legal status and practice of Sharia councils in the United Kingdom.

SHARIA AND ALTERNATIVE DISPUTE RESOLUTION

Before we delve in deeply in the practice at Sharia councils, I would like to clarify that Sharia councils are not arbitration or mediation tribunals. It is almost considered standard to refer to Sharia councils by using the terminology of Alternative Dispute Resolution (ADR).[71] It is my contention that this is incorrect. It is not merely erroneous because it fuses the concepts of *arbitration* (in which both parties agree to submit their dispute to a mutually agreeable third party for a decision to be made), and *mediation*, (when two parties voluntarily use a neutral third party to help them reach an agreement that is acceptable to both sides). Both concepts are not applicable.

England has a rich history of resolving disputes outside judicial institutions.[72] The United Kingdom has a clearly defined legal framework, the Arbitration Act of 1996, which authorises arbitration. The legal effect of an arbitration award is the same as any other judgement or order of the court and is thus binding. The 1996 Act does contain a number of safeguards, so state courts may modify or – partially – set aside the award, for example,

---

70 <http://www.islamic-sharia.org/aboutus/>.
71 See, *inter alia*, Rohe, Mathias, 'Alternative Dispute Resolution in Europe under the Auspices of Religious Norms', *Religare Working Paper* Number 6, 2011; Rohe, Matthias, 'Reasons for the Application of Shari'a in the West', pp. 25-46, in: Berger 2013; Boyd, Marion, 'Religion-Based Alternative Dispute Resolution: A Challenge to Multiculturalism', pp. 465-473, in: Banting, Keith *et al.* (eds.), *Belonging? Diversity, Recognition and Shared Citizenship in Canada*, Montreal: McGill-Queen's University Press 2007; Keshavjee, Mohamed, *Islam, Sharia and Alternative Dispute Resolution: Mechanisms for Legal Redress in the Muslim Community*, London: I.B. Tauris 2013; Shachar 2008, pp. 572-607; Yilmaz, Ihsan, 'Muslim Alternative Dispute Resolution and Neo-Ijtihad in England', *Turkish Journal of International Relations* 2003, pp. 117-139.
72 See: Maret, Rebecca, 'Mind the Gap: The Equality Bill and Sharia Arbitration in the United Kingdom', *Boston College International & Comparative Law Review* 2013, pp. 255-283 (261-263).

if the tribunal exceeded its powers, if an award relates to matters which are not capable of settlement via arbitration, if a party was under some incapacity, or if enforcing the award would be contrary to national law or public policy.[73]

In his speech, Phillips asserted that parties are already able to settle disputes by means of Sharia principles under the Arbitration Act 1996. He was referring to the stipulation that parties are free to choose the rules which are applicable to the substance of the dispute: "S46 (1): The arbitral tribunal shall decide the dispute – (a) *in accordance with the law chosen by the parties* as applicable to the substance of the dispute, or (b) if the parties so agree, in accordance with such *other considerations as are agreed by them or determined by the tribunal*". Sharia could thus function as a body of laws which the parties could use to resolve family disputes, as is the opinion of England and Wales' most important judge. Shaykh Suhaib Hasan of the London-based Islamic Sharia Council also uses the terminology of the Arbitration Act: "The existence of the ISC is legal under British law, based on legislation such as the Arbitration Act 1996 which permits disputants in civil matters to go for mediation and alternative dispute resolution. The ISC is bound by civil legislation, and so it cannot judge on issues of child custody, maintenance and especially on issues of criminal law. It is thus not a parallel legal system but a procedure granted by legislation".[74]

The Muslim Arbitration Tribunal (MAT), an umbrella organisation of Sharia councils under the leadership of Shaykh Faiz-ul-Aqtab Siddiqi, claims their main enterprise is arbitrating commercial disputes under the Arbitration Act 1996. Two private parties sign a binding agreement prior to the hearing and the tribunal consists of a minimum of two arbitrators – a UK qualified solicitor or barrister, and an Islamic scholar. This way, the outcome is in line with both "the Laws of England and Wales and the recognised Schools of Islamic Sacred Law" (article 8 (2) of the Procedure Rules of the Muslim Arbitration Tribunal), and leads to a contractually binding arbitration award.[75] Appeals are not possible under the MAT's statute: Article 23 of the procedural rules reads: "No appeal shall be made against any decisions of the Tribunal. This rule shall not prevent any party applying for Judicial Review with permission of the High Court". During an interview, Siddiqi told me there haven't been appeals as his clients are "satisfied customers who consider it a serious matter". Chief Crown Prosecutor Nazir Afzal stated later that the Muslim Arbitration Tribunal is known to deter parties from seeking appeal, even though individuals do have an inalienable right to challenge the award in court, which is codified in Article 58 of the Arbitration Act. Yet, when correctly regulated by the Arbitration Act, Afzal sees no problem

---

73   Arbitration Act 1996, S46 (1), S66 (1), S68, S103. 'Public policy' is the principle that no person or government official can legally perform an act that tends to injure the public.

74   <http://sheikhsuhaibhasan.blogspot.co.uk/2014/05/muslim-family-law-in-britain.html>.

75   See: www.matribunal.com. There has never been an arbitration award appealed. Appealing an arbitration award in general is quite rare, nevertheless it is peculiar that the MAT statute bans it. (Interviews with public prosecutor Nazir Afzal (phone interview, 11 July 2013) and barrister Elissa Da Costa-Waldman (phone interview, 11 July 2013).)

in the Muslim Arbitration Tribunal using alternative dispute resolution regarding local property disputes, especially when parties are equally matched.[76]

Yet, this is for the largest part theoretical, as Sharia councils are mainly involved in family law. A Sharia council's "core business" consists of dealing with women requesting an Islamic divorce and not commercial disputes. In fact, 95 per cent of the cases (hundreds per year per council) relate to divorce requests. Considering that mediation and arbitration are tools for extra-judicial decision-making for a minimum of *two parties* having a *legal dispute*, a *one-party* divorce *request* surely does not count as any form of alternative dispute resolution. But even if there were two parties, the Arbitration Act does not extend to divorce.[77]

Furthermore, using ADR terminology is incorrect by definition because Islamic judges have an agenda of their own.[78] This is a key difference compared to ADR. For example, president of the Islamic Sharia Council Shaykh Abu Sayeed said regarding granting divorces on women's request that "we don't break the marriage. As long as marriage is sacred, our job is to reconcile the marriage".[79] For an independent mediator or arbitrator – who should be neutral – to approach this task with such a clear personal agenda is entirely unacceptable.

It is also important that the basic requirement of arbitration, voluntary agreement, is not always met. The 'Sharia Law in Britain' report devotes a lot of attention to the involuntary nature of Sharia council proceedings. It contests the general assumption that those who attend Sharia councils do so voluntarily, and that unfair decisions can be redressed in state courts. As most principles of Sharia – contrary to what the proponents say – are contrary to British law and public policy, in theory they would be unlikely to be upheld in a secular court. Also, in reality, women are often pressured by their families to go to a Sharia council and to accept unfair decisions. British researcher Samia Bano, who visited Sharia councils and spoke to the women involved, found that, in reality, Sharia councils are "conceptualised in terms of a *duty* upon all Muslims to abide by the requirements of the sharia and the stipulations of the sharia councils".[80] Even more, there is evidence for the fact that refusal to settle a family dispute in a Sharia council can amount to threats and intimidation, or, at best, being excommunicated and labelled a disbeliever.[81]

Establishing the fact that the voluntary nature is, to say the least, questionable, is an essential part of the discussion, because if women are coerced into the frameworks of

---

76 Telephone interview with Nazir Afzal, 11 July 2013.
77 See also: Addison, Neil, 'Sharia Tribunals in Britain – Mediators or Arbitrators?', p. xi, in: MacEoin & Green 2009.
78 See also on this issue: Moore, Kathleen, *The Unfamiliar Abode: Islamic Law in the United States and Britain*, Oxford: Oxford University Press 2010, p. 119.
79 Interview with Abu Sayeed, London, 2 July 2013. See also: 'In the name of the law', *The Guardian* 14 June 2007, via <http://www.theguardian.com/world/2007/jun/14/religion.news>.
80 Bano 2008, p. 298.
81 'Sharia Law in Britain' 2010, p. 16.

Sharia councils, this severely impacts the rhetorical strength of arguing in favour of Sharia councils, which is founded on the notion of religious *freedoms*. Yet, even if Sharia councils – hypothetically – were accessed fully voluntarily, that does not end the discussion on the nature of Sharia law in the United Kingdom.

Concepts of mediation, arbitration and Alternative Dispute Resolution are used incorrectly. It is important to note that this is not a mix-up without consequences. Using the terminology of alternative dispute resolution as under the Arbitration Act creates a false impression that softens and obscures the reality that underlies the practice of Sharia councils. It is further implied that Sharia councils fall under a recognised regime that upholds legal standards, safeguards, and thus protects parties – which is not the case.[82] This means that most academic discussions about ADR, family law and Sharia councils are off base.

Sharia councils have no formally recognised legal jurisdiction over family law due to the sensitive nature of these disputes and their consequences. Some months after Phillips' speech, then minister of Justice Jack Straw confirmed this: "Arbitration is not a system of dispute resolution that may be used in family cases. Therefore no draft consent orders embodying the terms of an agreement reached by the use of a Sharia Council have been enforced within the meaning of the Arbitration Act 1996 in matrimonial proceedings".[83] The rulings coming from Sharia councils thus do not meet the legal system, they fall outside the Arbitration Act and the parties are thus not "protected" by legal safeguards. Nor are there any appeal procedures for parties that are confronted with unfair decisions.

It is a different issue when Sharia law is actually ingrained in state law, as is for instance the case with Iranian or Saudi Law. Then, national judges can encounter cases regarding international private law. There is some case law on English courts dealing with Sharia-based disputes. For instance, in one case, the House of Lords argued unanimously that sending a mother and a child back to Lebanon would be a flagrant breach of the Convention, as she would lose custody of her son because of Sharia-inspired family law.[84] In another case, parents fought a custody battle, where the father asked the court to grant him the right to have the child live with him in Saudi Arabia. The father had spread but had then withdrawn allegations that the mother had associated with another man, which would have had draconian consequences for the British woman and child under Saudi Sharia

---

82   See also on this discussion: MacEoin & Green 2009.
83   'Sharia Law in Britain: A Threat to One Law for All and Equal Rights', Published by One Law for All, June 2010, p. 13. Moreover, the Lawyer's Secular Society states that the jurisdiction of the family courts cannot be ousted by contractual agreement (*Edgar v. Edgar* [1980] 1 WLR 1410). At present inheritance disputes could in principle be the subject of a binding arbitration decision because they don't come under the jurisdiction of the Family Courts.
84   House of Lords, Opinions of the Lords of Appeal for Judgement in *M (Lebanon) v. Home Secretary* [2008] UKHL 64.

law. The judge refused to grant the order.[85] British courts ruled in favour of the mothers, because Sharia law would have had unacceptable consequences for them.

Yet, these cases had to deal with Sharia in foreign jurisdictions, for instance Lebanon and Saudi Arabia. With regard to cases in English courts which are asked to settle a dispute coming from a Sharia council's ruling, there are no such records. This could mean that these cases are swept under the carpet, or that there just are not many of these cases before the courts. This latter option seems more likely.[86] In fact, sociocultural anthropologist John Bowen, author of several publications on English law and Sharia, said in an interview that none of the judges and lawyers he had talked to, and he had asked many, said that they had ever seen an instance where a judge had enforced an agreement that came out of a "sharia council mediation".[87]

Interestingly, there is a case where the English court struck down a ruling by the London-based Islamic Sharia Council. In *Midani v. Midani* in 1999, in a dispute about an inheritance settlement, two of four heirs (Myrna and Omar) challenged the London-based Sharia council's ruling regarding their late father's estate. They disputed that the council had the authority to make binding decisions and protested its jurisdiction over the matter. Although the two heirs did not attend meetings voluntarily and had put their objections to the Council's jurisdiction in writing prior to any outcome, the Islamic Sharia Council ruled that half of Myrna's inheritance was to go to her brother Omar (as under Sharia men inherit more than women). The plaintiffs sought a declaration from the English court that the Sharia Council's ruling was not an arbitration award. The court ruled that it was unable to see how the ruling could be binding on the heirs without their consent. Moreover, the court held that: "The Shari'a Council is neither a national Court nor, in this instance at any rate, an arbitration tribunal. It does not derive its authority from any statute, nor from any consensus between the parties before me. Neither does it purport to. It describes its bench in terms of being a "quasi-Islamic Court" and its bench's decisions as "extra judicial". It would not seem even on its own opinion to be, therefore, a judicial body".[88]

With the exception of the Muslim Arbitration Tribunal (when it is legitimately functioning under the Arbitration Act – something which has also never been acknowledged by a British court), by far most of what is said about ADR and Sharia councils, is off the mark.[89] There is no overlap between British courts and the work of Sharia councils. Almost

---

85   House of Lords, Opinions of the Lords of Appeal for Judgement, in the Case *re J (a child) (FC)*, [2005] UKHL 40.

86   For example, there was a case on dower in *Uddin v. Choudhury*, [2009] EWCA (Civ) 1205.

87   Bangstad, Sindre, Leirvik, Oddbjorn, and Bowen, John, '"Anthropologists are talking", About Islam, Muslims and Law in Contemporary Europe', *Ethnos* 2013, pp. 1 – 20 (6).

88   See: *Al Midani and Another v. Al Midani and Others* [1999] 1 Lloyd's Rep 923, 22 February 1999.

89   See on the difference between MAT and other Sharia councils – such as the Islamic Sharia Council – Lepore, Christopher R., 'Asserting State Sovereignty over National Communities of Islam in the United States and

all Sharia councils, including the MAT, focus on Islamic family law. Moreover, it is unlikely that any Sharia council decision will be recognised as a binding arbitration award. In response to BBC's exposé on the Islamic Sharia Council, Helen Grant, Parliamentary Under-Secretary of State in 2013, said: "[S]haria law has no jurisdiction under the law of England and Wales and the courts do not recognise it. There is no parallel court system in this country, and we have no intention of changing the position in any part of England and Wales".[90] The Under-Secretary was right that the courts do not recognise the rulings of Sharia councils. However, it must be recognised that there are, in fact, two separate legal orders now functioning, of which one currently operates in the "shadow of the law".

WHAT HAPPENS AT SHARIA COUNCILS?

Multiculturalists assert that it is possible to integrate Islamic law in European societies and not come into conflict with secular human rights. Let us see if reality supports that assertion.

The focus is on family law. Regardless of statements that Sharia councils *should* not involve matters of criminal law, in practice it turns out they do.[91] Unfortunately, though, there is little research on this. In Germany, various cases have been found of Sharia judges and families claiming jurisdiction over criminal matters. Legal scholar and journalist Joachim Wagner (1943) found the "mediation of criminal disputes" in 16 cases in less than a year in Germany's large cities. In *Richter Ohne Gesetz* (Judges without Law, 2011), Wagner describes how the prosecution of crimes, such as drug deals, extortion, murder and manslaughter, fails as victims and witnesses do not cooperate with public prosecutors. Witnesses all of a sudden do not remember their testimony. Instead, families of victims and offenders had arranged to exchange blood money for freedom under the direction of Sharia judges.[92] Wagner warns against the rise of an Islamic parallel legal system that endangers the German rule of law.

In 2008, it became public that the Muslim Arbitration Tribunal handled six cases of domestic violence. In all six cases, MAT president Siddiqi said, Sharia judges ordered husbands to take anger management classes as well as mentoring from community elders, but issued no further punishment. All women subsequently withdrew their complaints to

---

Britain: Sharia councils as a Tool of Muslim Accommodation and Integration', *Washington University Global Studies Law Review* 2012, pp. 669-692 (680-685).

90   Grant, Helen, 'Sharia Law' Hansard 23 April 2013, Column 289WH.

91   Likewise, the Catholic Church has successfully managed to keep priests who were (are) suspected of child rape out of the secular penal jurisdiction by trying them according to canonical laws. See: Verhofstadt, Dirk, *Atheïsme als Basis voor de Moraal* (Atheism as Foundation for Morals), Antwerp: Houtekiet 2013, pp. 58-61.

92   Wagner, Joachim, *Richter Ohne Gesetz*, Berlin: Econ 2011.

the police, who halted investigations. The advantage was, according to Siddiqi, that marriages were saved and couples were given a second chance.[93]

Also within British Somali community, Sharia is used to settle criminal cases. Saynab Muhamad, leader of the Somali Family Support Centre, believes the involvement of community elders is more efficient than getting the police involved. In one case a few years ago, Sharia was used to resolve the case of knife attacks among teenagers. The victim's family and the assailant came together with Somali elders. During an informal hearing the two parties were reconciled under the leadership of an Islamic judge. "Forgiveness" was purchased by the attacker; the police were never involved.[94]

Yet, evading criminal liability (or commercial disputes) are not the main reason individuals go to Sharia councils – including the MAT.[95] Moreover, Sharia criminal law or diverting Muslims away from secular criminal law enforcement and justice cannot even count on multiculturalist support. Vocal support from multiculturalists is based on the assumption that family law should be the focus of Sharia – as is the case with fundamentalists. For reasons that are not particularly clear to me, both multiculturalists and Islamists present their case for Sharia *family* law as a "modest" demand. "We merely ask for family law to be recognised, and perhaps some commercial law", seems to be the basic idea. From a doctrinarian view, Sharia's hold on family law (e.g. marriage, divorce, maintenance) is particularly strong, especially compared to other branches, such as Islamic tax law or constitutional law.[96] But also from a practical point of view, wherever Islamists gain political power, it is Islamic *family law* that is pushed to the top of the agenda. For instance, when the Muslim Brotherhood was voted into parliament in Egypt after Mubarak's downfall, the first thing the Islamists did was roll back women's rights by means of legislating Sharia-based family law.[97] The process is witnessed all over the world where fundamentalists gain influence.[98] It is therefore with extreme caution and scepticism that calls for recognition or toleration of Islamic family laws should be assessed.

There are some multiculturalists who find a focus on negative aspects regarding the status of women discriminatory or racist. They find that criticism on minorities in light of sex discrimination is "used" to "portray" minorities negatively. Racism is taken as a

---

93 'Islamic Sharia councils in Britain are now "legally binding"', *Daily Mail Online* 15 September 2008, via <http://www.dailymail.co.uk/news/article-1055764/Islamic-sharia-courts-Britain-legally-binding.html>.

94 'Sharia law UK: Mail on Sunday gets exclusive access to a British Muslim court', *Daily Mail Online* 4 July 2009.

95 Although formally they claim to offer dispute settlements under a mixture of Sharia and the Arbitration Act, their income comes mainly from divorce requests just like any other Sharia council. (Interview with Shaykh Faiz-ul-Aqtab Siddiqi and Fiaz Hussein, 4 July 2013.)

96 Schacht 1982, p. 76.

97 See: Dyer 2013.

98 See: Bennoune 2013.

cause for exaggeration of problems.[99] Moreover, many multiculturalists advocate that Sharia family law should be possible, "as long as it does not endanger women's rights". But is that possible? Let us clarify what happens at Sharia councils to see whether criticism on the status of women is justified or not.

In Britain, much of the tension around the debate on Sharia councils arises out of concern for women. This is not strange: over 95 per cent of the applicants at Sharia councils are women seeking a religious divorce.[100] That is, women initiating a divorce for a marriage constituted under Islamic law. This is the *raison d'être* of these councils. Religious marriage and divorce are agreements wholly separate from civil marriage and civil divorce.

A Muslim marriage, or *nikah*, is a contract – "a solemn Qur'ānic covenant" – between a bride and a groom, which they, or their proxies, must *freely* enter into, writes Sonia Shah-Kazemi who published a detailed report on why women visit Sharia councils in 2001.[101] Shah-Kazemi here equates "the bride and groom" with "their proxies". That is because, under Sharia, the woman's marriage act can also be stipulated by her *wali*. A *wali* is the nearest male relative who acts on behalf of the woman as legal guardian. This makes it possible for a groom and the father of the bride to contract a marriage, leaving the woman out of the equation, especially if she is a minor.[102]

For the contract to be valid, the groom must provide a sum of money, the dower – to which both parties have agreed, which is known as the *mahr*. Theoretically, this sum belongs to the wife. The *nikah* needs to be witnessed by two competent – male – witnesses. Men are allowed to enter into polygamous marriages, and may marry up to four wives. Marital rights (or duties), *inter alia*, are "sexual availability", and the wife's entitlement to maintenance.[103]

Unfortunately, not all marriages are destined for eternal bliss. Under UK law, in order to dissolve civil marriages, one spouse needs to divorce the other on the basis of grounds stipulated by law. These grounds include adultery, desertion, having been separated for a

---

99 That is the position of Malik 2009, p. 9 and of Phillips, Anne, *Multiculturalism Without Culture*, Princeton: Princeton University Press 2007, p. 2, who wrote: "Overt expressions of racism were being transformed into a more socially acceptable criticism of minorities said to keep their women indoors, marry their girls off young to unknown and unwanted partners, and force their daughters and wives to wear veils".

100 Shah-Kazemi, Sonia Nûrîn, *Untying the Knot. Muslim Women, Divorce and the Shariah*, The Nuffield Foundation/Signal Press: London 2001, p. 18. Also: '[T]he overwhelming majority of cases are to do with divorce – 95 percent of the roughly 7,000 cases the council has dealt with since opening its doors in 1982', in: 'In the name of the law', *The Guardian* 14 June 2007.

101 Shah-Kazemi 2001, p. 7.

102 Schacht 1964, p. 161.

103 Shah-Kazemi 2001, p. 7. In classical Islamic law, the mahr is usually divided in a 'prompt' and a 'deferred' part, the prompt sum is due in connection with the consummation of the marriage, the deferred part in case of divorce or death. See: Menski, Werner, 'Immigration and multiculturalism in Britain: New Issues in Research and Policy', paper of a lecture delivered at Osaka University on 25 July 2002, pp. 1-20, (5-6), available via <www.casas.org.uk/papers/pdfpapers/osakalecture.pdf>.

certain period, and "unreasonable behaviour", which is as broad as having to watch boring TV programs all the time. The procedure and its outcome are sex neutral; it does not matter whether divorce is initiated by a man or a woman. All in all, it can take 6-8 months if both spouses cooperate, but one spouse can frustrate the divorce, stretching it for years.[104]

Yet, a secular judge cannot dissolve a religious marriage. This would not accepted under Islamic law, and needs to be dissolved by an imam or an Islamic judge, a qadi. Religious divorce thus requires a separate dissolution. Women are likely to want a divorce more than a man, since Muslim men may marry up to four wives.[105] This means that if a man is dissatisfied with his marriage to his wife, he can easily ignore that particular marriage and find up to three others. Because the state does not recognise religious marriages, *religious* polygamy is not illegal. Furthermore, historically, there is overlap between the way a woman is released from an Islamic marriage and the way a master frees a slave (manumission).[106] A husband can unilaterally – without spousal permission – divorce his wife by pronouncing the *talaq* ("I divorce you"), for which no grounds are needed. Rules differing per school of Islamic jurisprudence, the talaq needs to be said three times. He forfeits his right to return of the dower.

Remarriage with the same woman is possible. However, for that remarriage to be valid, the woman will first need a new marriage with a sort of "in between" husband, with whom she will have to have sexual intercourse with. After this has happened, she has to divorce him and can then remarry her first husband. This is for instance what happens if a man pronounces the talaq, but then changes his mind. All in all, it can be a very traumatising experience for the woman who is basically forced to have sex with a strange man in order to return to her husband. This is called "*nikah halala*".[107]

---

104 'Grounds for divorce', UK Government Website (last updated 5 February 2015), via <https://www.gov.uk/divorce/grounds-for-divorce>; Advicenow.org.uk, website by the charity Law for Life: the Foundation for Public Legal Education, see: <http://www.advicenow.org.uk/advicenow-guides/family/survival-guide-to-divorce-and-dissolution/what-you-cant-expect-the-law-to-do-html,682,FP.html>.

105 Sura 4:3 of the Koran states an explicit endorsement of the practice: "Marry of the women, who seem good to you, two or three or four; and if ye fear that ye cannot do justice to so many then one only".

106 Ali 2010.

107 "When a free man has pronounced a threefold divorce, the divorced wife is unlawful for him to remarry until she has married another man in a valid marriage and the new man has copulated with her, which at minimum means that the head of the erect penis fully enters her vagina." (n.7.7) Keller 1991. This is based on Koranic sura 2:230: "And if he has divorced her [for the third time], then she is not lawful to him afterward until [after] she marries a husband other than him. And if the latter husband divorces her [or dies], there is no blame upon the woman and her former husband for returning to each other if they think that they can keep [within] the limits of Allah. These are the limits of Allah, which He makes clear to a people who know." See on the Nikah Halala also: 'Nikah Halala – Sharia divorce law that demands the wife to sleep with another man', *The Muslim Issue* 2 November 2014, via <https://themuslimissue.wordpress.com/2014/11/02/crazy-islam-nikah-halala-sharia-divorce-law-that-demands-the-wife-to-sleep-with-another-man/>. See also Ficq Council Birmingham: "Irrespective of whether a man pronounced to his wife the words of Talaq in one statement (e.g. 'I give you Three Talaqs'), or in three separate statements (e.g. 'I give you Talaq, I give you Talaq, I give you Talaq.'), according to the unanimous verdict of all Schools of Islamic Law

However, just like for Jewish women under Jewish law, it is (very) difficult for Muslim women to get a divorce under Islamic law if they want one but the husband does not want to help by easily pronouncing the *talaq*. There are several ways in which a woman can obtain a divorce. For instance, the woman can initiate a *khulla* agreement. In that case, both parties must agree to the wife's release from the marriage contract, and in most cases she is expected to refund the sum of the dower to the husband. In a sense she "buys" a *talaq*. The wife forfeits her right to maintenance. Custody of the children can be put at stake. Although custody rulings fall under the sole jurisdiction of state courts and Sharia councils formally acknowledge this, there are known cases of the wife illegitimately losing custody in exchange for a divorce. In particular, women who lack knowledge of Britain's legal system run the risk of falsely believing Sharia councils have jurisdiction over custody matters.[108] From the BBC documentary "Secrets of Britain's Sharia councils" it has become clear that even women who have had a state court grant them sole custody of the children can face a subsequent ruling by Sharia judges reversing that ruling as Sharia has its own rules on custody.[109] Sharia's schools of jurisprudence have detailed custody settlements, which come down to the fact that the father is most likely to get custody of the child, especially if the woman remarries.[110] Furthermore, under a khulla contract, the couple can remarry without the wife needing to remarry and have sex with another man first.[111] Generally, husbands are known to frustrate the khul, which can be terribly dangerous if the husband is violent towards her and the children. Sharia councils can prolong this dangerous situation by siding with the husband, stretching the abusive marriage.[112]

Other possibilities for dissolving the religious marriage are if the marriage has not yet been consummated due to the fault of the husband. Here, both parties can agree, without payment, that the wife is released from the marriage contract. This is called *mubara'ah*.

(Hanafi/Shafi'i/Maliki/Hanbali) that these three Talaqs will be regarded in sharia law as being three Talaqs and a husband will cease to have the right to take back his wife without a sharia based Halalah. A Shariah based Halalah is whereby the wife freely marries someone else after having been divorced thrice and then after consummation of that second marriage is given divorce by the second husband or the second husband passes away, in this situation she may now remarry the first husband with a new marriage contract and with a new mahr (dowry)". Via <http://www.fiqhcouncilbirmingham.com/page/marriage_arbitration#Q21>.

108 Private interview with barrister Charlotte Proudman, who has represented women at Sharia councils, 18 June 2013. It is also a problem that academics repeat the Sharia Council's lie that they do not rule on custody issues. See for someone who does, for instance, Bowen 2009-10, p. 419.

109 "Secrets   of   Britain's   Sharia   Councils",   BBC   Panorama,   22   April   2013,   via <http://www.bbc.co.uk/iplayer/episode/b01rxfjt/Panorama_Secrets_of_Britains_Sharia_Councils/>.

110 A woman has no right to custody of a child from a previous marriage when she remarries ("because married life will occupy her with fulfilling the rights of her husband and prevents her from tending the child"). (m.13.4). If a child reaches the age of "discrimination" (mostly at the age of 7 or 8), it gets to choose the parent he wants to stay with, "though if a son chooses his mother, he is left with his father during the day so the father can teach and train him". m.13.5, Keller 1991.

111 Keller 1991, n.5.0.

112 Telephone interview with Chief Crown prosecutor Nazir Afzal, 11 July 2013.

Also, the woman, prior to the marriage, can adopt a clause in the contract in which the husband allows the wife the possibility of divorce.

Unlike under Jewish law, Sharia allows women to obtain a divorce without a husband's consent. This is called *faskh*, and it forms the bulk of divorce procedures at Sharia councils. Whereas in Western secular legal systems the grounds for divorce are very easily met, this is not the case under Sharia. A qadi will need to check whether the divorce request meets the conditions. These are, *inter alia*:

- The husband's renunciation of Islam, apostasy or return to his former religion.
- The husband has a sexual defect, is impotent, or has taken a vow to abstain from sexual relations.
- There has been a corruption of the marriage, for instance, if the husband is imprisoned for a specified period.
- The husband has not provided maintenance for his wife, as he is required to.
- The incapacity or refusal to fulfil marital obligations by either party may constitute the right to divorce.
- The husband has deserted or harmed the wife.
- Both parties have engaged in "mutual cursing", for instance, when adultery has been alleged by one party against the other.[113]

So, continuing with the Islamic Sharia Council as an example, when a woman files for an Islamic divorce, she fills out an application form provided by the Sharia council. She is required to sign the application, which stipulates "I promise to accept the decision of the Council irrespective of my own personal interests in order to maintain the supremacy of the Sharia over all other considerations [...] I also solemnly swear that at the moment I am not violating any of the matrimonial laws of the Sharia".[114] She pays a fee of £400 (which is peculiar as the Islamic Sharia Council is a registered charity).[115] She is either interviewed by a representative of the ISC, or the procedure will be conducted by means of written correspondence. The Sharia council will send three letters to the husband to inform him of his wife's decision to divorce him, and he may or may not reply, and he may or may not actually attend the hearing which the ISC schedules. The husband is invited to join his wife at the session(s).[116]

---

113 Shah-Kazemi 2001, pp. 7-8. The specific conditions depend on the interpretation of the different schools of law.

114 See: <www.shariacouncil.org>.

115 According to the annual report filed at the Charity Commission, the ISC held a reserve of £170,241 in 2014. via <http://apps.charitycommission.gov.uk/Accounts/Ends55/0001003855_AC_20131231_E_C.pdf>.

116 Which can be a traumatising experience. One woman interviewed by BBC's Panorama stated about being made to see her abusive husband at session: "I was shocked. Surely they can see that women who have been through this cannot be forced to meet up with someone who is abusing them." Samia Bano, a British scholar,

When one of the above stated grounds for divorce is accepted, or is assumed to be proven – by the *qadi* – a divorce is granted. The Islamic Sharia Council embraces all four schools of Sunni jurisprudence. Once a month, fifteen scholars – e.g. Haitham al-Haddad and Abu Sayeed – meet at Regent's Park Mosque and discuss the cases until consensus about the outcome is reached.[117] There is no transparency, nor is there the possibility of redress.

When it comes to delivering evidence for fulfilling the grounds for divorce, women are confronted with unequal burdens of proof compared to men. Islamists maintain that the sexes are naturally different which results in different rights, where women draw the shortest straw. Islamists find confirmation for this in Surah Al-Baqarah 2:282, that two female witnesses are required compared to one male witness: "[...] And bring to witness two witnesses from among your men. And if there are not two men [available], then a man and two women from those whom you accept as witnesses – so that if one of the women errs, then the other can remind her. [...]" The Islamic Sharia Council has now updated its website. It used to say the following about the testimony of women: "Man's mind is uni-focal while the women's mind is multi-focal. In other words, a man would be fully occupied with the task he is involved with; he may not be distracted by anything else while being engaged in his activity. On the other hand, a woman may be busy in kitchen work and she will be easily alert to a phone buzzer or her infants cry from the cradle. In a way she is found to be more sensitive and active in her dealings. Thus, she has got a very praise worthy character but that is not so good for a case of testimony which requires more attention and concentration. What is wrong then, if a second woman is needed, only to remind her is she fails to deliver her testimony completely. So it is a case of verification of the testimony, not that of degradation to the status of the women at all". And: "To deny the difference

---

researched the experiences of women at Sharia councils, and finds that: 'of the sample, ten women reported that they had been 'coaxed' into participating in the reconciliation sessions with their husbands even though they were reluctant to do so. More worrying still, four of these women reported that they had existing injunctions issued against their husbands on the grounds of violence and yet they were urged to sit only a few feet away from these violent men during the reconciliation sessions. Again, an extract of interviews reveals how potentially dangerous this may be for women and illustrates how husbands may use this opportunity to negotiate access to children and, in some cases, financial settlements, matters which are in effect being discussed under the 'shadow of the law'.' Bano writes: 'A woman reports: 'I told him [the imam] that I left him because he was violent but he started saying things like "Oh, how violent was that? Because in Islam a man is allowed to beat his wife!" I mean, I was so shocked. He said it depends on whether he really hurt me! I was really shocked because I thought he was there to understand but he was trying to make me admit that somehow I had done wrong." (Shazia, London), excerpt from: Bano, Samia, 'In Pursuit of Religious and Legal Diversity: A Response to the Archbishop of Canterbury and the 'Sharia Debate' in Britain', *Ecclesiastical Law Journal* 2008, pp. 283-309 (303). See also: Bano, Samia, 'Muslim Family Justice and Human Rights: The Experience of British Muslim Women', *Journal of Comparative Law* 2007, pp. 45-52.

117 'Sharia law UK: Mail on Sunday gets exclusive access to a British Muslim court', *Daily Mail Online* 4 July 2009.

between the two genders is a denial of truth. Allah who created us, gave us rulings according to our nature. And all is well as long as we go by the nature".[sic][118]

Nonetheless, the Islamic Sharia Council can administer the *faskh* (the divorce ruled by a qadi), although its qadis would rather see the marriage reconciled and are reluctant to dissolve it.[119] Thus, if the husband does not want to divorce his wife, it is very difficult for her to get divorced, even if there is (severe) abuse. He can keep her lingering in an abusive marriage for as long as he likes. Qadi Al-Haddad stated that a husband should not be asked about hitting his wife.[120] Qadi Suhaib Hasan has been filmed secretly on several occasions downplaying the severity of violence and deterring women from going to the police. In one instance, filmed by *The Guardian*, after a woman said her husband hit her once, he said: "Only once? So it's not a very serious matter".[121] In the BBC *Panorama* documentary, he asked: "He actually beats you? Severely, or just…", leaving that hanging in the air. "He hits me", the undercover reporter said, asking if she should go to the police. "The police, that is the very last resort", Hasan replied.[122] Qadi Abu Sayeed is fully aware that most of the women requesting divorce are on the receiving end of violence. However, testimonies by these women remain "allegations", if not confirmed by their husbands.[123]

Generally, it is not uncommon for a man to refuse cooperation regarding the divorce until he feels enough money has been paid by his wife, nor is it uncommon for women to plea before the qadi that she is a victim of domestic abuse, hoping that the "judge" will agree with her divorce request. I have witnessed these hearings. Women testify there has been emotional and/or physical abuse, that huge loans are taken out in her name which she will need to pay for, that the husband hasn't been seen for years, or that he has other wives besides her. No qadi appeared surprised when a woman told him or her about abuse, and the police are never mentioned.

---

118 This text is no longer available on the Islamic Sharia Council's website.
119 American professor of Law Robin Fretwell Wilson gives the example of *Ameena*: Ameena sought assistance from the Islamic Sharia Council to divorce her husband. Backed by testimony of her daughter and two women's shelter workers, Ameena told Dr. Hasan that her husband "beats me and the children." Hasan documented the abuse including the beating that caused a miscarriage. Although Ameena corroborated her claims of abuse, Hasan referred *Ameena*'s case to a council of seven qadis. The council decided Ameena's husband should be given another opportunity to reconcile with her before they would grant Ameena a divorce, if the council did so at all. As of July 2009, "Ameena's fate remain[ed] in limbo". See: Wilson, Robin Fretwell, 'Privatizing Family Law in the Name of Religion', *William & Mary Bill of Rights Journal* 2010, pp. 925-952 (931).
120 'Shaikh Haitham Al Haddad 'The family' Talk at Masjid Umar R.A. Part 2', YouTube clip, published on 15 May 2012, via <http://youtu.be/fST0Vmyim44?t=12m56s>.
121 "Inside a sharia divorce court", *The Guardian* 9 March 2011, via <http://www.the-guardian.com/law/video/2011/mar/09/islam-sharia-council-divorce>.
122 "Secrets of Britain's Sharia Councils", BBC Panorama, 22 April 2013.
123 Interview with Abu Sayeed, 2 July 2013.

In 2013, I was present at hearings at the Islamic Sharia council, where I spent two after-noons, and at the Birmingham Central Mosque Sharia Council, where I spent half a day. I was limited to that amount of time as extra time was not granted. Moreover, I was not allowed to look into any files. I took notes – there are no recordings. The following are abstracts from these notes. I believe it is valuable information, because it is not generally known what goes on at Sharia councils. Moreover, it has been brought to my attention that researchers are not allowed to be present at hearings anymore. That makes this kind of information increasingly scarce.[124] The following is what I have observed at the Islamic Sharia Council in London:

The first case I attend is with qadi-in-training Khola Hasan, daughter of qadi Suhaib Hasan. A young woman has been visiting the Islamic Sharia Council for two years now. She has brought a solicitor with her. She desperately seeks a religious divorce, a khul, in which a couple decide together that the husband will pronounce the divorce (talaq), often in exchange for return of the dower and sometimes – illegally – custody of the children. In this case, there was never a civil marriage, as, she explains, her mother-in-law discouraged her from getting one. Her husband now does not want to cooperate with the religious divorce until his wife has paid back the dower, the mahr, which consists of £10,000 worth of gold. She denies she ever received that sum in the first place. Her mother-in-law immediately took away the mahr. Another financial problem she has is that he took out a loan on her name the day they got married. Khola Hasan asks the woman if she is sexually active. The reason she asks, is because her husband has made allegations of adultery. The woman denies that is the case. In turn, she asks Hasan why it is that the last time she went to the Islamic Sharia Council, she was told she was not allowed to bring anyone with her, no solicitor, no friend, no family. She says that consequently, there was a hearing consisting of two male qadis interrogating her alone for quite some time about her sexual activities, in detail. She had found that very uncomfortable and unprofessional. Hasan asks her who had told her it was not allowed to bring anyone. The woman tells her the man on the phone did not want to give his name. Hasan says it should not have happened and that she will look into it. Some more questions are asked. Hasan: "We are sitting here under the eyes of God. Then the sin lies on you, if you lied". Soon, she will hear whether her divorce request will be granted. The woman does not have to come to the Islamic Sharia Council anymore. She looks as if she is ready to burst out in tears.

---

124 I was at the Islamic Sharia Council on 1 and 2 July, 2013. I was present at the Birmingham Central Mosque Sharia Council on 3 July, 2013. Other researchers state the experiences of the women themselves. See for that, *inter alia*, Shah-Kazemi 2001 and Bano 2008, pp. 283-309 (303). See also: Bano 2007, pp. 45-52. Lastly, there is the umbrella organisation called "The Muslim Arbitration Tribunal", located in Nuneaton under the leadership of Shaykh Faiz-ul-Aqtab Siddiqi. I interviewed Shaykh Siddiqi on 4 July 2013, but was not allowed to visit hearings at the Muslim Arbitration Tribunal, therefore the focus is on those where I have seen hearings.

The second case is with a young qadi named Furqan Mahboob. He has a beard and wears a white robe. His I-Phone continuously beeps as he deals with the couple sitting before him. They make a nervous impression. The married couple have an issue. The wife used to be married to another man. They had a civil divorce years ago. Now she remarried the man who is with her today, with whom she has children. There is no contact with her first husband whatsoever – she assumes he went back to his country of origin years ago. They ask Mahboob whether her civil divorce of the other man constituted a religious divorce as well. Did he pronounce the talaq? It is important, because if that is not the case, it means she is still married to her first husband, making her an adulteress. The conversation went as follows:

Qadi Mahboob: "He never gave you a divorce through his mouth?"

Wife: "No".

Qadi Mahboob: "Have you asked for one?"

Wife: "No".

Qadi Mahboob: "You as a Muslim female, you should have known that you need a Muslim judge or an Islamic court or council for a divorce. Who told you that it was enough?"

Wife: "My friends and family. The UK divorce does not count as anything?"

The qadi asks whether she now is remarried and has children. She confirms.

Qadi Mahboob: "Oh-oh-oh. It needs investigation. It sounds dodgy. (Turns to me) All the secular courts here are secular, right?"

Me: "Yes".

Qadi Mahboob: (Turns back to the wife) "Through your ignorance we need to take matters into account. It is going to be a difficult case. We are going to ask our scholars to give you the answers. A man is lost … is a ground to apply for divorce. Marriage is an act of worship".

Husband: "But I thought Muslims in a non-Muslim country need to abide by the laws of the land of the country they live in".

Qadi Mahboob: "A secular judge does not do religious divorces. We have Islam. Secular courts do not have Islamic laws. Can a kafr (non-Muslim, MZ) come in and judge Islamic matters?"

Husband: "No".

Qadi Mahboob: "Is marriage an act of worship?"

Husband: "Yes".

Qadi Mahboob: "Can a non-Muslim, "I, John, who don't believe in God, I grant you divorce", can he?"

Husband: "No".

Qadi Mahboob: "It is important to determine a possible double or singular intention of the secular divorce. Did he or did he not also want a religious divorce? We should ask him. Otherwise the secular divorce counts as nothing. A kafr cannot rule a religious divorce".

Mahboob tells them they will need to make a new appointment. He is not able to say how long this procedure will take. A copy of the secular divorce act is unnecessary. Then the woman tells him that, back then, her first husband contested the civil divorce.

Qadi Mahboob: "Oh no. That makes it more difficult. That makes it clear that he did not have the intention to divorce religiously. The scholars need to be asked about this".

The couple leave. I ask the qadi what will happen to them. He says: "If the first marriage stands, then the current marriage is void". I ask him what consequences there will be. He stalls a bit, and says: "What do you think, we are going to stone them to death or something?" I respond: "No, but surely, there must be consequences, because why else come all the way here and why ask the scholars?" He tells me there are several conditions for accountability for sins. Firstly, there has to be knowledge about the sin, secondly, one needs to be aware (other than asleep), and thirdly, the intentions are important. These are cumulative demands. If these demands of the sin are met, the couple will have to be separated, for it is considered adultery, he explains.[125]

---

125 Under Sharia, the scholars could decide to go for a "Nikah Halala", as described above. That means the couple should separate first by means of her current husband pronouncing the talaq. Then a qadi can pronounce a faskh: a divorce on the first marriage on grounds of him being absent. The old couple can then remarry under Sharia, but not before she has another marriage with another man with whom she will need

Mahboob says problems such as these could be prevented if Sharia councils had the authority to make judgements which are legally binding. He states it is a problem that courts do not accept religious marriages as marriages. "How can we help the females if our hands are tied?"

The last hearing that day is with qadi Suhaib Hasan, founder and secretary of the Islamic Sharia Council, and father of Khola. Before the new case starts, I ask him for his thoughts on the case I had just seen with his colleague. Hasan says: "She was not supposed to remarry before her divorce, that is the problem". It is statements like these that should erase any doubt regarding the fact that Sharia functions as a parallel legal system.

There are two more cases I was present at. Again, there is a woman who is seeking divorce. She has not seen her husband for four years. He is abroad. The khulla was almost a fact, but suddenly he is unwilling to proceed until she returns the gold that she received as dower. She tells Hasan she has left the gold in his house when she left him. Moreover, he is not stable, he is big-headed, arrogant and drinks alcohol. The reason he does not want to pronounce the talaq is for revenge, she says. Now she has to pay him again, she does not have the money and she has a job, so she does not have any time for these procedures. "How many times do I have to come back here until it's done already?" Hasan says the khulla is now a fact, and that she does not have to return the dowry.

The fourth case involves a young woman who is married to a fifty-year-old man. This time, it is not divorce that is sought after. Rather, the woman urges Hasan to contact her husband. She says: "He oppressed me to the maximum, he is violent, physically treats me like a dog". She wears a headscarf on his request. With "every little thing" he threatens to divorce her. He is abusive both verbally and physically. She says he might have ten wives for all she knows. He is currently in Tunisia. She needs qadi Hasan to be "a brother, a father, a Muslim" and wants him to reason with her husband. She wants to remain married to him, her husband should look after her. Hasan needs to explain to her husband that he should take Islamic marriage seriously. Hasan laughs a bit: "Why did you marry such a person?"

The next day I spent a second afternoon at the Islamic Sharia Council. That day qadi Abu Sayeed, president of the council, allows me to be present at three cases. For the first case, a man comes in alone. His wife is willing to remain married to him, but then there are four conditions that need to be met. Firstly, he needs to sell his shop. Secondly, he will have to take care of his children one day a week. Thirdly, after the shop has been sold, he will have to pay maintenance. Fourthly, then Sayeed pauses. He looks at me. They switch to another language. After a short while, they switch back to English. Sayeed tells the man that he

---

to have sex first, divorce him, wait three menstrual periods, and then she can return to the father of her children

needs to swear on the Koran not to mistreat her anymore. This case has been going on for four years. The man agrees to meet the conditions. The marriage is saved. He leaves the room.

Sayeed and I talk a bit, waiting for the next case. He tells me that most of the cases, about six to eight hundred a year, involve divorce-seeking women who are on the receiving end of violence or maltreatment. He tells me: "As long as marriage is sacred, reconciliation is our job". Although, he tells me, reconciliation is mostly not successful, but sometimes it is.

The second case starts as two men walk in. One of the men explains to Sayeed that he was in prison and could not stop by earlier. He is angry. He tells he still has a wife, however, she claims they are divorced. Now she has a boyfriend and is pregnant. The man says he never divorced his wife. His wife claims he signed a talaq certificate at the Islamic Sharia Council, which he denies. The man turns to me: "You know more about Sharia councils than I do. These councils are supposed to be an advantage, but not for me. My wife took full advantage". He seems aggravated. Abu Sayeed has a copy of the Islamic divorce certificate which the man signed. He asks the man: "If you never came here, then why do I have here a divorce certificate of the ISC?" The man responds: "You tell me. The ISC Company has destroyed my marriage. With that fake certificate my wife remarried". The man will now sign a new document that he never gave a talaq. This hearing ends as the men leave. Sayeed tells me afterwards that there has been made an allegation against the ISC and that it will be looked into. He thinks the man did sign the talaq certificate, but now regrets his decision and made up this story.

The last case begins. A woman comes in. She looks sad and tense. She has brought her sister. When she was 19, her family received a marriage proposal for her. She was not in a position to deny. They got married in 1999 in the United Kingdom. He was an illegal Bangladeshi, but back then it was still allowed to marry. She made him a British citizen through civil marriage. They have two children. In 2009, the family went to Bangladesh after he promised there would be a house and a private school for their daughters. But there was nothing. He had not arranged any of his promises, she tells Sayeed. She returned to the United Kingdom alone, with the children, and now she wants to divorce him. She is in the final stage of a civil divorce, to which he agrees, because he can then marry another woman he already found. It is a religious divorce she wants from the Islamic Sharia Council, but the husband refuses to cooperate with that. The woman has not seen him in four years. She already gave him back the dower of £8000. Next to that, she gave him £30.000.

Sayeed: "You have not had contact with him for four years. Why a divorce?"

Woman: "There was a lot of fighting. He threw stuff at me. He put me in debt".

Sayeed: "Debt is not a cause for divorce. You should help him. Why don't you pay him more?"

Woman: "Should I stay poor forever? Not have a pension when I'm old? My sister already paid him a lot. I am now poor because of him".

Sayeed: "You do not have more money to continue paying his debt?"

Woman: "I've got two kids to feed. And so much other problems. He has the wrong mentality. I was not allowed to wear a headscarf. He has an un-Islamic mentality".

Sayeed: "Did he pay something for you or the children?"

Woman: "No. And I get along fine with the in-laws. We got the families together, but reconciliation efforts failed".

Sayeed: "What does he do with the money?"

Woman: "I don't know".

Abu Sayeed tells her about the "scientific biologic reasons for polygamy" [sic]. Occasionally they switch to another language.

During these hearings, I got the impression that the qadis were steering the women away from divorce. In the last case, Abu Sayeed tried to persuade the woman towards acceptance of the marriage in polygamous form, rather than terminating her religious marriage. Public Prosecutor Nazir Afzal told me that he suspects Sharia councils discourage abused women from seeking help, which means they are perpetuating serious harm: "if a woman wants a divorce, they will say you will disgrace your family".[126]

The organisation Women Living under Muslim Laws wonders why "no research to date has questioned why Shariah councils do not automatically issue a certificate that following civil divorce, the religious marriage is also dissolved in the eyes of Muslim laws, and why instead they insist upon lengthy processes of calling husbands to 'give evidence'".[127] In fact, research shows that at this Sharia council 45 per cent of cases were decided in 6-8

---

126 Telephone interview Nazir Afzal, 11 July 2013.
127 'Recognising the Un-recognised' 2006, p. 72.

months, 45 per cent in 10-19 months, and 10 per cent took much longer, which, considering the potentially violent home situation can be very dangerous for the petitioners.[128]

It is a valid critique. The Sharia council connected to the Birmingham Central Mosque had faster procedures and did not wait for the husbands to respond. This council was founded in the late 1990s. The mosque serves around 4,000 worshippers for Friday prayers. It is one of Europe's largest mosques. Women can petition for a religious divorce, for which the Council asks a fee of £250; "administrative costs" was the explanation when I asked why. They do ten to fifteen cases per month.[129] When I visited in 2013, women had to back up their request in front of a panel of three qadis: Amra Bone, Muhammad Talha Bokhari, and chaired by Indian-born Mohammad Naseem, who died aged 89 in 2014. Naseem was a medical practitioner, mainly focused on male circumcisions. He was chairman of the mosque and executive member and home affairs spokesman for the Islamic Party of Britain until it was dissolved in 2006. The Islamic Party of Britain was an Islamist political party which never succeeded in getting elected.[130]

The following abstracts are an illustration of the setting and cases at the Birmingham Sharia Council.

A woman comes in and takes a seat in front of the panel. She tells the qadis that she wants a divorce in order to gain peace of mind. The husband harasses her and her children. He leaves the house for long periods of time without notice, and constantly texts or calls her in an accusatory tone. He stalks her and abuses her. When he does come home, the children are so scared that the oldest ones flee the house. There are rumours that he is married to someone else. She does not care whether that is true or not, she just wants a divorce. The panel asks the woman to leave the room, so that they can discuss her request. "This is not a valid marriage under the Koran, it is a sham. I have no interest in saving this. I just don't

---

128 Bowen, John, 'Panorama's exposé of sharia councils didn't tell the full story', *The Guardian* 26 April 2013.

129 That makes an average of £37,500 per year. The report 'Equal and Free? Evidence in support of Baroness Cox's Arbitration and Mediation Services (Equality) Bill', researched and drafted by Charlotte Rachael Proudman 2012, comes at a wider estimate. "The Sharia Council rule on at least 20 Islamic divorces in one day of each month, thus the minimum amount the Sharia Council earns per month is £4,000, equating to £48,000 per annum."(p. 71).

130 Its viewpoints were, for instance, that the existing political parties did not suffice as "Muslims can't rely on the secular system", that the banking system needed to be reformed into an Islamic system, and that homosexuality needed treatment, was not to be tolerated and that homosexuals should be put to death for a "public display of lewdness". See: Dabrowska, Karen, 'British Islamic Party spreads its wings', *New Straits Times* (Malaysia) 16 November 1989, via <https://news.google.co.uk/newspapers?id=TbY-TAAAAIBAJ&sjid=K5ADAAAAIBAJ&pg=6294,6124&hl=en> and 'Question Forum: Islamic View On Homosexuality', *Islamic Party of Britain* 9 March 2002 via <http://www.mustaqim.co.uk/ipb-archive/question/ans41.htm>. Birmingham MP Khalid Mahmood called for Naseem's resignation after he suggested the July 7 London bombings were a Government conspiracy. See: 'Chairman of Birmingham Central Mosque should quit over 7/7 bombings row says MP', *Birmingham Mail* 5 July 2009, via <http://www.birmingham-mail.co.uk/news/local-news/chairman-of-birmingham-central-mosque-should-241309>.

understand this marriage. It makes no sense", says Naseem, who is leading the panel. Amra Bone, at that time the only female qadi in the United Kingdom, agrees with him. "The husband hasn't taken the Islamic conception of marriage where man and wife are garments of each other. They have to take care of each other". They laugh a bit: "Some men just like to dominate". They call the woman back in. Mohammad Naseem tells her the marriage will be dissolved, as this is not the Koranic definition of marriage. The council will give her an official document and after three menstrual cycles she will be free. "He has the right to see his children, of course".

Other women come in, one after another. One woman got religiously married so that her Pakistani husband could get a visa to come and live in the United Kingdom. When the visa application failed, he used her for money. Now she is £4,000 in debt and she has not seen him since her wedding day. She is granted a divorce as well.

A 27-year-old woman comes in and tells the panel she has been married for five years, the last four years of which have consisted of physical and emotional abuse. One night, the abuse was so bad an ambulance had to come for her and the police arrested him. When he returned home, she went to a refuge where she stayed for seven months. When he is drunk he also beats their son. Now she wants a divorce. The council invited him to come to give him the opportunity to speak. He didn't want to come, but he did say there has never been violence and that he wants to reconcile the marriage. "If he would beg you to come back, would you?", Amra Bone asks the woman. The wife is not interested. "This is a fairly straightforward case", the female qadi continues, "In Islam, marriage is about love and affection, and having a responsibility towards each other". Yet, the husband retains access to his children, as Bone says: "In Islam, a man has a right to see his children". (Later she will say that they do not decide on custody.) The marriage is dissolved: she receives a document and is told that she has to wait three menstrual cycles and then she is free to find another husband.

Lastly, a woman comes in who wants a religious divorce from her Pakistani husband. The first year of the marriage, when she was twenty years old, everything was fine. Then her two sisters-in-law and mother-in-law, who all lived under the same roof in Pakistan, started beating her severely and abuse her emotionally. One day, her mother-in-law pushed her and her sister-in-law rammed her head against the marble floor. The staff was fired and the woman became the household drudge, having to cook and clean for the family. It was a very controlling family, she explains. The ingredients for the meals she was to prepare were kept in a fridge in the mother's bedroom. Every time she had to go to her mother-in-law and had to ask for those ingredients. The mother-in-law made her son beat his wife, too. She asked to leave the house, but her husband refused. She barely ate and did not do anything anymore. She returned to the United Kingdom. Here she is a full-time chemical engineer. She is never going back to Pakistan. The panel confer and award her a divorce. She asks whether this Sharia council's divorce certificate is valid for a Pakistani civil divorce.

It is not, she is told. As Naseem says: "In the United Kingdom this decision is only valid under Islamic law". Bone says: Some people will and some people will not accept our ruling.

The Birmingham Central Mosque stance, I was told, is that marriage requires mutual love, trust and consent: "In Islam you live in happiness. Religion is for ease, not for hardship", Amra Bone said. Divorce procedures here take about 2-3 months, which is a relatively fast procedure. They do not wait for the husband to respond.

I told them about the Islamic Sharia Council case where the qadi told a couple that kaffirs cannot rule on Islamic matters and that the woman's civil divorce means nothing under Islam. They seemed to be appalled. "We totally disagree. We cannot have two laws. This is totally wrong. We live as British citizens and accept the law of the land".

Their position is, as I was told, that they live as British citizens and accept the law of the land, that religious law can work with the civil courts on the basis that the law of the land is supreme. They believe in fast procedures, as "the Koran has made *talaq* and *khul* easy on purpose. Sharia has made very easy grounds for marriage and divorce. [...] Islam is not intrinsically discriminatory against women".[131]

Yet, that is the question. Some people, including qadi Amra Bone, argue that Sharia councils actually help women by releasing them from a situation of marital captivity when their husbands are unwilling to cooperate with a religious divorce. In reality it is shown that women succumb to community pressure and go to a Sharia council, where they have to accept unfair decisions. Or, as Professor of Law Shaheen Sardar Ali labels it, "their very existence [...] pressurises women to use such forums to obtain 'acceptance' from their families and communities".[132]

Although the Birmingham council does give out *faskhs* in a faster and easier manner than the London-based Islamic Sharia Council does, that has not settled the discriminatory nature of Sharia councils in general. Women still have to pay a large sum of money for their divorce request, especially considering they often lack sufficient means. This is all the more the case as their husbands (as I have heard most women testify at Sharia council hearings) have plummeted them into debt. Moreover, all Sharia councils condone violence against women. Especially the Islamic Sharia Council, which actively detracts women from seeking outside help or police protection.[133] The Birmingham Sharia Council passively ignores the fact that women are victims of (severe) physical abuse. Both councils are not the least bit concerned when women are in abusive domestic situations, even when there

---

131 This conversation took place on 1 July 2013 in between hearings at the Birmingham Central Mosques' Sharia Council.

132 Ali, Shaheen Sardar, 'Authority and Authenticity: Sharia Councils, Muslim Women's Rights, and the English Courts', *Child and Family Law Quarterly* 2013, pp. 113-137 (113).

133 See on victims of violence being detracted from seeking police protection also: Wilson, Robin Fretwell, 'The Overlooked Costs of Religious Deference', *Washington and Lee Law Review* 2007, pp. 1363-1383 (1375-1376).

are children involved. Victims are not advised, and sometimes even discouraged, from filing a police complaint against violent spouses. This is exacerbated by the fact that some applicants may lack knowledge of the English language and legal system, and their rights. Even more, there is evidence for the fact that refusal to settle a family dispute in a Sharia council can amount to threats and intimidation, being excommunicated and labelled an unbeliever, which is potentially dangerous.[134] Moreover, the councils make custody claims, although this is denied in public.

Besides these insurmountable problems, of which the scope differs per council and depends on those religious authorities pulling the strings, there is another prohibitive objection to positively evaluating the possibilities of Sharia councils. And that is that, ultimately, deference to these councils places religious authorities in the position to move women away from the national legal system, under which they are free to enter and exit relationships at will.

MARITAL CAPTIVITY

Sharia councils are thus mainly concerned with women requesting religious divorces. Islamic marriages are not registered and not recognised by British laws. One could think: why get a religious divorce in the first case? Why not just separate from your husband and leave it at that? Why is it important to get a religious divorce apart from a civil divorce (if there also was a civil marriage)?

Khola Hasan (daughter of Shaykh Suhaib Hasan), who was qadi in training when I spoke to her in 2013, told me that women want a religious divorce because their community expects them to get one, regardless of a civil divorce – if there ever was a civil marriage at all. Otherwise, members of the community will ostracise the women. It must be understood that in some Muslim communities, a secular divorce does not suffice when the religious marriage is not formally dissolved. Muslim women, who turn to Sharia councils for divorce, do so as a consequence of the shared conviction within the religious community that there is a distinct system of Muslim family law, to which these women feel compelled to abide by.[135] When a woman is still considered married under Islamic law, but no longer under civil law (or never had a civil marriage), one speaks of "marital captivity" or "limping marriages".[136] Women can get a civil divorce in a court, but for an Islamic religious divorce they require the cooperation of the husband or a cleric functioning as judge.

---

134 'Sharia Law in Britain: A Threat to One Law for All and Equal Rights', Published by One Law for All, June 2010.

135 Shah-Kazemi 2001, p. 5.

136 The term "marital captivity" is my translation of "huwelijkse gevangenschap", which I first used in a blog for the Leiden Law Blog. See: 'Femmes for Freedom: fighting against marital captivity', 14 June 2012, via <http://leidenlawblog.nl/articles/femmes-for-freedom-fighting-against-marital-captivity>. The term

The Dutch non-governmental organisation Femmes for Freedom specifically supports women trapped in marital captivity and lobbies for legislation against husbands leaving their wives in such a situation.[137] The issue can present itself in two forms: either women face the law of their religion – mainly Islamic and Jewish law, but also Catholic and Hindu – or religious family law of their country of origin, for instance, Pakistani law. Pakistan, like many other Islamic states, does not recognise Western civil divorces. In that case, a religious divorce needs to be registered under Pakistani law. The same goes for most Islamic countries.[138]

Being ostracised by one's community is one problem, but perhaps not the worst. As Femmes for Freedom states:

> As long as the wife is tied to her religious marriage, she lacks independence and is hampered in her participation in society. She may become socially isolated and will not be able to start a new relationship. If she does start a new relationship without having obtained, for example, an Islamic divorce, she will be considered an adulterous women in most Islamic cultures and countries.[139]

Other than the shame that a community brings upon a non-divorced yet separated woman, she is never really free from her husband, who remains entitled to sexual intercourse under Sharia, which can be a form of Sharia sanctioned rape. She cannot remarry as she is still married to her husband. There is the threat of having one's children abducted by their father. If she was to return to their country of origin, the woman can expect legal penalties under an Islamic criminal code.

An example of the problematic nature of marital captivity is the following: an Iranian woman is divorced under British law, but does not have an Islamic divorce. The Islamic Republic of Iran does not recognise her as divorced. Without her husband's consent, she cannot have her Iranian passport renewed. If her (ex-)husband abducts her children by taking them to Iran, she will probably never see them again. She is not able to travel without her husband's permission. And, if she chooses to start a new relationship or remarry, and she does manage to travel to Iran to see her children, she will be prosecuted for adultery for which the Iranian authorities award the death penalty.[140] As her (ex-) husband is

---

"limping marriages" is, for instance, used by Pearl, David and Menski, Werner, *Muslim Family Law*, London: Sweet & Maxwell 1998, p. 34.

137 See: <www.femmesforfreedom.com>.

138 The recognition of civil divorces under civil regimes between EU Member States is addressed in Brussels II Regulation (EC) No 2201/2003. There are no such agreements with the majority of Islamic states, which do not recognise, EU civil divorces.

139 <http://www.femmesforfreedom.com/english/>.

140 Musa, Shirin, 'Shariaraad houdt vrouwen gevangen in hun huwelijk' (Sharia council keeps women trapped inside their marriage), *NRC Handelsblad* 12 July 2012.

unwilling to cooperate with the religious divorce, this situation could continue for her entire life.

Muslim women who are still considered married, can either stay alone for the rest of their lives or may start a new relationship, but they risk grave consequences in countries where adultery is considered a crime. With the husband being in control of the woman's future, it "[...] leaves women vulnerable to extortion, manipulation and abuse. Women who live in marital captivity are trapped for long periods of time, even decades, in a state of limbo and unable to rebuild their lives".[141] As the husband is able to marry up to four wives, he can easily continue his life without consequences.

The need to obtain a religious divorce next to a civil divorce can be pressing. One Dutch-Pakistani woman told me she did not particularly feel the need to get an Islamic divorce next to her Dutch civil divorce. However, her parents who lived in Pakistan told her that the villagers threatened to set her parents' house on fire – with them in it – if she was to continue her life without a religious divorce.[142]

From one perspective, it can be argued that Sharia councils actually provide a solution for the problem of marital captivity. For, if a husband frustrates the divorce or is entirely absent, a qadi can pronounce the divorce nonetheless, thereby releasing the woman from marriage. This is a different approach to a multiculturalist one. A multiculturalist focuses on a "need" stemming from a "religious identity", experienced as "member of a community". The pragmatic approach to releasing women from a – not seldom abusive – marriage obviously does not have the romantic connotation of accommodating Sharia to fulfil the spiritual needs of a religious minority. Countering the multiculturalist narrative, Pragna Patel, director of non-profit organisation Southall Black Sisters and a founding member of Women Against Fundamentalism, speaks about the "fallacious construction of the needs of communities". She says: "religion is a private matter, a personal thing, what we do or how we pray and all that is our private matter. What we don't want is religion institution-alised in the provision of services, including legal services, because that is when your rights are violated".[143] This is particularly relevant. Sharia councils are not advisory institutions where co-religionists find each other in mutual faith. Sharia councils are constituting, fuelling and maintaining a parallel legal order that has real consequences for individuals.

In a toxic mix of religious fundamentalism, culture and tight-knit communities, Sharia councils uphold the theory and practice of the stronghold men have over women. Sharia councils may "help" women who want a divorce, but it is a solution to a problem that they fuel and one that they seek to preserve. Moreover, that religious divorces are Sharia councils' "core business" does not in the least bit mean that they are actually *willing* to

---

141 <http://www.femmesforfreedom.com/english/>.
142 Private interview with anonymous woman.
143 Interview with Pragna Patel, London, 25 June 2013.

help women obtain one. In fact, they are known to frustrate women in their requests, especially if the husband is unwilling to cooperate.

Sharia Councils and Human Rights

Unfortunately, in the spirit of Williams and Phillips, it is widely accepted in academic circles to state that Sharia is diverse and flexible, and it is also common to simply do away altogether with "negative" analyses which might reveal there is an inherent conflict between Sharia and individual rights as acknowledged in Western secular legal systems.

Are Sharia councils and human rights compatible? That depends on who you ask. The European Court of Human Rights says they are not, as I show below. Yet, multiculturalists have two choices when answering this question. A first option is simply stating that Sharia councils *should* operate within the boundaries of human rights, viz. not violate notions of sex equality (how this is to be done is never specified). I label this the "wishful thinking" option. A second strand of reasoning is that, since "Sharia cannot be defined" – in the way secular laws can be clearly defined – and its norms are "ever-changing" it is not possible to have a meaningful debate on the compatibility of Sharia and human rights.[144]

Take for instance this acceptance of the idea that Sharia law is not a concrete entity:

> From this it is clear that there is no exact answer as to the compatibility of sharia with human rights standards, nor is it possible to make an assessment of the precise treatment of women – sharia is flexible and can be adapted and developed along with the demands of modern society. While this is positive in that it goes against the presumption of sharia being archaic and sexist, it also means that it is difficult to regulate application of Islamic norms, as there is no uniform and defined body of 'accepted' laws.[145]

---

144 See, for instance, Lester, Shonda, 'The State and the Operation of Sharia councils in the United Kingdom A Critical Response to Machteld Zee', *Journal of Religion and Society* 2015, pp. 1-9 (3). A response to Lester is: Zee, Machteld, 'The State and the Operation of Sharia Councils in the United Kingdom: A Response to Shonda Lester', *Journal of Religion & Society* 2015, pp. 1-6. Also, Dutch Arabist Maurits Berger states that it is "[...] almost impossible to give definitions or general overviews of 'Islamic values' that European Muslims adhere to, since these values have been developing into a numerous forms of Islam, ranging from liberal and integrated to ultra-orthodox and isolationist interpretations of Islam". See: Berger, Maurits, 'The Third Wave: Islamisation of Europe, or Europanization of Islam?', *Journal of Muslims in Europe* 2013, pp. 115-136 (129).

145 See: Brechin, Jessie, 'A Study of the Use of Sharia Law in Religious Arbitration in the United Kingdom and the Concerns That This Raises for Human Rights', *Ecclesiastical Law Journal* 2013, pp. 293-315 (297-298); See also: Rehman, Javaid, 'Islam, "War on Terror" and the Future of Muslim Minorities in the United Kingdom: Dilemmas of Multiculturalism', *Human Rights Quarterly* 2007, pp. 831-878 (838), and Rehman, Javaid, 'The Sharia, Islamic Family Laws and International Human Rights Law: Examining the Theory and Practice of Polygamy and Talaq', *International Journal of Law, Policy and the Family* 2007, pp. 108-127:

Yet, is it not clear from the fact that British Sharia councils do manage to function, that at least Islamic judges themselves have no problem finding their way through "the forest of vagueness" every time they decide upon a case? Islamists in general have no trouble making decisions on how to treat people based on Sharia. This simple argument in itself makes it possible to say that, yes, there are diverse interpretations, but the core of Islamic family law is readily understandable and enforceable. It is perfectly possible to study and evaluate the practice of Sharia councils in the United Kingdom, despite diversity of Islamic laws and practices.

Rightfully so, there is growing concern over the development of a 'quasi-legal' system, which functions contrary to the principle of equality before the law, and which is eroding the United Kingdom's commitment to the eradication of discrimination. I laid out the *theory* on the grounds for Islamic divorce, which itself is discriminatory towards women. And the *practice* in Sharia councils confirms that.

Several reports confirm the experiences I have had at the Islamic Sharia council in London and the Sharia council hosted by the Birmingham Central Mosque. These Sharia institutions, according to the framers of the reports, are not merely offering a helping hand in granting women their religious divorces they so desperately seek in order to overcome the issue of marital captivity. Sharia councils operate outside their legal boundaries, where faith-based discrimination is institutionalised and women's dependence on Sharia and affiliated institutions is deepened by means of pressure and (the threat of) violence enforced upon them.

Regarding discrimination on grounds of sex, the most basic and fundamental issue is that it is by far mostly *women* who seek Sharia council services. This simple and basic finding deserves special attention. Men are not dependent on Sharia council rulings. As British Professor of Law Shaheen Sardar Ali states:

> If, being allowed to practise Islam in a non-Muslim jurisdiction is a matter of freedom of religion and minority rights, Muslim men and women ought to be equally keen to access such forums [...].[146]

That it is mainly women needing the service should raise concern in itself. Sharia family law consists of inherently discriminatory rules. It has become clear that the rules of the game are fundamentally more difficult for women than they are for men: something Islamists define as "justice" emanating from biological sex differences. Also, sexual obedi-

---

"[...] the hastiness in the condemnation of historic Islamic principles fails to take account of the contextual, and flexible nature of the Sharia and the rules of Islamic family law" (p. 114).
146 Ali 2013, p. 130.

ence in marriage is not questioned by qadis. Marital violence is accepted as ground for divorce, rather than a ground to start an intensive community campaign against it.

Lastly, Sharia councils exist so that Islamic fundamentalists can promote their ideology whilst at the same time making money by letting women buy their freedom.[147] A freedom not seldom denied, if husbands are set on remaining married – religiously – to their wives.[148] It should not come as a surprise that Muslim women "[…] remain extremely cautious of initiatives to accommodate sharia into English law", as British researcher Samia Bano is convinced.[149] Needless to say, the multiculturalist romantic view of the need Muslims have for Sharia is off beat.

Proponents of recognition of Sharia councils, such as Williams and Phillips, and many academics, are aware that Islamic laws can and do conflict with sex equality as codified in secular laws and treaties. But as multiculturalists, they simultaneously believe equality between Muslim minorities and the "indigenous" majority can be achieved by abandoning the universal nature of British laws. That means that Muslims should be able to resort to their "own" laws, but at the same time, this may not infringe upon sex equality. This is a condition set in most contributions to this particular debate: Sharia, yes, on the condition it is not discriminatory. Yet, it is never attempted to stipulate *how* this can be done. It is important to point this out. The problem multiculturalists ultimately have is that it is not possible.[150] Sharia is fundamentally discriminatory towards non-Muslims and women – as was also made clear in the previous chapter – while secular laws and human rights regimes explicitly denounce unlawful discrimination on grounds of sex and religion. Besides, multiculturalists overlook the fact that even in Islamic countries or countries with a majority of Muslims, there is a constant tussle to (re)define laws under the influence of competing religious fundamentalists and secularists.

These and other problems were dealt with by the European Court of Human Rights (ECtHR) in the well-known *Refah v. Turkey* case (2001). The ECtHR concurred with the decision by the Turkish constitutional court to ban the Refah Partisi ('Welfare Party').[151]

---

147 See also: Schwartz, Stephen and al-Alawi, Irfan, 'Our Survey shows British Muslims don't want sharia', *The Spectator* 9 July 2008: "The sharia divorce courts are in the hands of radicals who use them to promote extremist ideology while making money". Via <http://www.spectator.co.uk/features/825601/our-survey-shows-british-muslims-dont-want-sharia/>.

148 See, for instance, the testimony of "Sara" in: Cox, Caroline, 'A Parallel World. Confronting the abuse of many Muslim women in Britain today', *The Bow Group* 2015, p. 16.

149 Bano 2008, p. 309.

150 See also: Manea 2012: "[I]t is simply not possible to introduce Islamic law in family domain without violating human rights." Israeli law professor Frances Raday (1944) makes the argument that even in the hypothetical case that there be symmetry between religious and liberal values, then still this does not justify the accommodation and support for religious values. The outcome of symmetry, would logically and at the most lead to stalemate and not deference to religious values. (Raday, Frances, 'Secular Constitutionalism Vindicated', *Cardozo Law Review* 2008, pp. 2770-2798 (2773).)

151 *Refah Partisi (the Welfare Party) and Others v. Turkey*, (App nos 41340/98, 41342/98, 41343/98 and 41344/98), ECtHR 2001.

Refah operated in breach of Turkey's constitution, which stated that no political party may act counter to the state's secularist principle. *Refah*, an Islamist political party which expected to achieve a large number of votes at the coming election, aimed to establish a plurality of legal systems, in order to enable Sharia to function for the Islamic part of the population. The party stated that this proposed plurality actually intended to promote freedom to enter into contracts and the freedom to choose which court should have jurisdiction. However, Turkey's secular principle entailed the notion that it considered the rules of Sharia incompatible with the democratic regime, as Sharia does not comply with the democratic foundation of equality between citizens before the law.[152] The ECtHR explicitly denounced the possibility of a societal model that enables legal pluralism[153]:

> Firstly, it would do away with the State's role as the guarantor of individual rights and freedoms and the impartial organiser of the practice of the various beliefs and religions in a democratic society, since it would oblige individuals to obey, not rules laid down by the State in the exercise of its above-mentioned functions, but static rules of law imposed by the religion concerned. But the State has a positive obligation to ensure that everyone within its jurisdiction enjoys in full, and without being able to waive them, the rights and freedoms guaranteed by the Convention. [...] Secondly, such a system would undeniably infringe the principle of non-discrimination between individuals as regards their enjoyment of public freedoms, which is one of the fundamental principles of democracy. A difference in treatment between individuals in all fields of public and private law according to their religion or beliefs manifestly cannot be justified under the Convention, and more particularly Article 14 thereof, which prohibits discrimination. Such a difference in treatment cannot maintain a fair balance between, on the one hand, the claims of certain religious groups who wish to be governed by their own rules and on the other the interest of society as a whole, which must be based on peace and on tolerance between the various religions and beliefs.[154]

The ECtHR subscribed to the view that Sharia in itself is incompatible with the fundamental principles of democracy and human rights – ironically, a view Islamists agree with – as conceived in the Convention:

---

152 *Refah Partisi (the Welfare Party) and Others v. Turkey*, § 19-25.
153 See on Refah and legal pluralism also: Macklem, Patrick, 'Militant Democracy, Legal Pluralism, and the Paradox of Self-determination', *International Journal of Constitutional Law* 2006, pp. 488-516.
154 *Refah Partisi (the Welfare Party) and Others v. Turkey*, § 119.

It is difficult to declare one's respect for democracy and human rights while at
the same time supporting a regime based on sharia, which clearly diverges from
Convention values, particularly with regard to its criminal law and criminal
procedure, its rules on the legal status of women and the way it intervenes in
all spheres of private and public life in accordance with religious precepts.[155]

It was thus not *merely* legal pluralism that was problematic in itself, but the fact that *Sharia*
would function as the content of an autonomous, separate, legal system, that drove the
conclusion of the ECtHR. Citizens have religious freedom, including the right to manifest
religion by worship and observance. However, the Court reiterated that freedom is "primarily a matter of individual conscience which is quite different from the field of private
law, which concerns the organization and functioning of society as a whole."[156]

Yet, at the same time, multiculturalists in the United Kingdom defend the freedom to
choose to resort to Islamic law for Muslim minorities. Muslims should thus have the option
to choose jurisdictions, as the proponents argue. In general, those who favour accommodation of Sharia councils hold freedom of religion to be foundational to their position,
and find suspicions of intra-group discrimination remedied by its presupposed voluntary
nature. When it comes down to the degree to which Muslims may enact and enforce a
sub-legal system that is fundamentally at odds with the human rights framework of the
law of the land, multiculturalists suddenly start to question whether those involved do so
out of a sense of identity. However, this judgement shows the European Court understands
very well the importance of distinguishing between private religious convictions and the
Islamist desire to institutionalise religious laws for a minority of Muslims in the West.
From the argument developed in Refah, it is clear that all the considerations that the Court
presents are applicable in other legal orders that subscribe to the principles developed in
the Convention. If Sharia law contradicts the provisions of the Convention in Turkey, it
also contradicts the Convention in Italy, France or the United Kingdom. Two years after
the *Refah* ruling, the ECtHR confirmed its views on the incompatibility between democracy
and Sharia in the case of *Gündüz v. Turkey*.[157]

One could argue that the discussion about Sharia councils in the United Kingdom is
different from a ruling against a political party that wants to have Sharia officially instituted.
However, even if the demands of religious groups are mitigated in the sense that it should
be "merely" restricted to family matters, then the tension with democratic values is still
present. From the Refah case, as well as the discussion in the previous chapter, we can state
that Sharia encapsulates a theocratic state model. Even in a moderated form, such as

---

155 *Refah Partisi (the Welfare Party) and Others v. Turkey*, § 123.
156 *Refah Partisi (the Welfare Party) and Others v. Turkey*, § 128.
157 *Gündüz v. Turkey*, (Application no. 35071/97), ECTHR 4 December 2003, § 51.

informal Sharia councils, religious leaders have a position of leadership in religious communities whereby they exert tremendous power over individuals who happen to be pulled into a societal subsystem. As judges, fundamentalist leaders rule over the lives of people who depend on them without the possibility of redress or there being any form of accountability. It is difficult to harmonise this religious legal regime within the democratic structure.[158] Or, as British scholar Rumy Hasan states:

> Importantly, the establishment of even a minimal Sharia jurisdiction will enormously increase the power of the mullahs and imams, who will then inevitably push for more exemptions to the law, and more Sharia laws and courts. Moreover, it will give the green light for religious leaders of other 'faith communities' to push for their own separate legal jurisdictions, a vista that cannot at all be appealing to anyone seeking a more just, unified, cohesive society.[159]

Moreover, the idea against informal Islamic private law receives legal backing by the UN Convention on the Elimination of All Forms of Discrimination Against Women (CEDAW), which the United Kingdom ratified in 1966. CEDAW's *ratio legis* is to remedy the tension between religious freedoms and sex equality. States that have ratified the Convention are required to enshrine sex equality into their domestic legislation and enact new provisions to guard against discrimination against women. Professor of Law Frances Raday states that CEDAW creates a clear hierarchy of values by giving superior force to sex equality when there is a clash between customs and cultural norms, including religious norms.[160] Also, under Article 2 (c) of CEDAW, State parties agree by all appropriate means to "establish legal protection of the rights of women on an equal basis with men and to ensure through competent national tribunals and other public institutions the effective protection of women against any act of discrimination".

In fact, in 2013, the United Nations Committee on the Elimination of Discrimination against Women issued a general recommendation on Article 16 of CEDAW – which deals with discrimination against women at the inception of, and during, marriage and at its dissolution by divorce or death. The Committee recommended that all Member States adopt legislation to eliminate the discriminatory aspects of family law regimes, whether they are regulated by civil code, religious law, ethnic custom or any combination of laws

---

158 See also on this Cliteur, Paul and Rijpkema, Bastiaan, 'The Foundations of Militant Democracy', in Ellian, Afshin and Molier, Gelijn (eds.), *The State of Exception and Militant Democracy in a Time of Terror*, Dordrecht: Republic of Letters Publishing 2012, pp. 227-273 (264).

159 Hasan 2010, p. 253.

160 See on the intersection of culture, religion, and gender in the context of international and constitutional human rights law: Raday, Frances, 'Culture, Religion, and Gender', *International Journal of Constitutional Law* 2003, pp. 663-715 (678) and Raday 2008, p. 2779.

and practices. This thus also includes Sharia. Moreover, the Committee expressed "concern that identity-based personal status laws and customs perpetuate discrimination against women and that the preservation of multiple legal systems is in itself discriminatory against women".[161] From this point of view, it is bitter to see that Turkey has prohibited the unilateral divorce (talaq) by men under its secular civil code, while in the United Kingdom, multiculturalists are paying tribute to a system that embraces this religious construction.[162]

Sharia councils pose several problems. Firstly, it represents an encroaching influence of Islamism in Europe. Secondly, it is a problem that that expression of Islamism comes in an institutionalised form of legal pluralism. Thirdly, it is a problem that this pluralism does not entail, for instance, rivalry between two equally good systems, but rivalry between, on the one hand, a secular democratic system that sets out to protect the rights of members of (religious) minorities and women just like it does for every other citizen, and on the other hand, a system of Islamic laws that is clearly incompatible with freedom and equality. Muslim women who are part of tight-knit communities do not have the freedom and equal choice to decide to live their lives with or without marriage. This problem is a part of (sometimes tribal) group cultures, and exacerbated by Sharia councils. Sharia law is designed and intended to restrict and remove freedoms. But is that unique for *Muslim* women?

BATEI DIN: JEWISH COUNCILS

Multiculturalists assert that equality also means that, like Jewish and Catholic minorities, Muslim minorities may resort to their own institutionalised councils. Hindus also have informal religious councils. Is it indeed unfair to deny Muslims access to Sharia councils if other religious minorities have tribunals of their own?

Like the Muslim Arbitration Tribunal, the London-based United Synagogue offers faith-based arbitration as under the Arbitration Act. Yet, like Sharia councils, the problem lies in family law, specifically in divorce proceedings.

In 1857, the UK parliament passed the Matrimonial Causes Act, which reformed the law on divorce, moving litigation from the jurisdiction of the ecclesiastical courts to the civil courts.[163] In addition, amongst Christian believers, a civil divorce suffices when ending

---

161 "General recommendation on Article 16 of the convention on the elimination of all forms of discrimination against women", via <http://www2.ohchr.org/english/bodies/cedaw/docs/comments/CEDAW-C-52-WP-1_en.pdf>.

162 Otto, Jan Michiel (ed.), *A Comparative Overview of the Legal Systems of Twelve Muslim Countries in Past and Present*, Leiden: Leiden University Press, p. 631.

163 See on the Rota (Roman Catholic councils), Douglas, Gillian *et al.*, *Social Cohesion and Civil Law: Marriage, Divorce and Religious Courts* 2011, pp. 29-32, via <http://www.law.cf.ac.uk/clr/Social%20Cohesion%20and%20Civil%20Law%20Full%20Report.pdf>.

a marriage contract. When Lord Phillips and Archbishop Williams referred to other religious tribunals, the Jewish courts are more analogous to Sharia councils. Just like the Sharia divorce regime, in the Jewish tradition a civil divorce decree does not dissolve the religious marriage.

According to Jewish law, marriage is a contract of ownership, where the husband (ba'al in Hebrew, which means owner) 'acquires' his wife. Jewish law mandates both spouses' consent in a religious divorce. The termination of a Jewish marriage is executed by a writ of divorce (the get), delivered by the husband to his wife, out of his own free will.[164] The wife merely needs to accept the get. After 92 days, she can remarry. The Beth Din acts as a witness to this process of mutual consent and the writing of the get for the divorce to be lawful under Jewish law. Without a get, a Jewish woman cannot remarry under Jewish law and she is condemned as an adulteress if she has sexual relations with other men. In addition, if those relations lead to children, these offspring are branded *mamzerim* – a stigma that lasts for nine generations. A *mamzer* is prohibited from marrying any Jew other than another *mamzer* and is thus barred from marrying freely within the Jewish community. This prospect of being unable to remarry and jeopardising not only herself but her children, too, is devastating to observant Jewish women. If unable to divorce due to an unwilling or disappeared husband, a woman can be trapped in a "dead marriage" for years (or perhaps her whole life), and is labelled *agunah*, a "chained woman". She is left in marital captivity. However, a non-divorced man may cohabit with other women without the stigma of adultery, nor are his children born out of those relations considered mamzerim.[165]

Like Muslim women, Jewish women often find themselves at a disadvantage in the religious divorce process. Unlike Sharia councils, where a qadi can issue a divorce in the absence of a husband, it is not possible for a Jewish woman to obtain a get without her husband's cooperation (at least, not according to classis interpretations). In that vein, a Beth Din does not function as a 'court'; it is a witness to the dissolution of the marriage. The Islamic *faskh* thus offers a possibility for Muslim women to obtain a divorce from an absent or uncooperative husband, which Jewish women do not have. A Jewish husband, on the other hand, can frustrate the divorce even in cases of domestic abuse without a Beth Din being able to step in.[166]

In order for Jewish women not to be pressured to agree to unfair financial or (informal) custodial demands in order to obtain the get under the supervision of male-dominated

164 Westreich, Avishalom, 'The Right to Divorce in Jewish Law: Between Politics and Ideology', *International Journal of the Jurisprudence of the Family* 2010, pp. 177-196 (177).

165 Zornberg, Lisa, 'Beyond the Constitution: Is the New York Get Legislation Good Law?' *Pace Law Review* 1995, pp. 703-784 (703-704).

166 See also: Cares, Alison and Cusick, Gretchen, 'Risks and Opportunities of Faith and Culture: The Case of Abused Jewish Women', *Journal of Family Violence* 2012, pp. 427-435 (428).

Batei Din, the United Kingdom passed the Divorce (Religious Marriages) Act in 2002. This Act aims to remedy the unbalanced bargaining power of the husband. If a Jewish couple requests a divorce from a civil court, the civil judge can withhold the final legal civil dissolution of a marriage "until a declaration made by both parties that they have taken such steps as are required to dissolve the marriage in accordance with those usages". This means that the civil divorce will not be finalised until the woman has received the get.[167] Interestingly, the 2002 Act explicitly mentions the 'usages of the Jews', and 'any other prescribed religious usages'. 'Prescribed' means that any other religious group may subject itself to the Act by asking the Lord Chancellor to prescribe the religious group for that purpose. Yet, no application has been received from any Islamic group requesting such recognition.[168] It must be added that this 2002 Act is successful within the Jewish community, as almost all Jewish citizens have a civil marriage combined with a religious marriage, which is unfortunately not the case in the British Islamic community. This also means that despite the similarities between Jewish and Islamic tribunals, both carry on institutionalising marital captivity and upholding discriminatory religious laws. There are (legal) differences. These relate both to religious family law regarding the competence of the councils, and regarding British secular law which recognises 'Jewish usages'.

Another important difference is that, unlike Jewish women, Muslim women face grave penalties when they enter a new relationship if their previous religious marriage is not dissolved. There is honour violence involved, as well as the fact that Sharia attaches the death penalty to adulteresses. This can be carried out in the form of honour-based violence, or as a punishment under state law, for instance, in Pakistan and Saudi Arabia.[169] Violent family members are a problem cross-culture and religion. However, as American Emerita Professor of Psychology Phyllis Chesler (1940) states, the specific planning of murdering often young women is typical of Islam-rooted communities. Moreover, major religious and political leaders in developing Muslim countries keep silent and it is mostly Islamic communities that maintain an enforced silence on all matters of religious, cultural, or

---

167 Comparable to the 1983 New York Get Law, see: Broyde, Michael, 'New York's Regulation of Jewish Marriage. Covenant, Contract, or Statute?', pp. 138-163 (153), in: Nichols, Joel (ed.), *Marriage and Divorce in a Multicultural Context: Multi-tiered Marriage and the Boundaries of Civil Law and Religion*, Cambridge: Cambridge University Press 2011.

168 Hunt, Phillip, 'House of Lords (Written Answers): Justice: Sharia Law' Hansard 3 March 2008, Column WA154.

169 The Crown Prosecution Service states: "Honour based violence (HBV) can be described as a collection of practices, which are used to control behaviour within families or other social groups to protect perceived cultural and religious beliefs and/or honour. Such violence can occur when perpetrators perceive that a relative has shamed the family and/or community by breaking their honour code."See lemma 'Honour Based Violence and Forced Marriage' via <http://www.cps.gov.uk/legal/h_to_k/honour_based_violence_and_forced_marriage/#a04) See also the documentary: "Banaz: A Love Story" (2012), by Deeyah Khan>.

communal "sensitivity", thereby perpetuating violence.[170] The aspect of (life-threatening) violence gives Islamic, thus other than Jewish, marital captivity an even more problematic dimension.

Regarding Jewish courts, the state has made legislation in order to provide women with some leverage when husbands do not want to cooperate with a religious divorce. From interviews with rabbinic judges it was clear that it works in practice: women have been able to obtain the get more easily since the Divorce (Religious Marriages) Act. That means that there is a fundamental difference between the legal relationship between the UK and Jewish courts, where there is formal recognition of the Jewish practices regarding family law and state intervention; and the UK and Sharia councils, which have not received any formal recognition, nor are they the subject of state intervention. What these two systems do have in common, though, is that they function based on a system that is inherently discriminatory towards women. Their religious laws are the foundation of a system keeping women stuck in a situation of marital captivity. Religious leaders are not keen on reform. Furthermore, both Muslim as well as Jewish men are known to stall religious divorce and use their power to blackmail women to negotiate favourable financial and custodial settlements in the civil procedure.[171]

Religious tribunals calling upon divine laws concur with this system and support community convictions involving shame and honour that keep marital captivity alive as an issue. Different from a tolerant (denounce yet accept) or intolerant (denounce and intervene) position, multiculturalists support the system of women being dependent on religious councils and their husbands, based on a romanticised view on communal values. Yet, the romantic vision multiculturalists have regarding the possibility for Jewish and Muslim minorities to have access to their own laws is off beat.

THE ARBITRATION AND MEDIATION SERVICES (EQUALITY) BILL

There is an additional problem that marks another difference between Jewish women and Muslim women. That is, Jewish women – apart from a tiny minority – generally also have a civil marriage, and therefore the Divorce (Religious Marriages) Act actually works as a lever.[172] However, only about ten per cent of the United Kingdom's mosques are registered to conduct civil ceremonies under the 1949 Marriage Act.[173] It is believed that a high percentage of Muslim marriages are religious only, not civil. A further problem is that the

---

170 See: Chesler 2010, pp. 3-11.
171 Hamilton, Carolyn, *Family, Law and Religion*, London: Sweet and Maxwell 1995, pp. 118-120.
172 Interview with dayanim at the London Federation of Synagogues, London 18 November 2013.
173 See: Kuric, Lejla, 'Britain's sharia councils and secular alternatives', *Leftfootforward.co.uk* 2014, via <https://leftfootforward.org/2014/04/britains-sharia-councils-and-secular-alternatives/>.

criminal offence of performing a marriage ceremony that is not registered under the Marriage Act 1949 is not enforced.[174] This cements the false belief that the nikah (Islamic marriage contract) is registered under domestic law.[175] It is also problematic that – unlike Jewish women – Muslim women often have relatively little knowledge of the British legal system and are unaware of their rights.[176] It is this that the bill seeks to address.

In 2012, 4 years after the Archbishop and the Lord Chief Justice delivered their speeches, the Arbitration and Mediation Services (Equality) Bill was discussed in the House of Lords. The bill's aim is to prevent discrimination against Muslim women and "jurisdiction creep" in Islamic courts.[177] It addresses the concern that some Sharia councils apply Sharia principles that go well beyond their legal remit, such as dealing with criminal law (for example, pressure being placed on women to withdraw allegations of domestic violence) or family law; that some Sharia council rulings are being misrepresented as having the force of UK law; that some Muslim women are being coerced into agreeing to arbitration or mediation which ought to be voluntary; and that some proceedings of Sharia councils are discriminatory against Muslim women.

The bill does not aim to interfere in the internal theological affairs of religious groups, as the report 'A Parallel World. Confronting the abuse of many Muslim women in Britain today' states.[178] The report is drafted by a member of the House of Lords, Baroness Caroline Cox (1937), who initiated the bill. This aim is in line with the European Court of Human Rights' approach to Sharia. The bill explicitly makes it clear that sex discrimination law applies directly to 'Arbitration Tribunal' proceedings: the bill proposes to amend the Arbitration Act (1996) by stating that discriminatory rulings can be struck down under the bill. It also creates a new criminal offence of 'falsely claiming legal jurisdiction' under the Courts and Legal Services Act 1990. The maximum penalty would be seven years in prison.[179] In addition, the Equality Act would be amended so as to impose a statutory duty

---

174 As under Section 75, see also: Addison, Neil, 'Lady Cox's bill is not so controversial', *The Guardian* 23 June 2011.

175 Proudman, Charlotte, 'A practical and legal analysis of Islamic marriage, divorce and dowry', *Family Law Week* 31 January 2012, via <http://www.familylawweek.co.uk/site.aspx?i=ed95364>.

176 In June 2014 Justice Minister Simon Hughes told the House of Commons: "The Government is committed to the protection and promotion of the rights of women, families and children. This includes raising awareness of the legal consequences of 'religious only' marriages and encouraging mosques to register in order to be able to carry out legally recognised marriages in their various facilities." See: 'Muslim 'wives' discover that they have no marriage rights', *Family Law Week* 11 December 2014, via <http://www.family-lawweek.co.uk/site.aspx?i=ed137790>. See also Jaan, Habiba, 'Equal and Free? 50 Muslim Women's Experiences of Marriage in Britain Today', Aurat Research Report 2014, via <https://www.secular-ism.org.uk/uploads/aurat-report-dec2014.pdf>.

177 See, for instance, 'Bill limiting sharia law is motivated by 'concern for Muslim women'', *The Guardian*, 8 June 2011. The Bill was announced in 2011, and debated in the House of Lords in 2012.

178 See: Cox 2015.

179 The Bill extends to England and Wales only. See: Arbitration and Mediation Services (Equality) Bill [HL] 2012-13).

on public institutions, such as the police, social workers, and health care personnel, to inform women they come into contact with about the rights they have under domestic laws.[180]

If this bill were passed, the opponents of Williams' and Phillips' plea in favour of Sharia councils would have clearly established that the state stands firm on its position regarding sex equality and the law: no state court may enforce an arbitration award that is discriminatory towards women. It also creates a positive equality duty on public bodies, which need to actively inform women of their rights, and Sharia councils would need to make explicit to their applicants that they have no jurisdiction whatsoever.

This addresses for instance the practices of the Muslim Arbitration Tribunal. The MAT – at least formally – functions in a different way to other Sharia councils in the sense that they perform Islamic divorces as well, but they claim their main focus is on arbitrating financial disputes under the Arbitration Act. For example, the MAT adjudicated on an inheritance dispute between three sisters and two brothers. In accordance with Sharia law principles, the men were given double the inheritance of the women.[181]

The bill is a laudable goal to curtail Sharia councils. Nonetheless, the question is whether the bill also addresses Sharia councils in their essence. The bill aims to restrict the (discriminatory) practices of Sharia councils under the Arbitration Act. However, I question whether it will sort effect in practice. The *raison d'être* of Sharia councils is one-party divorce requests, with either an absent husband or one frustrating the process (and thus disagreeing with the procedure as such). It would only count as arbitration if there was a married couple giving decision-making power to an independent arbiter (which is not the case). A second step would be, hypothetically, if one of the parties is unsatisfied with the outcome and decides to go to a secular court to strike down the arbitration award based on the amended Arbitration Act. This is even more unlikely considering the repercussions that would follow from challenging a "divine ruling".

Sharia councils do not arbitrate – with the exception of the Muslim Arbitration Tribunal. In general, they are divorce councils. Their products are registered *talaqs*, *khuls*, and *faskhs*, they are not arbitration awards considering a decision on a dispute between two parties. Therefore, the Arbitration and Mediation Services (Equality) bill misses the mark for the largest part.

There is one important exception to this. Barrister Charlotte Proudman (1988), who has represented many women during their divorce procedures at Sharia councils, explained

---

180 Duffet, Rebecca, 'Baroness Caroline Cox and the Sharia Bill', *Cross Rythms* June 30 2011, via <http://www.crossrhythms.co.uk/articles/life/Baroness_Caroline_Cox_And_The_Sharia_Bill/43747/p1/>

181 Cox 2015, p. 6. The new MAT website addresses concerns regarding sex discrimination. It now says it offers: A platform through which women are included as part of the expert panel and ensure that there is no bias within the organisation against genders. The active role of women professionals provides a sense of support and guidance for the client and also offers re-assurance that the sensitivity of the matter is appreciated, see <http://www.matribunal.com/why-MAT.php>. There is no updated research on the MAT's practice.

to me how the creation of the criminal offence could be effective.[182] The biggest improvement would be in the elimination of illegitimate custody rulings. Proudman has experience with clients who have been made to surrender custody of their children to their (sometimes abusive) husbands based on Sharia council rulings, although the councils formally deny this. These women did not know that custody rulings were the sole remit of secular courts. When these women finally learned about their rights, they would go to a secular judge to seek custody of their children after this had been denied by qadis. However, as is custom in many secular legal systems, the secular judge would turn down this request based on the ground that the children had been accustomed to the situation of living with their father and that disruption to a child's life should be kept to a minimum.[183] It is at this point that the proposed criminal offence for falsely claiming legal jurisdiction may actually work. Charges could be pressed against the qadi(s) ruling on custody. If the criminal court were to convict the qadi(s), this could have a positive effect on restricting the *de facto* remit of Sharia councils.[184] General and special prevention could benefit the wellbeing of children and restrict the effects of the inherent sex discrimination of these councils.

The Islamic Sharia Council responded to the bill. It is believed that the deficiency of the bill lies in "its failure to appreciate cultural sensitivities". Suhaib Hasan argued that the bill "made no attempt to understand the workings of the shariah councils", and that "it [was] morally wrong to comment on [the issue of the testimony of a woman being half of that of a man] without any knowledge of [it]". He also stated that Baroness Cox merely "regurgitated common myths about the role of women in Islam in an effort to undermine the work of the shariah councils", and that "she deserves little praise" for doing so.[185]

SECULAR ALTERNATIVES TO SHARIA COUNCILS

Valuable as this bill could actually be in keeping the public debate on religious tribunals going, it unfortunately does not address the problems arising from the fact that for at least a part of the British Muslim community, Sharia law is inevitable when dealing with issues regarding marriage and divorce.

Rather than, for instance, outlawing Sharia councils, it is very important to study alternatives for women who seek religious divorce, be it Jewish, Muslim or whatever religious denomination. Is it possible to keep women independent from religious authorities

---

182 Interview with Charlotte Proudman, London, 18 June 2013.

183 See also: 'Multiculturalism and Child Protection in Britain: Sharia Law and Other Failures' Published by One Law for All, June 2013, via <http://www.onelawforall.org.uk/wp-content/uploads/Multiculturalism-and-Child-Protection-in-Britain.pdf>.

184 The same goes for Batei Din, yet it is very unlikely that Jewish women in Britain think a Beth Din holds formal jurisdictional powers.

185 See: Maret 2013, p. 276.

yet at the same time be able to resolve the issue of uncooperative husbands who leave the women in marital captivity?

I believe this approach is better than to wrongly refer to arbitration, and remaining vague about Sharia and the fact that "it should not frustrate women's rights"; yet leave the question *how* that should be organised unanswered. The United Kingdom could consider the following legal alternatives.

The Netherlands has two secular alternatives for women who have been put into a situation of marital captivity by their husbands. The first important alternative to Sharia councils was established by the Dutch-Pakistani Shirin Musa in 2010. After years of failed attempts to get her husband to cooperate with the religious divorce, she took the civil route: the judge imposed damages upon the husband for each day of non-compliance with the court's ruling that he had to release her from the religious marriage. He instantly did. The Dutch civil court established that it was important for women to carry on with their lives, including remarriage, and not have to face penalties in Islamic countries, often the woman's country of origin.[186]

After her religious divorce – for which Musa principally refused to go to a Sharia council – Musa founded Femmes for Freedom. This NGO sets out to help, financially and otherwise, women of all denominations in marital captivity. In 2013, Femmes for Freedom successfully lobbied to extend the law against forced marriage to include marital captivity – being forced to *remain* married – as a criminal offence (in case of complaint).[187] According to Musa, after years of marital captivity, a woman finally pressed charges, which caused her husband to immediately cooperate with a religious divorce. If the United Kingdom were to create this criminal offence as well, British Muslim women who are refused a religious divorce could not only press charges against their uncooperative husbands, but potentially also against the qadi. The qadi could be held accountable for acting as an accessory to marital captivity. Religious authority holders who have the power to pronounce divorce yet refuse to do so could thus be held criminally liable.

Moreover, rather than the woman not being able to travel to her country of origin in fear of being prosecuted, it is now the husband who risks prosecution in secular states for the crime of leaving his wife in a state of marital captivity.

---

186 See: Rechtbank Rotterdam, 08-12-2010, 364739 / KG ZA 10-1018; ("Vordering tot medewerking aan ontbinding van het religieuze huwelijk na echtscheiding naar Nederlands recht toewijsbaar. Door zijn weigering daaraan mee te werken houdt de man de vrouw gevangen in wat zij ervaart als een religieus huwelijk. De man gedraagt zich aldus in strijd met hetgeen volgens ongeschreven regels in het maatschappelijk verkeer van hem kan worden gevergd".) See also: Rechtbank Amsterdam 22 May 2014, case number/rolnummer: c/13/563478 / KG ZA 14-495 HJ/NRSB; Rechtbank Den Haag 11 January 2013, case number/rolnummer 431258/KG ZA 12-1273.

187 Under Article 284 of the Dutch Criminal Code. See for the amendment: *Kamerstukken II* 2012/13, 32840, 8.

This basically means that if Muslim women were to resort to secular courts to make their husbands cooperate, they would no longer be dependent on religious tribunals for their religious divorces.

Unfortunately, these Dutch secular alternatives do not solve the problem of *absent* husbands and marital captivity. In the case of Jewish law, for instance, there are no ways out of the religious marriage when the husband is untraceable.

There are interpretations of Sharia where marriage to an absent husband after a certain period automatically constitutes a "divine divorce". That is, for an automatic religious divorce, no Sharia councils are needed. More fundamentalist interpretations, however, state that there always needs to be a *talaq* or a qadi ruling on divorce.[188] If important state actors, such as an archbishop and the most senior judge call for the accommodation of Sharia as a basis for "dispute settlement", the fundamentalist interpretation is favoured. A greater recognition of Sharia councils means a greater acceptance of the unofficial regime of marital captivity. When multiculturalists and Islamic fundamentalists call for the recognition of Sharia councils, women's dependence on these institutions is deepened, and the secularisation process of fundamentalist Sharia rules is weakened.

The (potentially grave) consequences of a woman continuing with her life – for instance, remarrying without a religious divorce, possibly causing shame or violating "honour" – ultimately depend on family members, (ex-)in-laws, and tribe and/or community members. This means that for many Muslim women with missing husbands, the reality is that some will turn to Sharia councils in search of freedom.

It will take immense global community reform, education, secularisation, laws and enforcement, (police) protection, and emancipation to counter this social, cultural and religious problem of marital captivity and honour based violence. Only the future can tell how this develops. Surely, promoting the institutionalisation of Sharia councils – run by Islamists, backed by multiculturalists – will halt this development. As Yemeni-Swiss political scientist Elham Manea writes:

> In fact, these voices are actually calling for the legitimisation of systematic dis-crimination against women and children. And such discrimination will certainly not help any successful integration of migrants' communities of Islamic faith. Indeed, it will only lead to the cementation of closed parallel societies, with two types of women, Western women who enjoy their rights according to the state's laws, and migrants' women who do not.[189]

---

188 '11681: Does leaving one's wife for a long time count as divorce?', *Islam Question and Answer*. Quoting the Saudi Grand Mufti Bin Baz: "So long as the husband has not uttered the word of divorce to her, and the wife has not gone to the qaadi to seek a divorce, then divorce has not taken place. She is still his wife and divorce does not take place automatically". <http://islamqa.info/en/11681>.

189 Elham 2012.

CONCLUSION

While downplaying the problems faced by individuals under the increasing influence of Islamism, former Archbishop Williams and Lord Chief Justice Phillips made statements about Sharia as embodying "universal principles". These high-profile public figures argued that Sharia could and should be accommodated for the sake of equality and in light of the need to recognise Muslim identity, a discourse also adopted by Islamic fundamentalists.

Contemporary multiculturalism incorporates the need for (some degree of) legal autonomy for "communities". Since it is religious codes that provide such laws, multiculturalists, like fundamentalists, place religion in the core of one's identity. Multiculturalists believe that such accommodation is possible within the (legal) norms of the host society.

Multiculturalists do not want a Sharia state, but what they *do* want is vague, remains unaddressed, and is mostly limited to emphasising a communal need for shared values and rejecting what is deemed a "too negative" focus on Sharia. Clarity is key to any debate. The vagueness of what Sharia should hold for British society has the result that people postpone their negative judgement whilst hoping that it can't be all that bad. This is how multiculturalists create space. This space is readily consumed by fundamentalists who claim Muslims are entitled to Sharia, like multiculturalists argue as well.

The lack of functional content in multiculturalists' claims should be met with caution. Islamic fundamentalists, such as the leaders behind the Islamic Sharia Council, are influential. They reach a wide audience of susceptible Muslims in Britain and beyond its borders, and are pursuing more Sharia in the United Kingdom and elsewhere in Europe. The frequent plea that Sharia should be allowed as long as it does not conflict with equal rights is wishful thinking at best and perilous at worst. It detracts from the truth: that Sharia is a competing body of laws on British territory, and that these laws are hostile towards non-Muslims and towards women, to say the least. Moreover, Sharia is incompatible with democracy: a conviction shared by secularists, Islamists, and the European Court of Human Rights.

The well-meant mitigation that it is merely Islamic *family* law that requires recognition is, other than multiculturalists – also in academic circles – believe, not a modest demand. Wherever Islamists gain political power, it is Islamic family law that is pushed to the top of the agenda. Sharia councils are not institutions where Islamic individuals go to whenever they experience an identity-driven need for a psychological commitment to their community. Instead they are revived anachronisms cementing women's secondary and dependent position.

Unfortunately, some women actually do depend on these councils if their husbands are set on keeping them in a situation of marital captivity. Rather than cementing the continuance of this international problem of marital captivity, for instance, by espousing false and romantic notions of community cohesion and religious needs, the United Kingdom would do well to offer its citizens secular alternatives to Sharia councils. The Netherlands offers women who are kept in marital captivity the possibility of pressuring husbands into cooperation by means of civil and criminal liability. Future litigation will tell whether this will release Muslims from the pressure of being ruled by Islamic laws at a larger scale.

Concluding Remarks

This book revolved around the question what the implications are of the political ideologies of multiculturalism and Islamic fundamentalism, and, more in particular, what the interaction is between these ideologies when it comes to the debate on the legitimacy of Sharia councils in the United Kingdom.

The rhetoric of multiculturalists and fundamentalists combined results in a reactionary movement with religious identity politics at its core. Multiculturalists promote the ideology that members of minorities value community membership and that this is constitutive of their identity. This minority cultural identity should not be harmed by nonrecognition in order to avoid psychological harm. The focus should be on either respect or toleration, and that minority cultures must not be criticised by the dominant majority which has the obligation to preserve these minority cultures. Preservation is achieved by calling for accommodation of a Muslim minority legal order that stands apart from the host society's. Islamic fundamentalists undermine and re-order the secular and democratic character of European nation-states.

Like multiculturalists, they want Islamic communities to be able to live under Sharia. Multiculturalists aim to do so out of a presumably well-meant gesture towards minorities, whereas fundamentalists do so driven by divine command.

Multiculturalist sensitivities still detract many from studying the underlying foundations of Islamist ideology. There is a wide range of Islamist ideologies and movements, but there are significant commonalities among fundamentalists. They believe in the imposition of Islamic laws, also called Sharia. The core of this Islamic fundamentalism is a theologically justified political goal of saving and purifying society by means of establishing a Sharia state in which the Umma – all Muslims worldwide – is unified. This Sharia state can be achieved by means of terror, by a political takeover, or by a bottom-up approach. In the West, the aim is to form disciplined diasporic communities ruled by these laws.

It needs to be acknowledged that Islamic fundamentalism exists, that it is increasingly present, and that it is something that deserves to be rejected. Especially as Islamic fundamentalism is increasingly gaining ground among European Muslims.

Since the 1980s, in the United Kingdom, Islamic family law has been informally institutionalised in the form of Sharia councils. These councils falsely operate under the flag of mediation and arbitration.

Contemporary multiculturalists advocate the position that accommodation of these councils is possible within the (legal) norms of the host society – either by stating that unacceptable parts of Sharia "have nothing to do with Islam", which is not true, or that parts of Sharia should not clash with human rights, which is not possible – particularly with regard to family law.

Both political ideologies challenge the state's sovereignty when it comes to laws for Muslim minorities in the West. In doing so, they cooperate closely in achieving, *de facto*, fewer rights for individuals, regardless of the amount of time spent on claiming otherwise.

The multiculturalist argument trades on a simple idea: namely, that "[...] being able to choose what to believe and how to live [...] makes for a better life. Being told what you must believe and how you must live, conversely, make lives worse".[1] It remains unconvincing why the "liberty of free choice" for Islamic fundamentalism in the form of Sharia councils should go uncontested. Moreover, the multiculturalist ideology aims to support emancipation and integration. It misses the mark. Multiculturalism as an ideology is not merely theoretically questionable, but also practically. For: if Muslim fundamentalists in Europe seek to enhance the goal of *more* fundamentalist Sharia for *more* Muslims through preaching and ideology, the multiculturalist ideology of not judging Muslim identity is nurturing just that.

The development of increasing Islamic fundamentalism worries many across the globe, and rightfully so. This development imparts the task of clear moral judgement on governments, (academic) elites, and citizens. Multiculturalism with its focus on identity, not wanting to "cause offence", and its resort to relativism to rectify that what is wrong, is still an important force in the Western debate on Islamic fundamentalism. That is why it is important to take a critical stance towards both multiculturalism and Islamic fundamentalism.

It is right that fundamentalists *choose* to live under Sharia. Yet, multiculturalists tend to overlook the fact that they may tend to increasingly choose for that, if not challenged adequately. Moreover, if in the future the better part of society has voluntarily chosen for Islamic fundamentalism, we will see that free choice will cease to exist, as is more than ever the case in countries where Islamisation has gained territory. Or, in other words, the reason men and women in the West have the luxury of debating in terms of "free choice" is precisely because they live in a liberal society that is committed to protecting freedom.[2]

Coming at the end of this book it may be useful to position the view on Sharia councils as developed in this book against the broader background of five constitutional models on the relationship between state and religion.

Generally speaking, a state can deal with religion, religious believers, and religious communities in five ways. Firstly, there is the ambition to radically destroy every influence

---

1   Leiter 2008, p. 7-8.
2   See also: Dunlap, Bridgette, 'Protecting the Space to Be Unveiled: Why France's Full Veil Ban Does Not Violate the European Convention on Human Rights', *Fordham International Law Journal* 2011, pp. 968-1026 (1025).

of religion in the social and political sphere. This model was popular in the Soviet Union between 1917 and 1989. This may be called "political atheism". It is mirrored by the equally radical approach to force one specific religion upon all others. This may be called "theocracy", a political interpretation of religious fundamentalism. The second chapter of this book is dedicated to the Islamist brand of religious fundamentalism.

Next to political atheism and theocracy, there is the model of a state church. This commonly implies an orientation on one specific religion to which the state has contributed a special task in politics without making overriding infringements on the rights of others. This is the model of a state church. Needless to say, compared to the other two models, the model of a state church is the least objectionable. But also this alternative is far from satisfactory.[3] The model of a state church is based on an inherently unequal treatment of all citizens – only those who happen to adhere to the state religion are represented.

The remaining two models are multiculturalism and political agnosticism. Multiculturalism is extensively described and analysed in the first chapter of this book, while political agnosticism is implicitly defended in all three chapters. The idea of political agnosticism is that the state should principally defend neutrality towards the religious choices of its citizens. The state is literally "agnostic" ("it does not know" in the sense of "it does not *want* to know") what its citizens believe with respect to religion. That also means the state has no positive or negative opinions or policies towards religious communities. However, still, it is one of the state's core duties to develop and maintain a cohesive legal order that has similar consequences for all of its citizens alike, regardless of cultural or religious liaisons. Pushing for, or allowing, minority legal orders conflicts with the state's neutrality regarding religion. Within the multiculturalist and Middle Way Islamic fundamentalist doctrine there is space for independent and conflicting legal orders within state borders. Yet, it is the politically agnostic state that aspires to maintain one law for all.

We may call this position *political* agnosticism because it describes the attitude of the state and not the attitude of the individual. The notion of "agnosticism" arose within the context of the religious choices of the human individual.[4] An individual who considers him- or herself "agnostic" means that he or she does not make a choice between various religious options. The reasons for this may vary. One of the reasons often advanced by agnostics is that the arguments for the existence of God are not better but also not weaker than the arguments against the existence of God.[5] Individual agnosticism usually tries to steer a middle course between atheism on the one hand and theism on the other.

---

3   Although not rejected by the European Court in Strasbourg. See: *Lautsi v. Italy*, (Application no. 30814/06), ECtHR 3 November 2009 and *Lautsi and others v. Italy*, (Application no. 30814/06), ECtHR 18 March 2011.

4   See: Cliteur, Paul, 'Atheism, Agnosticism, and Theism', pp. 14-68, in: Cliteur 2010, pp. 14-69.

5   See also: Poidevin, Robin Le, *Agnosticism. A Very Short Introduction*, Oxford: Oxford University Press 2010 and Vernon, Mark, *How To Be An Agnostic*, Houndmills: Palgrave MacMillan 2011.

Beyond this specific agnostic stance regarding not being able to know whether there is a deity, the state should not decide whether individuals are better off (or not) as members of religious communities. Thus, for instance, regarding pleas on behalf of accommodating assumed needs of minority religious cultures, the state has no opinion on whether adherence to a religion or membership of a religious community is either worthy of respect and should be nurtured, or that it is something that should be loosened and considered detrimental for personal development.

Whatever may be true about individual agnosticism, for the *state* this suspension of judgement seems a perfectly sensible course to take. Especially in a pluralist society the state can best adopt a religiously neutral attitude, as we have seen in the elaborate analysis of the dangers of religious fundamentalism or problems of encouraging and wanting to preserve minority cultures under multiculturalism.

Modern-day multiculturalists steer towards accommodating a minority legal order for religious minorities. Pleas of this sort are supported by religious fundamentalists, who also believe minorities should be ruled over by an independent body of religious laws. One of the most important consequences of political agnosticism was the focus of this book: the necessity to stick to a monocultural legal order, regardless of, or better put, *especially* in a culturally and religiously diverse society.

Bibliography

'1st Oic Observatory Report on Islamophobia May 2007 To May 2008', via <http://www.oic-oci.org/uploads/file/Islamphobia/islamphobia_rep_may_07_08.pdf>.

'2008 Update: Saudi Arabia's Curriculum of Intolerance. With Excerpts of Saudi Ministry of Education Textbooks for Islamic Studies', Center for Religious Freedom of Hudson Institute with Gulf Institute 2008, via <http://www.hudson.org/content/researchattachments/attachment/656/saudi_textbooks_final.pdf>.

'40% of British Muslims want Sharia Law', ICM poll 20 February 2006, via <ukpollingreport.co.uk/blog/archives/146>.

'40% of young UK Muslims want sharia law', Poll by UK think tank Policy Exchange 31 January 2007, via <www.wnd.com/2007/01/39942/>.

'A look at the writings of Saudi blogger Raif Badawi – sentenced to 1,000 lashes', *The Guardian* 14 January 2015, via <http://www.theguardian.com/world/2015/jan/14/-sp-saudi-blogger-extracts-raif-badawi>.

'Abused women battle Saudi injustice', *Financial Times* 14 October 2006, via <http://www.ft.com/intl/cms/s/0/d9ee5a5a-d7b0-11df-b478-00144feabdc0.html#axzz3Q1TFiDV9>.

'Archbishop on Radio 4 World at One - UK law needs to find accommodation with religious law codes', 7 February 2008, via <http://rowanwilliams.archbishopofcanterbury.org/articles.php/707/archbishop-on-radio-4-uk-law-needs to find accommodation-with-religious-law-codes>.

'Backlash over call for Sharia', *Birmingham Mail* 8 February 2008.

'Bill limiting sharia law is motivated by "concern for Muslim women"', *The Guardian* 8 June 2011.

'Britain's underage Muslim marriage epidemic', *Gatestone Institute* 15 October 2013, via <http://www.gatestoneinstitute.org/4017/uk-muslim-underage-marriage>.

'Cameron steps into Sharia law row', *news.bbc.co.uk* 26 February 2008.

'Chairman of Birmingham Central Mosque should quit over 7/7 bombings row says MP', *Birmingham Mail* 5 July 2009, via <http://www.birminghammail.co.uk/news/local-news/chairman-of-birmingham-central-mosque-should-241309>.

'Controversial Muslim cleric banned from Britain', *The Guardian* 7 February 2008.

'Council of Islamic Ideology declares women's existence anti-Islamic', *Pakistan Today* 15 March 2014, via <http://www.pakistantoday.com.pk/2014/03/15/comment/coucil-of-islamic-ideology-declares-womens-existence-anti-islamic/>.

'Equal and Free? Evidence in support of Baroness Cox's Arbitration and Mediation Services (Equality) Bill', researched and drafted by Charlotte Rachael Proudman 2012.

'Five Reasons To Ban the Burqa', *Frontpage Mag* 11 July 2011, via <http://www.front-pagemag.com/2011/dgreenfield/five-reasons-to-ban-the-burqa/>.

'General recommendation on article 16 of the convention on the elimination of all forms of discrimination against women', via <http://www2.ohchr.org/english/bodies/cedaw/docs/comments/CEDAW-C-52-WP-1_en.pdf>.

'Growing Islamic fundamentalism seen pushing Malays to quit country', *Malay Mail Online* 30 October 2014, via <http://www.themalaymailonline.com/malaysia/article/growing-islamic-fundamentalism-seen-pushing-malays-to-quit-country#sthash.TD5Jb1f0.dpuf>.

'Happy clappy Rowan repents in Sharia storm', *Daily Mail*, 12 February 2008.

'I will fight Islamic authorities till the end, vows Kassim Ahmad', *The Malaysian Insider* 18 January 2015, via <http://www.themalaysianinsider.com/malaysia/article/i-will-fight-islamic-authorities-till-the-end-vows-kassim-ahmad>.

'In full: Rowan Williams interview', *bbc.co.uk* 11 February 2008, via <http://news.bbc.co.uk/2/hi/uk_news/7239283.stm>.

'In the name of the law', *The Guardian* 14 June 2007, via <http://www.the-guardian.com/world/2007/jun/14/religion.news>.

'Islamic sharia courts in Britain are now "legally binding"', *Daily Mail Online* 15 September 2008, via <http://www.dailymail.co.uk/news/article-1055764/Islamic-sharia-courts-Britain-legally-binding.html>.

'Just How Moderate is Iqbal Sacranie?', *MCBWatch* 4 August 2005, via <http://mcb-watch.blogspot.co.uk/2005/08/just-how-moderate-is-iqbal-sacranie.html>.

'Kweekschool van het kalifaat' (Breeding Ground for the Caliphate), *NRC Handelsblad* 28 March 2015.

'Leading Sunni Sheikh Yousef Al-Qaradhawi and Other Sheikhs Herald the Coming Conquest of Rome', MEMRI Special Dispatch Series No. 447, 6 December 2002, via <http://www.memri.org/bin/articles.cgi? Area=sd&ID=SP44702>.

'Moderate Malaysia has so many fatwas there's a website to keep track of them', *Global Post* 5 January 2015, via <http://www.globalpost.com/dispatch/news/regions/asia-pacific/141222/moderate-malaysia-has-so-many-fatwas-there-s-website-keep->.

'Multiculturalism "a big failure": Spain's ex-prime minister Aznar', 27 October 2006, via <http://www.freerepublic.com/focus/f-news/1726950/posts>.

'Multiculturalism and Child Protection in Britain: Sharia Law and Other Failures' Published by One Law for All, June 2013, via <http://www.onelawforall.org.uk/wp-content/uploads/Multiculturalism-and-Child-Protection-in-Britain.pdf>.

'Multiculturalism has failed, says French president', *Daily Motion* 11 February 2011 <http://www.dailymotion.com/video/xgzqs8_Multiculturalism-has-failed-says-french-president_news>.

'Muslim gangs enforce Sharia law in London', *Gatestone Institute* 25 January 2013, via <http://www.gatestoneinstitute.org/3555/sharia-law-london>.

'Muslim "wives" discover that they have no marriage rights', *Family Law Week* 11 December 2014, via <http://www.familylawweek.co.uk/site.aspx?i=ed137790>.

'Nikah Halala – Sharia divorce law that demands the wife to sleep with another man', *The Muslim Issue* 2 November 2014, via <https://themuslimissue.word-press.com/2014/11/02/crazy-islam-nikah-halala-sharia-divorce-law-that-demands-the-wife-to-sleep-with-another-man/>.

'Our survey shows British Muslims don't want sharia', *The Spectator*, 12 July, 2008.

'Pleidooi voor sharia-raad' (Plea for a Sharia council), *nos.nl* 11 June 2012, via <http://nos.nl/artikel/382618-pleidooi-voor-shariaraad.html>.

'Radicals who spread message of brutality, hate and intolerance', *The Times* 13 May 2013, via <http://www.thetimes.co.uk/tto/faith/article3763189.ece>.

'Raif Badawi: Saudi blogger is spared public flogging for a second week', *The Independent* 23 January 2015, via <http://www.independent.co.uk/news/world/middle-east/saudi-blogger-raif-badawi-is-spared-public-flogging-for-a-second-week-9997804.html>.

'Rape in marriage is no crime says cleric', *Daily Express* 15 October 2010, via <http://www.express.co.uk/news/uk/205474/Rape-in-marriage-is-no-crime-says-cleric>.

'Reaction in quotes: Sharia law row', *news.bbc.co.uk*, 8 February 2008.

'Recognising the Un-recognised: Inter-Country Cases and Muslim Marriages & Divorces in Britain', published by Women Living Under Muslim Laws in 2006.

'Rise of strict Islam exposes tensions in Malaysia', *bbb.co.uk* 26 August 2011, via <http://www.bbc.co.uk/news/world-radio-and-tv-14649841>.

'Rushdie in hiding after Ayatollah's death threat', *The Guardian* 18 February 1989, via <http://www.theguardian.com/books/1989/feb/18/fiction.salmanrushdie>.

'Saudi Arabia: Five beheaded and "crucified" amid "disturbing" rise in executions', *Amnesty.org* 21 May 2013, via <http://www.amnesty.org/en/news/saudi-arabia-five-beheaded-and-crucified-amid-disturbing-rise-executions-2013-05-21>.

'Saudi Arabia: Men 'Behaving Like Women' Face Flogging', *Human Rights Watch* 7 April 2005, via <http://www.hrw.org/news/2005/04/06/saudi-arabia-men-behaving-women-face-flogging>.

'Saudi human rights activist in prison for "annoying others"', *The National* 20 July 2010, via <http://www.thenational.ae/news/world/middle-east/saudi-human-rights-activist-in-prison-for-annoying-others>.

'Saudi Publications on Hate Ideology Invade American Mosques', Center for Religious Freedom, New York: Freedom House 2005.

'Schweigen, Fragen, unerwünschtes Lob. Ruud Koopmans über die Reaktionen auf seine Fundamentalismus-Studie', *WZB Mitteilungen* 2014, pp. 53-55.

'Sharia council: same pitch, same rules', Webmagazine Maastricht University 30 October 2012, via <http://webmagazine.maastrichtuniversity.nl/index.php/research/society/item/357-sharia-council-same-pitch-same-rules>.

'Sharia Law in Britain: A Threat to One Law for All and Equal Rights', Published by One Law for All, June 2010.

'Sharia law not welcome here, says PM Brown', *Birmingham Post* 9 February 2008.

'Sharia law row: Archbishop is in shock as he faces demands to quit and criticism from Lord Carey', *London Evening Standard* 7 February 2008.

'Sharia law UK: Mail on Sunday gets exclusive access to a British Muslim court', *Daily Mail Online* 4 July 2009, via <http://www.dailymail.co.uk/news/article-1197478/Sharia-law-UK--How-Islam-dispensing-justice-side-British-courts.html#ixzz3ZMpBmrBz>.

'Sheikh Qaradawi's First Interview with Onislam.net', *OnIslam.net* 18 October 2010, via <http://www.onislam.net/english/shariah/contemporary-issues/interviews-reviews-and-events/449388-sheikh-qaradawis-first-interview-with-onislamnet.html?Events=>.

'The Beth Din: Jewish law in the UK', *The Centre for Social Cohesion* 2009.

'The British child brides: Muslim mosque leaders agree to marry girl of 12… so long as parents don't tell anyone' *Dailymail.co.uk* 9 September 2012, via <http://www.dailymail.co.uk/news/article-2200555/The-British-child-brides-Muslim-mosque-leaders-agree-marry-girl-12--long-parents-dont-tell-anyone.html>.

'The Church should have the guts to sack the Archbishop…and pick a man who truly treasures British values', *Daily Mail* 11 February 2008.

'The Global Terrorism Index 2014' report by The Institute for Economics and Peace (IEP), via <http://www.visionofhumanity.org/sites/default/files/Global%20Terrorism%20Index%20Report%202014_0.pdf>.

'The Kingdom in the Closet', *The Atlantic* 1 May 2007, via <http://www.theatlantic.com/magazine/archive/2007/05/the-kingdom-in-the-closet/305774/>.

'We want to offer sharia law to Britain', *The Telegraph* 20 January 2014, via <http://www.telegraph.co.uk/news/uknews/1576066/We-want-to-offer-sharia-law-to-Britain.html>.

'Why we should oppose Islamic Sharia courts in Britain', *Liberal Conspiracy* 16 August 2013, via <http://liberalconspiracy.org/2013/08/16/why-we-should-oppose-islamic-sharia-courts-in-britain/>.

'Williams "shocked" at Sharia row', *news.bbc.co.uk* 8 February 2008.

'World Report 2012: Saudi Arabia', *Human Rights Watch*, via <http://www.hrw.org/world-report-2012/world-report-2012-saudi-arabia>.

Abiad, Nisrine, *Sharia, Muslim States And International Human Rights Treaty Obligations: A Comparative Study*, London: British Institute of International and Comparative Law 2008.

Addison, Neil, 'Sharia Tribunals in Britain – Mediators or Arbitrators?', in: MacEoin, Denis and Green, David (eds.), *Sharia Law or 'One Law for All?*, London: Civitas: Institute for the Study of Civil Society 2009.

Addison, Neil, 'Lady Cox's bill is not so controversial', *The Guardian* 23 June 2011.

Ahdar, Rex and Aroney, Nicholas (eds.), *Shari'a in the West*, Oxford: Oxford University Press 2010.

Al-Azm, Sadi Jalal, 'The Importance of Being Earnest about Salman Rushdie', *Die Welt des Islams* 1991, quoted in: Mayer, Ann Elizabeth, 'Universal versus Islamic Human Rights: A Clash of Cultures or Clash with a Construct', *Michigan Journal of International Law* 1994, pp. 307-404.

Ali, Kecia, *Marriage and Slavery in Early Islam*, Cambridge: Harvard University Press 2010.

Ali, Shaheen Sardar, 'Authority and Authenticity: Sharia Councils, Muslim Women's Rights, and the English Courts', *Child and Family Law Quarterly* 2013, pp. 113-137.

An-Na'im, Abdullahi, *Islam and the Secular State: Negotiating the Future of Shari'a*, Cambridge, Massachusetts: Harvard University Press 2008.

Aufderheide, Patricia (ed.), *Beyond PC. Toward a Politics of Understanding*, Minnesota: Graywolf Press 1992.

Bale, Jeffrey, 'Denying the Link between Islamist Ideology and Jihadist Terrorism: "Political Correctness" and the Undermining of Counterterrorism', *Perspectives on Terrorism* 2013, via <http://www.terrorismanalysts.com/pt/index.php/pot/article/view/290/html>.

Bangstad, Sindre, Leirvik, Oddbjorn and Bowen, John, '"Anthropologists are talking", About Islam, Muslims and Law in Contemporary Europe', *Ethnos* 2013, pp. 1-20.

Bano, Samia, 'Muslim Family Justice and Human Rights: The Experience of British Muslim Women', *Journal of Comparative Law* 2007, pp. 45-52.

Bano, Samia, 'In Pursuit of Religious and Legal Diversity: A Response to the Archbishop of Canterbury and the "Sharia Debate" in Britain', *Ecclesiastical Law Journal* 2008, pp. 283-309.

Baron, B., 'Tolerable Intolerance?' Silence on Attacks on Women by Fundamentalists', *Contention* 1996, in: Moghissi, Haideh (ed.), *Feminism and Islamic Fundamentalism. The Limits of Postmodern Analysis*, London and New York: Zed Books 1999.

Barry, Brian, *Culture and Equality: An Egalitarian Critique of Multiculturalism*, Cambridge: Polity Press 2001.

Benn, Piers, 'On Islamophobia-phobia', *New Humanist* 2002, via <https://newhumanist.org.uk/524>.

Bennet, Dashiel, 'Look Who's on Al Qaeda's Most-Wanted List', *The Wire* 1 March, 2013, via <http://www.thewire.com/global/2013/03/al-qaeda-most-wanted-list/62673/>.

Benson, Ophelia and Stangroom, Jeremy, *Does God Hate Women?*, London: Continuum 2009.

Berger, Maurits, 'Juist blokkeren van shariaraad is dom' (Actually, blocking a Sharia council is stupid), *NRC Handelsblad* 15 June 2012.

Berger, Maurits (ed.), *Applying Shari'a in the West. Facts, Fears and the Future of Islamic Rules on Family Relations in the West*, Leiden: Leiden University Press 2013.

Berger, Maurits, 'The Third Wave: Islamisation of Europe, or Europeanization of Islam?', *Journal of Muslims in Europe* 2013, pp. 115-136.

Berlin, Isaiah, *Four Essays on Liberty*, Oxford: Oxford University Press 1975 (1969).

Berlinski, Claire, 'Moderate Muslim watch: How the term "Islamophobia" got shoved down your throat', *Ricochet* 24 November 2010, via <https://ricochet.com/archives/moderate-muslim-watch-how-the-term-islamophobia-got-shoved-down-your-throat/>.

Berman, Paul, *The Flight of the Intellectuals*, New York: Melville House 2010.

Bielefeldt, Heiner, 'Muslim Voices in the Human Rights Debate', *Human Rights Quarterly* 1995, pp. 587-617.

Bin Ladin, Carmen, *Inside the Kingdom: My Life in Saudi Arabia*, New York: Warner Books 2005.

Blum, Lawrence, 'Recognition, Value, and Equality: a Critique of Charles Taylor's and Nancy Fraser's Accounts of Multiculturalism', *Constellations* 1998, pp. 51-68.

Blum, Lawrence, 'Recognition and Multiculturalism in Education', *Journal of Philosophy of Education* 2001, pp. 539-559.

Bodin, Jean, *On Sovereignty. Four Chapters from the Six Books of the Commonwealth.* Edited and translated by Julian H. Franklin, Cambridge: Cambridge University Press 1992.

Bowen, John, 'How Could English Courts recognise Shariah?', *University of St. Thomas Law Journal* 2009-10, pp. 411-435.

Bowen, John, 'Panorama's exposé of sharia councils didn't tell the full story', *The Guardian* 26 April 2013.

Boyd, Marion, 'Religion-Based Alternative Dispute Resolution: A Challenge to Multiculturalism', pp. 465-473, in: Banting, Keith *et al.* (eds.), *Belonging? Diversity, Recognition and Shared Citizenship in Canada*, Montreal: McGill-Queen's University Press 2007.

Brague, Rémy, *The Law of God. The Philosophical History of an Idea*, Chicago: The University of Chicago Press 2007.

Brechin, Jessie, 'A Study of the Use of Sharia Law in Religious Arbitration in the United Kingdom and the Concerns that This Raises for Human Rights', *Ecclesiastical Law Journal* 2013, pp. 293-315.

British Runnymede Trust, 'Islamophobia: A Challenge For Us All', *Commission on British Muslims and Islamophobia* (1997), via <http://www.runnymedetrust.org/uploads/publications/pdfs/islamophobia.pdf>.

Brown, Alexandra, 'Constructions of Islam in the Context of Religious Arbitration: A Consideration of the "Shari'ah Debate" in Ontario, Canada', *Journal of Muslim Minority Affairs* 2010, pp. 343-356.

Brown, Eric, 'After the Ramadan Affair: New Trends in Islamism in the West', *Current Trends in Islamist Ideology* 2005, pp. 7-29.

Browne, Anthony, *The Retreat of Reason. Political Correctness and the Corruption of the Public Debate in Modern Britain*, London: Civitas 2006.

Broyde, Michael, 'New York's Regulation of Jewish Marriage. Covenant, Contract, or Statute?', pp. 138-163, in: Nichols, Joel (ed.), *Marriage and Divorce in a Multicultural Context: Multi-tiered Marriage and the Boundaries of Civil Law and Religion*, Cambridge: Cambridge University Press 2011.

Bruckner, Pascal, *The Tyranny of Guilt*, Princeton: Princeton University Press 2010.

Budziszewski, J., 'Natural Law, Democracy, and Shari'a', pp. 181-206 (183), in: Rex Ahdar and Nicholas Aroney (eds.), *Shari'a in the West*, Oxford: Oxford University Press 2010.

Buruma, Ian, *Murder in Amsterdam*, London: Penguin Books 2006.

Buttner, Friedemann, 'The Fundamentalist Impulse and the Challenge of Modernity', pp. 57-79, in: Stauth, Georg (ed.), *Islam – Motor or Challenge of Modernity. Yearbook of the Sociology of Islam (1)*, Hamburg: Lit Verlag 2008.

Caeiro, Alexandre and Gräf, Bettine, 'The European Council for Fatwa and Research and Yusuf al-Qaradawi', pp. 119-121 (120), in: Peter, Frank and Ortega, Rafael (eds.), *Islamic Movements of Europe*, London: I.B. Tauris 2014.

Caldwell, Christopher, *Reflections on the Revolution in Europe: Can Europe be the Same with Different People in It?*, London: Allen Lane 2009.

Campbell, Andrew, '"Taqiyya": How Islamic Extremists Deceive the West', *National Observer* 2005, pp. 11-23.

Cares, Alison and Cusick, Gretchen, 'Risks and Opportunities of Faith and Culture: The Case of Abused Jewish Women', *Journal of Family Violence* 2012, pp. 427-435.

Cartwright, Richard, 'Some Remarks on Essentialism', *The Journal of Philosophy* 1968, pp. 615-626.

Chaudhry, Ayesha, *Domestic Violence and the Islamic Tradition*, Oxford: Oxford University Press 2013.

Chervel, Thierry and Seeliger, Anja, *Islam in Europa. Eine internationale Debatte*, Frankfurt am Main: Suhrkamp Verlag 2007.

Chesler, Phyllis, *The Death of Feminism*, New York: Palgrave MacMillan 2006.

Chesler, Phyllis, 'Worldwide Trends in Honor Killings', *Middle East Quarterly* Spring 2010, pp. 3-11.

Chesler, Phyllis, *An American Bride in Kabul: A Memoir*, New York: Palgrave Macmillan 2013.

Cliteur, Paul, 'Van etnisch naar kosmopolitisch multiculturalistisme' (From ethnic to cosmopolitan Multiculturalism), pp. 61-76, in: Manen, N.F. van (ed.), *De multiculturele samenleving en het recht* (The Multicultural Society and the Law), Nijmegen: Ars Aequi Libri 2002.

Cliteur, Paul, *Moderne Papoea's – Dilemma's van een Multiculturele Samenleving* (Modern Papuans – Dilemmas of a Multicultural Society), Amsterdam: De Arbeiderspers 2002.

Cliteur, Paul, *The Secular Outlook. In Defense of Moral and Political Secularism*, Chicester: Wiley-Blackwell 2010.

Cliteur, Paul, 'Female Critics of Islamism', *Feminist Theology* 2011, pp. 154-167.

Cliteur, Paul, 'State and Religion Against the Backdrop of Religious Radicalism', *International Journal of Constitutional Law* 2012, pp. 127-152.

Cliteur, Paul and Rijpkema, Bastiaan, 'The Foundations of Militant Democracy', pp. 227-273, in Ellian, Afshin and Molier, Gelijn (eds.), *The State of Exception and Militant Democracy in a Time of Terror*, Dordrecht: Republic of Letters Publishing 2012.

Cohen, Joshua, Howard, Matthew and Nussbaum, Martha (eds.), *Is Multiculturalism Bad For Women?*, Princeton: Princeton University Press 1999.

Cox, Caroline, 'A Parallel World. Confronting the abuse of many Muslim women in Britain today', *The Bow Group* 2015.

Cumper, Peter, 'Multiculturalism, Human Rights and the Accommodation of Sharia Law', *Human Rights Law Review* 2014, pp. 31–57.

Dabrowska, Karen, 'British Islamic Party spreads its wings', *New Straits Times* (Malaysia) 16 November 1989, via <https://news.google.co.uk/newspapers?id=TbY-TAAAAIBAJ&sjid=K5ADAAAAIBAJ&pg=6294,61245&hl=en>.

Dankowitz, Aluma, 'Tariq Ramadan – Reformist or Islamist?', The Middle East Media Research Institute (MEMRI) Inquiry & Analysis Series Report No. 266, 17 February 2006.

Desai, Meghnad, *Rethinking Islamism. The Ideology of the New Terror*, London: I.B. Tauris 2007.

Douglas, Gillian *et al.*, *Social Cohesion and Civil Law: Marriage, Divorce and Religious Courts* 2011, via <http://www.law.cf.ac.uk/clr/Social%20Cohesion%20and%20Civil%20Law%20Full%20Report.pdf>.

Duffet, Rebecca, 'Baroness Caroline Cox and the Sharia Bill', *Cross Rythms* June 30 2011, via <http://www.crossrhythms.co.uk/articles/life/Baroness_Caroline_Cox_And_The_Sharia_Bill/43747/p1/>.

Dunlap, Bridgette, 'Protecting the Space to Be Unveiled: Why France's Full Veil Ban Does Not Violate the European Convention on Human Rights', *Fordham International Law Journal* 2011, pp. 968-1026.

Dyer, Emily, *Marginalising Egyptian Women. The Restriction of Women's Rights Under the Muslim Brotherhood*, London: The Henry Jackson Society 2013.

El Fadl, Khaled Abou, *Speaking in God's Name. Islamic Law, Authority and Women*, Oxford: OneWorld 2010.

Ellian, Afshin, 'Emancipation and Integration of Dutch Muslims in Light of a Process Polarization and the Threat of Political Islam', *Middle East Program Occasional Paper Series Summer* 2009, pp. 15-23.

Ellian, Afshin, 'The Legal Order of Political Religion', pp. 187-232, in: Molier, Gelijn, Ellian, Afshin and Suurland, David (eds.), *Terrorism, Ideology, Law and Policy*, Dordrecht: Republic of Letters 2011.

Ellian, Afshin and Molier, Gelijn (eds.), *Freedom of Speech Under Attack*, The Hague: Eleven International Publishing 2015.

Eltahawy, Mona, 'Why do they hate us?', *Foreign Policy* 23 April 2012.

Engin, Serkan, 'Why we must ban Islam', *The Conservative Papers* 23 March 2015, via <http://conservativepapers.com/news/2015/03/23/why-we-must-ban-islam/#.VRD-mfmsWT8>.

Erikson, Erik, 'The Problem of Ego Identity', *Journal of the American Psychoanalytic Association* 1956, pp. 56-121.

Euben, Roxanne Leslie and Zaman, Muhammad Qasim (eds.), *Princeton Readings in Islamist Thought: Texts and Contexts from al-Banna to Bin Laden*, Princeton: Princeton University Press 2009.

Fairclough, Norman, '"Political Correctness": The Politics of Culture and Language', *Discourse & Society* 2003, pp. 17-28.

Fatah, Tarek. *Chasing a Mirage: The Tragic Illusion of an Islamic State*, Mississauga, Ontario: Wiley & Sons Canada 2008.

Fennema, Meindert, *Van Thomas Jefferson tot Pim Fortuyn. Balans van de Democratie* (From Thomas Jefferson to Pim Fortuyn. Democracy's Balance), Apeldoorn: Spinhuis Uitgevers 2012.

Fourest, Caroline, *Brother Tariq: The Doublespeak of Tariq Ramadan*, New York: Encounter Books 2008.

Fowers, Blaine and Richardson, Frank, 'Why is Multiculturalism Good?', *American Psychologist* 1996, pp. 609-621.

Gaede, Stan, *When Tolerance Is No Virtue*. 'Political Correctness, Multiculturalism & the Future of Truth & Justice', Downers Grove, IL: InterVarsity Press 1993.

Glazer, Nathan, *We Are All Multiculturalists Now*, Cambridge: Harvard University Press 1998.

Gold, Dore, *Hatred's Kingdom: How Saudi Arabia Supports the New Global Terrorism*, Washington, DC: Regnery Publishers 2003.

Grant, Helen, 'Sharia Law' Hansard 23 April 2013, Column 289WH.

Guiora, Amos, *Freedom from Religion: Rights and National Security*, Oxford: Oxford University Press 2013.

Guiora, Amos, *Tolerating Extremism. To What Extent Should Intolerance be Tolerated?*, dissertation Leiden University 2014, p. 74, available via <https://openaccess.leide-nuniv.nl/handle/1887/21977>.

Hamilton, Carolyn, *Family, Law and Religion*, London: Sweet and Maxwell 1995.

Hasan, Rumy, 'Critical Remarks on Cultural Aspects of Asian Ghettos in Modern Britain', *Capital & Class* 2003, pp. 103-134.

Hasan, Rumy, *Multiculturalism. Some Inconvenient Truths*, London: Politico's Publishing 2010.

Hasan, Suhaib, 'Muslim family law in Britain. A paper submitted to the international family law conference on 14 may 2014 at the University of Islamabad', 20 May 2014, via <http://sheikhsuhaibhasan.blogspot.co.uk/2014/05/muslim-family-law-in-britain.html>.

Hasan, Suhaib, 'My memoirs: Early days of my life, Part 1', 27 January 2015, via <http://sheikhsuhaibhasan.blogspot.co.uk/2015/01/my-memoirs-early-days-of-my-life-part-1.html>.

Helfand, Michael, 'Religious Arbitration and the New Multiculturalism: Negotiating Conflicting Legal Orders', *New York University Law Review* 2011, pp. 1231-1305.

Herman, Arthur, *The Idea of Decline in Western History*, New York: The Free Press 1997.

Herrenberg, Tom, 'Denouncing Divinity: Blasphemy, Human Rights, and the Struggle of Political Leaders to Defend Freedom of Speech in the Case of *Innocence of Muslims*', *Ancilla Iuris* 2015, pp. 1-19.

Higham, John, 'Multiculturalism and Universalism: A History and Critique', *American Quarterly* 1993, pp. 195-219.

Hirsi Ali, Ayaan, *Heretic. Why Islam Needs a Reformation Now*, New York: Harper Collins 2015.

Hirsi Ali, Ayaan, *Mijn Vrijheid* (Infidel), Amsterdam: Augustus 2006.

Horowitz, David and Spencer, Robert, *Islamophobia. Thought Crime of the Totalitarian Future*, David Horowitz Freedom Center 2011.

Hudelson, Patricia, 'Culture and Quality: An Anthropological Perspective', *International Journal for Quality in Health Care* 2004, pp. 345-346.

Huntington, Samuel P., *The Clash Of Civilizations and The Remaking of World Order*, New York: Simon and Schuster Paperbacks 1996 (2003).

Ibn Warraq, *Why I Am Not a Muslim*, Amherst: Prometheus 1995.

Ibn Warraq, *Why the West is Best. A Muslim Apostate's Defense of Liberal Democracy*, New York: Encounter Books 2011.

Ibrahim, Raymond (ed.), *The Al Qaeda Reader: The Essential Texts of Osama Bin Laden's Terrorist Organization*. Portland: Broadway Books 2007.

Ibrahim, Raymond, 'How Taqiyya Alters Islam's Rules of War. Defeating Jihadist Terrorism', *Middle East Quarterly* 2010, pp. 3-13.

Ivison, Duncan, 'Introduction: Multiculturalism as a Public Ideal', in: Ivison, Duncan (ed.), *The Ashgate Research Companion to Multiculturalism*, Surrey: Ashgate 2010.

Jaan, Habiba, 'Equal and Free? 50 Muslim Women's Experiences of Marriage in Britain Today', Aurat Research Report 2014, via <https://www.secularism.org.uk/uploads/aurat-report-dec2014.pdf>.

Johnson, James, 'Why Respect Culture?', *American Journal of Political Science* 2000, pp. 405-418.

Joppke, Christian, 'The Retreat of Multiculturalism in the Liberal State: Theory and Policy', *The British Journal of Sociology* 2004, pp. 237-257.

Kaplan, David E., Monica Ekman, and Latif, Aamir, 'The Saudi Connection How Billions in Oil Money Spawned A Global Terror Network; Karachi', *US News & World Report* 2003.

Karima Bennoune, *Your Fatwa Does Not Apply Here: Untold Stories from the Fight Against Muslim Fundamentalism*, New York: Norton & Company 2013.

Keller, Nuh Ha Mim, *Reliance of the Traveller: A Classic Manual of Islamic Sacred Law*; 'Umdat al-Salik, by Ahmad ibn Naqib al-Misri (d. 769-1368) in Arabic with Facing English Text, Commentary, and Appendices. Edited and translated by Nuh Ha Mim Keller, Beltsville: Amana 1991.

Kepel, Gilles, *The War for Muslim Minds: Islam and the West*, Cambridge, Massachusetts: The Belknap Press of Harvard University Press 2004.

Keshavjee, Mohamed, *Islam, Sharia and Alternative Dispute Resolution: Mechanisms for Legal Redress in the Muslim Community*, London: I.B. Tauris 2013.

Koopmans, Ruud, 'Religious Fundamentalism and Hostility against Out-groups. A Comparison of Muslims and Christians in Western Europe', *Journal of Ethnic and Migration Studies* 2015, pp. 33-57.

Koopmans, Ruud and Veit, Susanne, 'Cooperation in Ethnically Diverse Neighborhoods: A Lost-Letter Experiment', *Political Psychology* 2014, pp. 379-400.

Kramer, Martin, *Islam Assembled: The Advent of the Muslim Congresses*, New York: Columbia University Press 1986, in: Gold, Dore, *Hatred's Kingdom: How Saudi Arabia Supports the New Global Terrorism*.

Kristol, Irving, 'The Tragedy of Multiculturalism', in: Kristol, Irving (ed.), *Neo-conservatism. Selected Essays 1949-1995*, New York: The Free Press, pp. 50-53.

Kuric, Lejla, 'Britain's sharia councils and secular alternatives', *Left Foot Forward* 2014, via <https://leftfootforward.org/2014/04/britains-sharia-councils-and-secular-alternatives/>.

Kymlicka, Will, *Liberalism, Community and Culture*, Oxford: Oxford University Press 1989.

Kymlicka, Will, *Multicultural Citizenship*, Oxford: Oxford University Press 1995.

Kymlicka, Will, 'Testing the Liberal Multiculturalist Hypothesis: Normative Theories and Social Science Evidence', *Canadian Journal of Political Science* 2010, pp. 257-271.

Kymlicka, Will, 'The Rise and Fall of Multiculturalism? New Debates on Inclusion and Accommodation in Diverse Societies', *International Social Science Journal* 2010, pp. 97-112.

Lacey, Robert, *Inside the Kingdom, Kings, Clerics, Modernists, Terrorists, and the Struggle for Saudi Arabia*, New York: Viking 2009.

Laes, Willy, *Mensenrechten in de Verenigde Naties. Een verhaal over manipulatie, censuur en hypocrisie* (Human Rights in the United Nations. A story on manipulation, censorship and hypocrisy), Antwerpen: Garant 2011.

Landes, Richard, 'From Useful Idiot to Useful Infidel. Meditations on the Folly of 21st-Century "Intellectuals"', *Terrorism and Political Violence* 2013, pp. 621-634.

Laycock, Douglas, 'Equal Access and Moments of Silence: The Equal Status of Religious Speech by Private Speakers', *Northwestern University Law Review* 1986, pp. 1-67.

Laycock, Douglas, 'Religious Liberty as Liberty', *Journal of Contemporary Legal Issues* 1996, pp. 313-356.

Lefort, Claude and Thompson, John, 'Totalitarianism without Stalin', pp. 52-88 (79), in: Lefort, Claude, *The Political Forms of Modern Society: Bureaucracy, Democracy, Totalitarianism*, Cambridge: Polity, 1986.

Leiter, Brian, 'Why Tolerate Religion?', *Constitutional Commentary* 2008, pp. 1-27.

Lepore, Christopher R., 'Asserting State Sovereignty over National Communities of Islam in the United States and Britain: Sharia Courts as a Tool of Muslim Accommodation and Integration', *Washington University Global Studies Law Review* 2012, pp. 669-692.

Lester, Shonda, 'The State and the Operation of Sharia Councils in the United Kingdom. A Critical Response to Machteld Zee', *Journal of Religion and Society* 2015, pp. 1-9.

Levy, Jacob, *The Multiculturalism of Fear*, Oxford: Oxford University Press 2000.

Lia, Brynjar, *The Society of the Muslim Brothers in Egypt*, Reading: Ithaca Press 1998.

Lichter, Ida, *Muslim Women Reformers. Inspiring Voices Against Oppression*, Amherst: Prometheus Books 2009.

London, Alex John, 'The Independence of Practical Ethics', *Theoretical Medicine and Bioethics* 2001, pp. 87-105.

MacEoin, Denis and Green, David (eds.), *Sharia Law or 'One Law for All?*, London: Civitas: Institute for the Study of Civil Society 2009.

Malik, Kenan, *Strange Fruit: Why Both Sides are Wrong in the Race Debate*, Oxford: Oneworld 2008 (2009).

Malik, Maleiha, 'Muslim Legal Norms and the Integration of European Muslims', EUI Working Paper 2009/29, via <http://cadmus.eui.eu/bitstream/han-dle/1814/11653/RSCAS?sequence=1>.

Malik, Maleiha, *Minority Legal Orders in the UK. Minorities, Pluralism and the Law*, London: The British Academy 2012.

Manea, Elham, 'Introducing Sharia in Western Legal Systems. When States Legally Sanction Discrimination, *Qantara.de* 19 March 2012, via <http://en.qantara.de/content/introducing-sharia-in-western-legal-systems-when-states-legally-sanction-discrimination>.

Manji, Irshad, *The Trouble with Islam. A Muslim's Call for Reform in her Faith*, New York: St. Martin's Press.

Maret, Rebecca, 'Mind the Gap: The Equality Bill and Sharia Arbitration in the United Kingdom', *Boston College International & Comparative Law Review* 2013, pp. 255-283.

Marsh, Christopher, *Religion and State in Russia and China. Suppression, Survival, and Revival*, New York: Continuum 2011.

Mayer, Ann Elizabeth, *Islam and Human Rights: Tradition and Politics*, Boulder, Colorado: Westview Press 2007.

McGoldrick, Dominic, 'Accommodating Muslims in Europe: From Adopting Sharia Law to Religiously Based Opt Outs from Generally Applicable Laws', *Human Rights Law Review* 2009, pp. 603-645.

McHale, T.R., 'A Prospect of Saudi Arabia', *International Affairs* 1980, pp. 622-647.

Menski, Werner, 'Immigration and multiculturalism in Britain: New Issues in Research and Policy', paper of a lecture delivered at Osaka University on 25 July 2002, pp. 1-20.

Mill, John Stuart, *On Liberty*, (1859) Cambridge: Cambridge University Press 2003.

Miller, Christian, 'Moral Relativism and Moral Psychology', pp. 346-367 (346-347), in: Hales, Steven (ed.), *A Companion to Relativism*, Chicester: Wiley-Blackwell 2011.

Mirza, Munira *et al.*, *Living Apart Together: British Muslims and the Paradox of Multiculturalism*, London: Policy Exchange, 2007.

Moghissi, Haideh, *Feminism and Islamic Fundamentalism. The Limits of Postmodern Analysis*, London and New York: Zed Books 1999.

Moore, Kathleen, *The Unfamiliar Abode: Islamic Law in the United States and Britain*, Oxford: Oxford University Press 2010, p. 119.

Muhammad, Abdur-Rahman, 'Whether or not Ground Zero mosque is built, U.S. Muslims have access to the American Dream.' *The Investigative Projecton Terrorism*, 5 September 2010, via <http://www.investigativeproject.org/2164/whether-or-not-ground-zero-mosque-is-built-us>.

Murray, Douglas and Verwey, Johan Pieter, 'Victims of Intimidation. Freedom of Speech within Europe's Muslim Communities', The Centre for Social Cohesion 2008.

Musa, Shirin, 'Shariaraad houdt vrouwen gevangen in hun huwelijk' (Sharia council keeps women trapped inside their marriage), *NRC Handelsblad* 12 July 2012.

Nawaz, Maajid, *Radical*, London: WH Allen 2012.

Nomani, Asra, 'Meet the honor brigade, an organised campaign to silence debate on Islam', *Washington Post* 16 January 2015, via <http://www.washingtonpost.com/opinions/meet-the-honor-brigade-an-organised-campaign-to-silence-critics-of-islam/2015/01/16/0b002e5a-9aaf-11e4-a7ee-526210d665b4_story.html>.

Okin, Susan Moller, 'Is Multiculturalism Bad for Women?', pp. 7-24, in: Cohen, Joshua, Howard, Matthew and Nussbaum, Martha (eds.), *Is Multiculturalism Bad For Women?*, Princeton: Princeton University Press 1999.

Othman, Norani, 'Muslim Women and the Challenge of Islamic Fundamentalism/Extremism: An Overview of Southeast Asian Muslim Women's Struggle for Human Rights and Gender Equality', *Women's Studies International Forum* 2006, pp. 339-353 (342).

Otto, Jan Michiel (ed.), *A Comparative Overview of the Legal Systems of Twelve Muslim Countries in Past and Present*, Leiden: Leiden University Press.

Otto, Jan Michiel, 'The Compatibility of Shari'a with the Rule of Law. Fundamentalist Conflict: Between Civilisations? Within Civilisations? Or Between Scholars?', pp. 137-154, in: Groen, Adriaan in 't *et al.* (eds.), *Knowledge in Ferment, Dilemmas in Science, Scholarship and Society*, Leiden: Leiden University Press 2007.

Parekh, Bhikhu, 'A Varied Modern World', pp. 69-75, in: Cohen, Joshua, Howard, Matthew and Nussbaum, Martha, *Is Multiculturalism Bad For Women?*, Princeton: Princeton University Press 1999.

Parekh, Bhikhu, 'What is Multiculturalism?' Seminar Contribution (Multiculturalism: a symposium on democracy in culturally diverse societies), December 1999, via <http://www.india-seminar.com/1999/484/484%20parekh.htm>.

Parekh, Bhikhu, *Rethinking Multiculturalism: Cultural Diversity and Political Theory*, London: Macmillan Press 2000.

Parekh, Bhikhu, *A New Politics of Identity: Political Principles for An Interdependent World*, New York: Palgrave Macmillan 2008.

Pearl, David S., *Islamic Family Law and Its Reception by the Courts in England*, Cambridge: Islamic Legal Studies Program, Harvard Law School 2000.

Pearl, David and Menski, Werner, *Muslim Family Law*, London: Sweet & Maxwell, 1998.

Phillips, Anne, *Multiculturalism Without Culture*, Princeton: Princeton University Press 2007.

Phillips, Melanie, *Londonistan. How Britain Created a Terror State Within*, London: Gibson Square 2012.

Phillips, Nicholas, 'Equality before the Law', pp. 309-318, Keynote speech at the East London Muslim Centre, 3 July 2008, transcript in: Ahdar, Rex and Aroney, Nicholas (eds.), *Shari'a in the West*, Oxford: Oxford University Press 2010.

Poidevin, Robin Le, *Agnosticism. A Very Short Introduction*, Oxford: Oxford University Press 2010.

Polanz, Carsten, 'The Legal Theory for Muslim Minorities and the Islamic Dream of Conquering the West', *Islam and Christianity* 2/2012, pp. 18-28.

Pospielovky, Dimitry, *Soviet Anti-Religious Campaigns and Persecutions*. Volume 2 of A History of Soviet Atheism in Theory and Practice, and the Believer, Houndmills: MacMillan 1988.

Proudman, Charlotte, 'A practical and legal analysis of islamic marriage, divorce and dowry', *Family Law Week* 31 January 2012, via <http://www.family-lawweek.co.uk/site.aspx?i=ed95364>.

Putnam, Robert, 'E pluribus unum: Diversity and Community in the Twenty-first Century' (the 2006 Johan Skytte Prize Lecture), *Scandinavian Political Studies* 2007, pp. 137-174.

Qaradawi, Yusuf al-, *Priorities of the Islamic Movement in the Coming Phase*, Cairo: Dar Al-Nashr for Egyptian Universities 1992.

Qutb, Sayyid, *Milestones* (1964), Translated in Andrew G. Bostom (ed.), *The Legacy of Jihad: Islamic Holy War and the Fate of Non-Muslims*, Amherst: Prometheus Books 2005.

Rachels, James, *The Elements of Moral Philosophy*, New York: McGraw-Hill 2003.

Raday, Frances, 'Culture, Religion, and Gender', *International Journal of Constitutional Law* 2003, pp. 663-715.

Raday, Frances, 'Secular Constitutionalism Vindicated', *Cardozo Law Review* 2008, pp. 2770-2798.

Ramadan, Tariq, 'Following shari'a in the West', pp. 245-255, in: Griffith-Jones, Robin (ed.), *Islam and English Law. Rights, Responsibilities and the Place of Shari'a*, Cambridge: Cambridge University Press 2013.

Rehman, Javaid, 'Islam, "War on Terror" and the Future of Muslim Minorities in the United Kingdom: Dilemmas of Multiculturalism', *Human Rights Quarterly* 2007, pp. 831-878.

Rehman, Javaid, 'The Sharia, Islamic Family Laws and International Human Rights Law: Examining the Theory and Practice of Polygamy and Talaq', *International Journal of Law, Policy and the Family* 2007.

Riccardi, Letizia, 'Women at Crossroads between UK Legislation and Sharia Law', Journal of Law and Social Sciences 2014, pp. 86-91.

Riddell, Peter, 'Islamisation and Partial Shari'a in Malaysia', pp. 135-160, in: Marshall, Paul (ed.), *Radical Islam's Rules: The Worldwide Spread of Extreme Shari'a Law*, Lanham, Maryland: Rowman & Littlefield Publishers 2005.

Ridley, Yvonne, 'How I Came to Love the Veil', *The Washington Post*, 22 October 2006.

Roex, Ineke, Stiphout, Sjef van and Tillie, Jean, *Salafisme in Nederland* (Salafism in The Netherlands), Universiteit van Amsterdam, Instituut voor Migratie-en Etnische Studies 2010.

Rohe, Mathias, 'Alternative Dispute Resolution in Europe under the Auspices of Religious Norms', *Religare Working Paper* Number 6, 2011.

Rohe, Matthias, 'Reasons for the Application of Shari'a in the West', pp. 25-46, in: Berger, Maurits (ed.), *Applying Shari'a in the West. Facts, Fears and the Future of Islamic Rules on Family Relations in the West*, Leiden: Leiden University Press 2013.

Rokeach, Milton, *The Nature of Human Values*, New York, NY: Free Press 1973.

Roosevelt, Eleanor, *The Autobiography of Eleanor Roosevelt*, London: Hutchinson 1962, p. 253, in: Laes, Willy (ed.), *Mensenrechten in de Verenigde Naties. Een verhaal over manipulatie, censuur en hypocrisie* (Human Rights in the United Nations. A story on manipulation, censorship and hypocrisy), Antwerpen: Garant 2011.

Roy, Olivier, *The Failure of Political Islam*, Cambridge: Harvard University Press 1994.

Saleh, Walid, 'Ibn Taymiyya and the Rise of Radical Hermeneutics: An Analysis of "An Introduction to the Foundation of Quranic Exegesis"', pp. 123-162, in: Ahmed, Shahab and Rapport, Yossef (eds.), *Ibn Taymiya and His Times*, Oxford University Press 2010.

Sartori, Giovanni, *Pluralismo, multiculturalistismo e estranei*, Milano: Rizzoli 2000, in: Joppke, Christian, 'The retreat of Multiculturalism in the liberal state: theory and policy', *The British Journal of Sociology* (2004): 237-257.

Saudi Arabia 2013 Human Rights Report; Country Reports on Human Rights Practices for 2013 by the United States Department of State, Bureau of Democracy, Human Rights and Labor, via <http://www.state.gov/documents/organization/220586.pdf>.

Schacht, Joseph, *An Introduction to Islamic Law*, Oxford: Clarendon Press 1982.

Schirrmacher, Christine, 'Sharia Judges, Parallel Legal System, Justices of the Peace – A Commentary to Joachim Wagner's "Outlaw Judges: The Threat Posed by Islamic Parallel Jurisprudence to the Rule of Law"', *Islam und Christlicher Glaube* 2012, pp. 35-40.

Schwartz, Seth, 'The Evolution of Eriksonian and Neo-Eriksonian Identity Theory and Research: A Review and Integration', *Identity. An International Journal of Theory and Research* 2001, pp. 7–58.

Schwartz, Stephen, '*Shari'a* in Saudi Arabia, Today and Tomorrow', pp. 19-40, in: Marshall, Paul (ed.), *Radical Islam's Rules: The Worldwide Spread of Extreme Shari'a Law*, Lanham, Maryland: Rowman & Littlefield Publishers 2005.

Schwartz, Stephen and al-Alawi, Irfan, 'Our Survey shows British Muslims don't want sharia', *The Spectator* 9 July 2008, via <http://www.spectator.co.uk/features/825601/our-survey-shows-british-muslims-dont-want-sharia/>

Sen, Amartya, *Identity and Violence. The Illusion of Destiny*, London: Allen Lane 2006.

Shachar, Ayelet, *Multicultural Jurisdictions: Cultural Differences and Women's Rights*, Cambridge: Cambridge University Press 2001, pp. 4-5.

Shachar, Ayelet, 'Privatizing Diversity: A Cautionary Tale from Religious Arbitration in Family Law', *Theoretical Inquiries in Law* 2008, pp. 572-607.

Shah-Kazemi, Sonia Nûrîn, *Untying the Knot. Muslim Women, Divorce and the Shariah*, The Nuffield Foundation/Signal Press: London 2001.

Sifaoui, Mohamed, *Pourquoi l' islamisme séduit-il?*, Paris: Armand Colin 2010.

Sniderman, Paul and Hagendoorn, Aloysius, *When Ways of Life Collide: Multiculturalism and its Discontents in the Netherlands*, Princeton: Princeton University Press 2007.

Sparrow, Andrew, 'Cameron attacks "State Multiculturalism"', *The Guardian* 26 February 2008, via <http://www.guardian.co.uk/politics/2008/feb/26/conservatives.race>.

Spinner-Halev, Jeff and Eisenberg, Avigail (eds.), *Minorities within Minorities. Equality, Rights and Diversity*, Cambridge: Cambridge University Press 2005.

Straub, Detmar *et al.*, 'Toward a Theory-based Measurement of Culture', *Journal of Global Information Management* 2002, pp. 13-23.

Strindberg, Anders and Wärn, Mats, *Islamism: Religion, radicalisation, and Resistance*, Cambridge: Polity 2011.

Sultan, Wafa, *A God Who Hates. The Courageous Woman Who Inflamed the Muslim World Speaks Out Against the Evils of Islam*, New York: St. Martin's Press 2009.

Suurland, David, 'Totalitarianism and Radical Islamic Ideologies', pp. 257-309, in: Labuschagne, Bart and Sonnenschmidt, Reinhard (eds.), *Religion, Politics and Law: Philosophical Reflections on the Sources of Normative Order in Society*, Leiden: Brill 2009.

Suurland, David, *Secular Totalitarian and Islamist Legal-Political Philosophy*, dissertation Leiden University 2011, available via <https://openaccess.leidenuniv.nl/handle/1887/19888>.

Szczesniak, Boleslaw, *The Russian Revolution and Religion. A Collection of Documents Concerning the Suppression of Religion by the Communists, 1917-1925*, Notre Dame: University of Notre Dame Press 1959.

Tamimi, Azzam, 'Islam and democracy from Tahtawi to Ghannouchi', *Theory, Culture & Society* 2007, pp. 39-58.

Taylor, Charles, 'The Politics of Recognition', pp. 25-73 (39), in: Taylor, Charles, *Multiculturalism. Examining the Politics of Recognition*. Edited and introduced by Amy Gutman, Princeton: Princeton University Press 1994.

Taylor, Charles, *Sources of the Self. The Making of the Modern Identity*, Cambridge: Harvard University Press 1989.

The Holy Qur'an, translated by Abdullah Yusuf Ali, Worldsworth Editions Limited 2000.

Tibi, Bassam, 'The Politization of Islam into Islamism in the Context of Global Religious Fundamentalism', *Journal of Middle East and Africa* 2010, pp. 153-170.

Tibi, Bassam, *Islamism and Islam*, New Haven & London: Yale University Press 2012.

Tibi, Bassam, *The Shari'a State. Arab Spring and* Democratization, London: Routledge 2013.

Tierney, P.J., *Theocracy: Can Democracy Survive Fundamentalism?* Bloomington: iUniverse 2012.

Tsaoussi, Aspasia and Zervogianni, Eleni, 'Multiculturalism and Family Law: The Case of Greek Muslims', pp. 209-239, in: Boele-Woelki, Katharina and Sverdrup, Tone (eds.), *European Challenges in Contemporary Family Law*, Antwerp: Intersentia 2011.

Turner, Terence, 'Anthropology and Multiculturalism: What is Anthropology That Multiculturalists Should Be Mindful of It?', *Cultural Anthropology* 1993, p. 411-429.

Tylor, Edward, *Primitive Culture*, London: John Murray, Albemarle Street 1871.

Verhofstadt, Dirk, *Atheïsme als Basis voor de Moraal* (Atheism as Foundation for Morals), Antwerp: Houtekiet 2013.

Verhofstadt, Dirk, De Derde Feministische Golf (The Third Feminist Wave), Antwerp: Houtekiet 2006.

Vernon, Mark, *How to Be an Agnostic*, Houndmills: Palgrave MacMillan 2011.

Vertovec, Steven and Wessendorf, Susanne (eds.), *The Multiculturalism Backlash: European Discourses, Policies and Practices*, London: Routledge 2010.

Vidino, Lorenzo, 'Aims and methods of Europe's Muslim brotherhood', *Current Trends in Islamist Ideology* November 2006, via <http://www.hudson.org/research/9776-aims-and-methods-of-europe-s-muslim-brotherhood>.

Vidino, Lorenzo, *The New Muslim Brotherhood in the West*, New York: Columbia University Press 2010.

Vidino, Lorenzo, 'Hisba in Europe? Assessing a murky phenomenon', *European Foundation for Democracy* 2013, via <http://www.europeandemocracy.org/images/stories/Media/Hisba/Hisba_in_Europe.pdf>.

Wagner, Joachim, *Richter Ohne Gesetz*, Berlin: Econ 2011.

Waldron, Jeremy, 'Mill and the Value of Moral Distress', *Political Studies* 1987, pp. 410-423.

Waldron, Jeremy, 'Minority Cultures and the Cosmopolitan Alternative', *University of Michigan Journal of Law Reform* 1991, pp. 751-793.

Waldron, Jeremy, 'Cultural Identity and Civic Responsibility', pp. 155-174 (158), in: Kymlicka, Will and Norman, Wayne (eds.), *Citizenship in Diverse Societies*, Oxford: Oxford University Press 2000 (2003).

Walzer, Michael, *Spheres of Justice: A Defense of Pluralism and Equality*, New York: Basic Books 1983.

Weaver, Matthew, 'Angela Merkel: German multiculturalism has "Utterly Failed,"' *The Guardian* 17 October 2010, via <http://www.guardian.co.uk/world/2010/oct/17/angela-merkel-german-Multiculturalism-failed>.

West, Patrick, *The Poverty of Multiculturalism*, London: Civitas 2005.

Westreich, Avishalom, 'The Right to Divorce in Jewish Law: Between Politics and Ideology', *International Journal of the Jurisprudence of the Family* 2010, pp. 177-196 (177).

Wiedl, Nina, 'Dawa and the Islamist Revival in the West', *Current Trends in Islamist Ideology* 2009, via <http://www.hudson.org/research/9789-dawa-and-the-islamist-revival-in-the-west#>.

Wiegers, Gerard, 'Dr. Sayyid Mutawalli ad-Darsh's Fatwas for Muslims in Great Britain: The Voice of Official Islam?', pp. 178-191, in: Maclean, Gerald, (ed.), *Britain and the Muslim World*, Cambridge: Cambridge Scholars Press 2011.

Wilkinson III, Harvie J., 'The Law of Civil Rights and the Dangers of Separatism in Multi-culturalist America', *Stanford Law Review* 1995, pp. 993-1026.

William, Arsani, 'An Unjust Doctrine of Civil Arbitration: Sharia Courts in Canada and England', *Stanford Journal of International Relations* 2010, pp. 40-47.

Williams, Rowan, 'Civil and Religious Law in England: A Religious Perspective', transcript in: Ahdar, Rex and Aroney, Nicholas (eds.), *Shari'a in the West*, Oxford: Oxford University Press 2010, pp. 293-303.

Wilson, Robin Fretwell, 'The Overlooked Costs of Religious Deference', *Washington and Lee Law Review* 2007, pp. 1363-1383.

Wilson, Robin Fretwell, 'Privatizing Family Law in the Name of Religion', *William & Mary Bill of Rights Journal* 2010, pp. 925-952.

Yilmaz, Ihsan, 'Muslim Alternative Dispute Resolution and Neo-Ijtihad in England', *Turkish Journal of International Relations* 2003, pp. 117-139.

Yousef, Ahmed Bin and Jobain, Ahmad Abul, *The Politics of Islamic Resurgence: Through Western Eyes: A Bibliographic Survey*, North Springfield: United Association for Studies and Research 1992.

Zee, Machteld, 'Femmes for Freedom: fighting against marital captivity', *Leiden Law Blog* 14 June 2012, via <http://leidenlawblog.nl/articles/femmes-for-freedom-fighting-against-marital-captivity>.

Zee, Machteld, 'Five Options for the Relationship between the State and Sharia Councils: Untangling the Debate on Sharia Councils and Women's Rights in the United Kingdom', *Journal of Religion & Society* 2015, pp. 1-18.

Zee, Machteld, 'The State and the Operation of Sharia Councils in the United Kingdom: A Response to Shonda Lester', *Journal of Religion & Society* 2015, pp. 1-6.

Zimmerman, Jonathan, 'Brown-ing the American Textbook: History, Psychology, and the Origins of Modern Multiculturalism', *History of Education Quarterly* 2004, pp. 46-69.

Zornberg, Lisa, 'Beyond the Constitution: Is the New York Get Legislation Good Law?' *Pace Law Review* 1995, pp. 703-784.

VIDEO MATERIAL

'Dispatches – Undercover Mosque', Channel 4 Documentary, 5 February 2011, via <https://vimeo.com/19598947>.

'Divorce: Sharia Style', Channel 4 Documentary, 10 January 2011, via: <https://www.youtube.com/watch?v=OB34_zrB2to>

'Secrets of Britain's Sharia Councils', BBC Panorama, 22 April 2013, via <http://www.bbc.co.uk/iplayer/episode/b01rxfjt/Panorama_Secrets_of_Britains_Sharia_Councils/>.

'Senior UK Imam Suhaib Hasan reveals "Jewish Conspiracy"', YouTube clip, published on 16 December 2013, via <https://www.youtube.com/watch?v=XGIjh47kP3w>.

'Shaikh Haitham Al Haddad "The family"' Talk at Masjid Umar R.A. Part 2', YouTube clip, published on 15 May 2012, via <http://youtu.be/fST0Vmyim44?t=12m56s>.

CASE LAW

The Netherlands

Rechtbank Rotterdam 8 December 2010, 364739/KG ZA 10-1018.
Rechtbank Den Haag 11 January 2013, 431258/KG ZA 12-1273.
Rechtbank Amsterdam 22 May 2014, c/13/563478/KG ZA 14-495 HJ/NRSB.

United Kingdom

Edgar v. Edgar [1980] 1 WLR 1410.
Al Midani and Another v. Al Midani and Others [1999] 1 Lloyd's Rep 923.
Re J (A Child) [2005] UKHL 40.

M (Lebanon) v. Home Secretary [2008] UKHL 64.
Uddin v. Choudhury & Ors [2009] EWCA Civ 1205.

United States of America

Plessy v. Ferguson, 163 U.S. 537 (1896).
Brown v. Board of Education of Topeka, 347 U.S. 483 (1954).

European Court of Human Rights

Refah Partisi (the Welfare Party) and Others v. Turkey, (App nos 41340/98, 41342/98, 41343/98 and 41344/98), ECtHR 2001.
Gündüz v. Turkey, (Application no. 35071/97), ECtHR 4 December 2003.
Lautsi v. Italy, (Application no. 30814/06), ECtHR 3 November 2009.
Lautsi and others v. Italy, (Application no. 30814/06), ECtHR 18 March 2011.

Acknowledgements

I am grateful to the many people who were there for me to discuss ideas and findings, who generously read drafts and offered thoughts and support. These are Paul Cliteur, Afshin Ellian, Dirk Verhofstadt, Rumy Hasan, Amos Guiora, Meindert Fennema, Gelijn Molier, Frits Bolkestein, Marcel Maussen, Emmy Bergsma, Shirin Musa, David Suurland, Simon Admiraal, Diederik Boomsma, Machteld Allan, Masua Sagiv, Boudewijn Niels, Evert Faber van der Meulen, Bastiaan Rijpkema, Jonathan Price, Sarah Strous, Zhang Tu, Roy van Keulen, Jamaseb Soltani, Janneke Vink, Tom Herrenberg, Jasper Doomen, Claudia Bouteligier, Yoram Stein, Mirjam van Schaik, Arie-Jan Kwak, Caroline de Ruijter, Lorike Waldus, Lisette Pluimgraaff, Alan Mendoza, Emily Dyer, Hannah Stuart, Svi Freedman, Elliot McArdle, Daniel Tuhrim, and lastly, Selma Hoedt, Mariska Duindam, and Jolien Honings of Eleven International Publishing.

My gratitude also extends to those who contributed to the research on Sharia councils that underpins this book. I would like to thank the following people who I have interviewed: Baroness Cox, Baron Phillips of Worth Matravers, Professor of Philosophy Anthony Grayling, barristers Charlotte Proudman and Elissa Da Costa-Waldman, Tehmina Kazi of British Muslims for Secular Democracy, Professor of Law Maleiha Malik, Maryam Namazie of One Law for All, Anne Marie Waters of ShariaWatch UK, Chief Crown Prosecutor Nazir Afzal, writer and journalist Gita Sahgal, Pragna Patel of the Southall Black Sisters, Charlie Klendijan of the Lawyers' Secular Society, dayanim Lichtenstein and Elzas of the London Federation of Synagogues, qadis Faiz-ul-Aqtab Siddiqi and Fiaz Hussein of the Muslim Arbitration Tribunal in Nuneaton, qadis Khola Hasan, Suhaib Hasan, Abu Sayeed and Furqan Mahboob of the Islamic Sharia Council in Leyton, London, and qadis Amra Bonc, Muhammad Talha Bukhari and the late Mohammad Naseem of the Sharia Council of the Birmingham Central Mosque.

Index

A

Abd al-Fattah Abu Ghudda, 114

Abduh, Muhammad, 59

Abdullah, Daud, 111

Abu Sayeed, Maulana, 114, 120, 129, 130, 134, 136

ad-Darsh, Sayyid Mutawalli, 97, 112, 113, 114

Afzal, Nazir, 97, 119, 136

Ahmad, Kassim, 77

al-Azm, Sadiq Jalal, 24

al-Banna, Hassan, 60, 61, 89, 91, 110

al-Bukhari, Muhammad, 55

al-Haddad, Haitham, 113, 116, 117, 129, 130

Ali, Shaheen Sardar, 139, 144

al-Qaradawi, Yusuf, 88, 89, 91, 92, 101, 109, 114

al-Zawahiri, Ayman, 72

Annan, Kofi, 82

Aristotle, 19

Audah, Abdul Qadir, 115

Aznar, Jose Maria, 1

B

Badawi, Raif, 65, 66

Bano, Samia, 120, 129, 145

Barry, Brian, 31

Bennoune, Karima, viii, 93

Benson, Ophelia, 38

Berger, Maurits, 23, 143

Bin Baz, Abd al-Aziz, 69, 116

Bin Laden, Carmen, 68

Bin Laden, Osama, 60, 68

Bin Mohamad, Mahatmir, 74

Bodin, Jean, ix, 95

Bokhari, Muhammad Talha, 137

Bone, Amra, 137, 138, 139

Bowen, John, 122

Brown, Gordon, 96, 98

Bruckner, Pascal, 27, 32

Buruma, Ian, 23

C

Cameron, David, 1, 96, 98

Carmichael, Stokely, 9

Charbonnier, Stéphane, 87

Chesler, Phyllis, 38, 151

Cliteur, Paul, 23, 37, 40

Cox, Caroline, 98, 153, 155

D

Du Bois, W.E.B., 9

E

Eichmann, Adolf, 60

Ellian, Afshin, ix, 23

Erikson, Erik, 7, 10, 22

F

Fourest, Caroline, 91

Freud, Sigmund, 6, 22

G

Gaede, Stan, 35, 36

Gandhi, Mahatma, 110

Glazer, Nathan, 10

Grant, Helen, 123

Guiora, Amos, 3

H

Hasan, Khola, 131, 140

Hasan, Rumy, 30, 38, 43, 148

Hasan, Suhaib, 97, 112, 113, 115, 119, 130, 131, 134, 140, 155

Hegel, Georg Wilhelm Friedrich, 11

Helfand, Michael, 100

Herder, Johann Gottfried von, 6, 16, 31

Higham, John, 35

Hirsi Ali, Ayaan, 23, 87

Hitler, Adolf, 61

Huxley, T.H., ix

I

Ibn Abd-al-Wahhab, Muhammad, 56, 57, 58, 59, 71

Ibn Abdullah, Muhammad, 54

Ibn Saud, Muhammad, 57, 59, 71

Ibn Taymiyya, Ahmad, 57, 58, 63

Ibn Warraq, 33, 67

Ibrahim, Raymond, 63

J

Johnson, James, 17, 25

K

Kaprawi, Norhayati, 78

Keller, Nuh Ha Mim, 54

Khan, Deeyah, 111

Kymlicka, Will, xi, 2, 10, 14, 15, 16, 17, 18, 21, 22, 25, 27, 34, 45

L

Lacey, Robert, 67

Laes, Willy, 80

Leiter, Brian, 36

M

Mahboob, Furqan, 132, 133

Mahboob, Shaaz, 98

Mahmood, Khalid, 98

Malik, Kenan, 10

Malik, Maleiha, 100, 103

Mandela, Nelson, 110

Manea, Elham, 99, 157

Mawlawi, Faisal, 114

Mayer, Ann Elizabeth, 83, 84

Merkel, Angela, 1

Mill, John Stuart, 37, 45, 46

Moghissi, Haideh, 39, 40, 41, 52, 101

Mubarak, Hosni, 124

Muhammad, Abdur-Rahman, 86

Musa, Shirin, 156

Mutahhari, Murtaza, 64

N

Naseem, Mohammad, 137, 138, 139

Nomani, Asra, 86

O

Okin, Susan Moller, 3

Othman, Norani, 76, 78, 86

P

Parekh, Bhikhu, xi, 6, 12, 13, 14, 16, 17, 18, 20, 25, 37, 41

Patel, Pragna, 142

Phillips, Nicholas, x, 95, 97, 99, 104, 105, 106, 110, 111, 115, 118, 119, 143, 150, 154, 158

Plessy, Homer, 7

Proudman, Charlotte, 127, 154

Putnam, Robert, 33

Q

Qutb, Sayyid, 61, 62, 87

R

Rachels, James, 38

Raday, Frances, 145, 148

Rahman, Tunku Abdul, 73

Ramadan, Tariq, 89, 91, 101, 110

Rida, Muhammad Rashid, 59, 60

Roosevelt, Eleanor, 80

Rushdie, Salman, 110, 117

Russell, Bertrand, ix

S
Sacranie, Iqbal, 110
Sarkozy, Nicholas, 1
Sartori, Giovanni, 31
Schacht, Joseph, viii, 53, 101
Sen, Amartya, 21
Shachar, Ayelet, 105
Shah-Kazemi, Sonia, 125
Siddiqi, Faiz-ul-Aqtab, 119, 123, 131
Stangroom, Jeremy, 38
Suurland, David, 58, 60, 62

T
Taylor, Charles, xi, 2, 11, 12, 13, 14, 16, 17,
    18, 20, 25, 29, 42, 95
Tibi, Bassam, 52, 87
Tolstoy, Leo, 23
Tylor, Edward Burnett, 4, 5

V
Vidino, Lorenzo, 90

W
Wagner, Joachim, 123
Waldron, Jeremy, 18, 22, 29, 45, 46, 47
West, Patrick, 35
Wilders, Geert, 87
Williams, Rowan, x, 95, 97, 99, 102, 103,
    104, 106, 110, 111, 113, 115, 117, 118,
    143, 150, 154, 158

X
X, Malcolm, 9